DENSITY
BY DESIGN

edited by
James W. Wentling, AIA
and
Lloyd W. Bookout

ULI–the Urban Land Institute
in cooperation with the
Housing Committee,
American Institute of Architects

 THE URBAN LAND INSTITUTE

ABOUT ULI–THE URBAN LAND INSTITUTE

ULI–the Urban Land Institute is an independent, nonprofit research and educational organization incorporated in 1936 to improve the quality and standards of land use and development.

The Institute is committed to conducting practical research in the various fields of real estate knowledge; identifying and interpreting land use trends in relation to the changing economic, social, and civic needs of the people; and disseminating pertinent information leading to the orderly and more efficient use and development of land.

ULI receives its financial support from membership dues, sale of publications, and contributions for research and panel services.

David E. Stahl
Executive Vice President

ULI PROJECT STAFF

Director of Publications
Frank H. Spink, Jr.

Project Director
Lloyd W. Bookout

Editor
Nancy H. Stewart

Art Director
Betsy VanBuskirk

Artists
Helene Y. Redmond
Kim Rusch

Production Manager
Diann Stanley

Watermark Tower photo credit (cover, bottom):
Sandy Farrier

Recommended bibliographic listing:
James W. Wentling and Lloyd W. Bookout, eds. *Density by Design.* Washington, D.C.: ULI–the Urban Land Institute, 1988.

ULI Catalog Number D49

© 1988 by ULI–the Urban Land Institute
1090 Vermont Avenue, N.W.
Washington, D.C. 20005

ISBN 0-87420-677-4
Library of Congress Catalog Card Number 88-50774
Printed in the United States of America

At its October 1986 meeting, the Housing Committee of the American Institute of Architects (AIA) discussed the growing emphasis on higher-density housing in the residential marketplace. Committee members raised concerns about the long-term consequences that some of the new higher-density products would bring; all agreed that as residential densities increase, extra attention must be paid to design quality. Seeking a forum in which to explore contemporary, higher-density housing forms and to promote design quality, the committee contacted ULI about collaborating on a book. Thus, *Density by Design* was born.

Although many must be acknowledged for their contributions, James W. Wentling deserves special recognition for his determination in writing, collecting, assembling, and organizing the material for this book. Without his fortitude, the ideas of so many would not be preserved in these pages. Recognition must also be given to the more than 20 architects (most of whom are members of the AIA Housing Committee) who contributed to the case studies that form the essence of this book.

The review committee, composed of ULI Residential Development Council Members, contributed greatly with their detailed review of the draft manuscript and suggestions for organization, content, and format. Special thanks also to Jeanne Whyte, AIA, for her assistance in organizing text and graphic materials, and to Rebecca Hardin of Open Line for her help in editing the case studies and collecting data.

Finally, thanks to Frank Spink, Nancy Stewart, and Betsy VanBuskirk of the ULI staff for their extraordinary efforts in bringing all of these diverse ideas and styles into a single publication.

Density by Design marks the second occasion in which ULI and the AIA Housing Committee have joined forces to study important trends in the planning and design of housing. In 1984, they collaborated on the highly successful publication, *Housing for a Maturing Population*. It is through such cooperative efforts that these organizations hope to realize their mutual objective of improving the built environment.

Lloyd W. Bookout

REVIEW COMMITTEE

Jack D. Bloodgood, FAIA
President
John D. Bloodgood Architects, P.C.
Des Moines, Iowa

James M. DeFrancia
President
Lowe-Weston Enterprises
Sterling, Virginia

Thomas L. Hodges
President
Greenbelt Companies
Little Rock, Arkansas

David R. Jensen
President
David Jensen Associates, Inc.
Denver, Colorado

Gerald M. McCue
Dean, Graduate School of Design
Harvard University
Cambridge, Massachusetts

Shirley F. Weiss
Professor of City and Regional
Planning
University of North Carolina
Chapel Hill, North Carolina

Leonard W. Wood
Regional Partner
Trammell Crow Company
Atlanta, Georgia

In the United States, higher-density housing is often perceived negatively. Unimaginative design, lack of amenities, and overcrowding might come to the minds of many Americans when the term "high-density" is mentioned. During the 1980s, American homebuyers, builders, and architects have come face-to-face with the need to provide housing at higher densities in spite of this common, though generally unjustified, perception. Some might consider the result a step toward the future: homebuyers are redefining what they consider necessary and desirable in housing, and higher densities are part of this new definition. Ironically, this step forward has been taken, in part, by looking to the past and reshaping it to meet today's economic and lifestyle requirements.

Density by Design builds on the premise that change is an evolutionary process (rather than a purely creative one) and that current trends in housing design are based on values, traditions, and prototypes handed down from previous generations. The book's case studies are organized around the theory that each contemporary housing type has an ancestor, no matter how distantly related. The case examples are not arranged to suggest any chronological order in the development of housing types, and, admittedly, some of them do not fall neatly into one particular category, while others may overlap categories. The structure of the book intends only to highlight the qualities inherent in historical housing forms that today's

buyers continue to seek, and to demonstrate ways of providing these qualities in housing products that can be used at higher densities.

Clearly, density is a relative term that will evoke different images for different people and communities. This book examines a large range of densities—from a few units per acre to several hundred units per acre—and housing types that may be applicable to suburban, urban infill, and downtown sites. There is, however, one constant: in virtually all urban and suburban settings—and in virtually all geographic regions—densities are increasing.

In recent years, suburban environments, once a haven for low-density, detached housing, have seen the greatest increase in overall density. Lack of available land, rising costs, and an increasing desire on the part of residents to reduce home-to-work commutes have changed the nature of the suburbs. Higher residential densities in the suburbs correspond with the emergence of new "suburban activity centers" growing around the original downtown cores.

Although many of the case studies examined in this book are types that lend themselves best to suburban settings, their selection should not be construed as bias on the part of the editors or publisher. Rather, it reflects the fact that the majority of houses in this country are being built and will continue to be built in large communities developing around existing metropolitan areas. These new communities will face the greatest challenge—that of preserving the market-driven traditions so in demand (for example, privacy, security, and open spaces) at perhaps four times the density of that only 20 years ago.

Already this challenge is being met. Far from extinct, the single-family house, which has remained the "American dream," has evolved into new and often complex forms—

Z lots, zipper lots, wide-shallow lots and a host of others. Time will tell whether these new variations will continue to be a trend; for now, they have proved highly successful in the marketplace.

It can be argued that none of the housing types featured in this book represents a major design breakthrough. For example, most of the case study projects are built in patterns and at densities that still require the automobile as the primary means of transportation, and most still seek to identify with the historical image of the detached house. Such a breakthrough would require a substantial change in the values and traditions so esteemed by most homebuyers. And perhaps therein lies the major point: such a change has not occurred, although the realities of affordability and lifestyle are dictating changes. Builders, planners, and architects, in turn, must become more creative in balancing what homebuyers perceive as valuable with what is, in fact, realistic.

Through this assembly of case studies and recollection of past housing forms, *Density by Design* attempts to reinforce the need for design quality in contemporary higher-density housing. As densities increase, so too does the need to be aware of design quality and the long-term livability of what is built.

Lloyd W. Bookout
James W. Wentling

From High-Rise Slab Buildings to . . .   153

The Continuing Evolution

EVOLVING FORMS OF HIGHER-DENSITY HOUSING

James W. Wentling

Our national housing stock is in a state of metamorphosis. A virtual retooling of housing forms is underway in the central cities and suburban communities. While recent urban settlement patterns are affecting *where* we live, lifestyle preferences, changing demographics, affordability, and revised concepts of the family unit are changing *how* we live. A new definition of what we require—and desire—in shelter is emerging.

Perhaps more than any other possession, one's house is an expression of one's values. In today's era of limitations, values are increasingly in conflict with the realities of affordability and availability. As a result of rising land and labor costs, higher interest rates, and myriad other reasons, housing prices have skyrocketed, generating demand for higher-density housing forms. In response, developers and designers have scurried to invent product types that satisfy today's density requirements while maintaining qualities traditionally held in high esteem.

James W. Wentling, AIA, is the principal of James Wentling/Architects, in Philadelphia, Pennsylvania. He is a member of the Urban Land Institute— where he serves on a Residential Development Council—and a member of the National AIA Housing Committee. Wentling is a frequent speaker at housing industry events and the author of numerous housing-related publications. He chaired the AIA Housing Committee effort in the publication of Density by Design.

It would be inaccurate to suggest that higher-density housing forms are emerging simply in response to affordability issues and against the will of the market. Lifestyle choices of a major segment of today's housing market reflect not just an acceptance, but a preference, for higher densities. This stems from the desire of many households to live within the city or close to urban services, to reduce the home-to-work commute, and to increase leisure time.

Using 25 case studies, this book explores some of the new housing forms developed over the last decade that have dealt successfully with the reality of density while sustaining qualities of livability handed down through previous housing forms. The case studies are organized under eight historical prototypes, each of which was designed for a different user group or urban location: 1) estate homes, 2) bungalows, 3) cottages, 4) duplexes, 5) townhouses, 6) breezeway buildings, 7) mid-rise block buildings, and 8) high-rise slab buildings.

Although these eight prototypes may no longer be practical in their traditional forms, certain qualities of each remain viable and desirable. The case studies of contemporary projects that follow each prototype accomplish objectives similar to those of their predecessors but do so with a greater consideration for density or design.

To review the ancestors of contemporary housing, it seems appropriate to consider the popular theory that the United States has experienced three major occupa-

Phillips Brandt Reddick

tional "eras"—those of the farmer, the laborer, and the clerk.[1] America's housing chronicles those eras.

Beginning with the agricultural age of the early settlers, the nation evolved into an industrial state through the 19th century and eventually into today's information society midway through the 20th century. Each of these eras had major impacts on the evolution of housing in terms of typology, tenure, delivery system, and density.

AGRICULTURAL AGE

During the agricultural age of colonial America, housing was predominantly owner-occupied and owner-built. Land grants were made available at reasonable prices as an incentive to populate the new land. Using natural, on-site materials, settlers constructed their earliest shelters with their own hands. Building forms were simple, with the basic goal of providing a means of protection from the seasonally harsh climates.

After the Revolutionary War, the agricultural age flourished, establishing the family farm as an American symbol. The farmhouse was to become an idealized housing form, strong to this day as a bastion of tranquility, open space, and self-sufficiency. Estate homes of vast plantations such as Mt. Vernon or Monticello epitomized the American concept of gracious living for over two centuries.

Thus, the modern homebuyer's overwhelming preference for the single-family detached home is rooted in the country's heritage as an independent, agrarian nation. The popular view of "the American Dream" as a single, freestanding dwelling is most likely a response to idyllic memories of the farmhouse.

[1]John Naisbitt, *Megatrends* (New York, N.Y.: Warner Books, 1982), p. 5.

Current activity in the higher-density detached category reflects the tremendous demand for this housing form.

During the agricultural era, towns and cities evolved primarily as mercantile centers. Most dominant were port cities accessible by water to major trade routes. The predominant higher-density housing type produced for city dwellers was the townhouse, a residential prototype that also remains quite common today.

Unlike rural homes, townhouses were less likely to be owner-built. The urban sites and more complex building techniques accelerated the evolution of specialized trades, such

". . . The popular view of the American Dream as a single, freestanding dwelling is most likely a response to idyllic memories of the farmhouse."

". . . The predominant higher-density housing type produced for city dwellers was the townhouse, a residential prototype that also remains quite common today."

"... The new manufacturing centers were often developed in the old colonial port cities, exerting extreme pressure on existing housing stock.... Vertical living in the form of stacked flats [sometimes over storefronts] became common."

as masonry and carpentry, within the colonial economy. Because of higher land and construction costs, inhabitants of early townhomes were also less likely to be owner-occupants. Although many luxurious city homes were built for the wealthy, tenancy and shared housing were more common for the average urban dweller. Speculative development of townhouses as "income property" was common. Among his multitude of achievements, Benjamin Franklin was also one of the early builders of rental housing.[2]

Since colonial times, traditional two- and three-story townhouses built within efficient grid street patterns often provided housing at densities of 30 to 40 units per acre. In spite of these densities, the town-

[2]Sam Bass Warner, *The Private City, Philadelphia in Three Periods of Growth* (Philadelphia, Pa.: University of Pennsylvania Press, 1968), p. 15.

houses generally had grade-level entrances and individual back yards. Interestingly, contemporary suburban townhouse programs that include attached garages commonly achieve only 10 units per acre.

INDUSTRIAL PERIOD

While townhouses became the high-density prototype for the agricultural age, the coming of the industrial era modified the role of the townhouse and introduced new housing forms. The gradual shift of the national economy to manufacturing required even higher densities near factories to house the vast labor force.

The new manufacturing centers were often developed in the old colonial port cities, exerting extreme pressure on existing housing stock. Townhomes were subdivided vertically and horizontally and building heights crept upward, raising effective density above the standard 30 to 40 units per acre. Vertical living in the form of "stacked flats" became common. Because many of the laborers were immigrant families of modest means, tenancy became the major form of tenure during the industrial era.

Images from early 19th century northern industrial centers render a negative portrait of housing conditions. The vast influx of European immigrants settled in ethnic ghettos, well documented in the history of cities such as Boston, New York, Philadelphia, and Baltimore. The legacy of housing from the early industrial revolution was largely one of overcrowded living spaces in tenement buildings. This negative image of high-density housing still influences today's housing market.

Although the conditions of urban centers like Boston and New York may shape our image of housing during the industrial period, other low-density "company towns" like

4

Pullman, Illinois, were built on new lands outside the central city.[3] Some of these early new communities experimented with prefabricated construction, primarily in the single-family detached category. During the industrial era, delivery systems for housing moved further from the owner-builder methodology. At company towns, the sponsor was likely not only to build but also to retain ownership of housing units, providing subsidized tenancy as part of the compensation for its employees.

Housing for company towns needed to be mass-produced and rapidly built; from this necessity came the concept of "production housing." The delivery of large quantities of substantially similar housing units by professional homebuilders became the urban norm by the late 19th century and remains so today.

Streetcar transportation also allowed major residential subdivisions to emerge outside the central cities. Independent contractors mass-produced uniform "tract" homes from stock or "pattern book" plans. Housing forms in these early close-in suburbs were diverse. Along with detached homes, the side-by-side twin house became popular. Elegant large brownstone townhouses were built for the wealthy, and higher-density apartment houses appeared on very desirable sites.

During the industrial era, suburban housing for the middle classes often could be distinguished by the transportation network that allowed its development. While early "garden" communities were built in response to the railroad or streetcar, the automobile and regional transportation authorities would later influence housing form and density.

Housing built in "streetcar" subdivisions such as Forest Hills, New York, and Roland Park outside Balti-

more did not contend with the automobile as a major design issue. Later suburban communities like Radburn, New Jersey, or Greenbelt, Maryland, attempted to resolve the automobile's growing influence on the planning and design of housing, although the most influential prototype was probably found in the Levittown subdivisions in New York and Pennsylvania. In the affordable Levittown communities, carports **were** standard features along the front elevations of houses.[4]

Levittown and the myriad similar communities developed during the 1950s and 1960s were encouraged by one of the most significant congressional land use acts of the century—the Federal Aid Highway Act of 1956. This regulation created the Highway Trust Fund, which was financed by taxing gasoline at a rate of $0.04 per gallon. The revenues were used to construct the interstate highway system, a transportation network composed of 42,500

[4]Ibid, p. 151.

". . . In the affordable Levittown communities, carports were standard features along the front elevations of houses."

[3]Robert A. M. Stern, *Pride of Place, Building the American Dream* (Boston, Mass.: Houghton Mifflin Company, 1986), p. 147.

miles, the largest public works project undertaken by the federal government. With the new interstate highways, the national landscape was soon transformed into a series of bedroom communities made up of closely spaced detached homes.[5]

As outlying land was made increasingly accessible through a major highway network, the urban population continued to disperse to low-density subdivisions. On the heels of housing, retail facilities followed, moving away from the central core of cities and into regional shopping centers.

---

[5]Peter Wolf, *Land in America, Its Value, Use and Control* (New York, N.Y.: Pantheon Books, 1981), p. 221.

". . . As outlying land was made increasingly accessible through a major highway network, the urban population continued to disperse to low-density subdivisions."

INFORMATION SOCIETY

The decentralization of our cities, which began after World War II, was concurrent with the advent of what today has become the "information society."[6] While industrial cores were based on trade and shipment of bulky goods, new centers were free to develop away from major railroad lines or waterways. This new economy was service-based, with job growth in the white-collar sector exceeding employment in agriculture and industry.

In response to this continued decentralization, housing changed further in terms of typology, density, and tenure. It moved deeper into the suburbs into new, even lower-density communities accessible to offices by automobile and, to a lesser extent, by public transportation. Volume construction of single-family detached homes was unprecedented, and homeownership was on the rise, aided by FHA and VA mortgage programs. Suburbanization was in full bloom through the 1960s and early 1970s. Toward the latter part of the 1970s, however,

---

[6]John Naisbitt states that the information age began in 1956, the year when clerical positions first outnumbered industrial occupations. *Megatrends*, p. 4.

early warning signs signaled that this sprawling, low-density pattern would have to be modified.

The Arab oil embargo of the late 1970s reminded suburban commuters of their dependency on inexpensive gasoline to keep transportation costs in balance. With the interstate highway system nearly completed, funding for new road improvements could not keep up with the continual suburban expansion. Traffic was to become a major issue for communities and "gridlock" a household word. Political sentiment began to favor residential growth management of development in outlying areas. Also, planning efforts were implemented to strengthen the home/work/shop relationship.

City "subcenters" or "suburban activity centers" gradually evolved around major retail malls, which in some cases were later expanded into mixed-use centers including office, hotel, and cultural facilities. The Post Oak area of Houston, for example, depends on the Galleria, a prototype suburban shopping mall, to provide additional business and community needs. Entirely new subcenters are now being master-planned for outlying areas as self-sufficient business, commercial, and residential districts.

On an even larger scale, vast planned communities such as Las Colinas near Dallas, Texas, or Pelican Bay outside Naples, Florida, were built on outlying tracts with a balance of office, residential, retail, and recreational uses. Other new communities are being constructed in urban settings as infill development. Battery Park City, a 92-acre site off lower Manhattan will eventually comprise 14,000 housing units and 6 million square feet of office space with appropriate public amenities and open space.

Although infill housing, rehabilitation, and mixed-use developments are progressing in the traditional urban centers, most of the new housing stock is still being built in outlying, master-planned communities. Planners and developers alike have embraced the planned unit development (PUD) concept, which allows different housing products within a master circulation and open space network. In most PUDs, the urban grid pattern has been largely abolished. Typically, diverse, mixed-density housing forms are used to capture the varied market segments of the population.

Whether occurring on urban infill sites or in new master-planned communities, contemporary housing is continuing its higher-density trend. The subdivisions of the 1950s and 1960s are no longer practical. It is pertinent to review some of the key factors influencing residential densities before exploring how developers and designers are meeting today's housing challenges.

DEMOGRAPHICS

Housing supply and demand are stimulated by many demographic factors, including new household formations, changes in household size, family income and affordability indexes, and regional employment growth. From the resettlement of GIs after World War II through the maturation of baby boomers, tremendous demographic changes have influenced the evolution of contemporary housing forms.

The number of American households grew 37 percent between 1970 and 1985, to a total of 86.6 million families. The largest increase occurred among households whose heads were 35 to 54 years old, reflecting the aging baby boom population. As baby boomers reached the

" . . . Traffic was to become a major issue for communities and 'gridlock' a household word."

" . . . Planners and developers alike have embraced the planned unit development (PUD) concept, which allows different housing products within a master circulation and open space network."

"... As baby boomers reached the age of independence, they entered the housing market very differently from the way in which their parents had a generation earlier."

age of independence, they entered the housing market very differently from the way in which their parents had a generation earlier. Most notably, their average household size was much smaller.

As of 1985, the average household consisted of only 2.67 people. The U.S. Census Bureau has forecast a decline in this number by the year 2000 to perhaps as low as 2.32 members. "Nonfamily households" (largely individuals living alone), are expected to represent a larger proportion of all American households in the future. Currently accounting for 28 percent of the total, this group may increase to 37 percent of the population by the year

2000.[7] Overall, household formation growth rates of 18 to 27 percent are predicted through this century, which would result in a total of 102.4 to 110.2 million households by the year 2000. During this period, the composition of homebuyers will be segmented into two major groups: the young and the mature. Each will have very distinct subcategories of specialty housing needs and preferences.

The current most populous group comprises the baby boomers who are 21 to 39 years old. This segment of the population includes 78 million people, whose members will head 50 percent of the households in the United States by 1990. In terms of housing needs, the baby boomers can be further divided into two categories. The older baby boomers, age 30 to 39, constitute approximately 46 percent of the total. For the most part, they are involved with their first or second homes and will fuel the "move-up" housing market of the 1990s. Younger baby boomers, age 21 to 29, make up the remaining 54 percent, and are expected to fuel the "starter" or first-time buyer market. Of the total baby boom group, approximately 56 percent are married and 44 percent are single.[8]

The baby boomers have diverse lifestyles and are highly segmented. Although often categorized together, they comprise many subgroups that will demand varied housing forms, with diverse locational preferences. The ability to define special subcategories within the baby boom generation—such as singles, mingles, DINKS (double incomes, no

kids), and others—gave birth to the concept of target marketing and created a new trend in the development of specialized housing products.[9]

The second major group of potential homebuyers may be called the "mature" market. They total 51 million people and can be segmented into four age categories: preretirees (55 to 64), 43 percent; retirees (65 to 74), 33 percent; elderly (age 75 to 84), 17 percent; and advanced elderly (85 and older), 5 percent. The unique needs of those in each of these categories will also require specialized housing as a major market focus through the 1990s and beyond.

The demographic shifts in both the "fair hair" and "gray hair" markets will generate tremendous demands for new housing units not readily found in the existing housing stock. The bulk of this housing is likely to be built in suburban or urban areas where services are in place. To accommodate this housing growth, densities are also likely to increase due to a variety of factors, one of them being affordability.

AFFORDABILITY

More housing units are available today than ever before in American history. Although the Census Bureau reported that the national housing stock reached 100 million units in March 1987, housing affordability continues to decline. Through the 1980s, housing costs rose at a faster pace than the overall consumer price index. From 1980 through 1983, monthly housing costs rose 26 percent for homeowners and 31 percent for renters, compared to the CPI increase of 17 percent.[9]

[7]U.S. Bureau of the Census, as abstracted in *The Wall Street Journal*, "Average Size of Households Is Likely to Fall, U.S. Says," May 29, 1986.

[8]For further discussion of market segmentations, see *Development Trends: 1986* (Washington, D.C.: Urban Land Institute, 1986), pp. 5–7.

[9]U.S. Bureau of the Census, as reported by *The Wall Street Journal*, "U.S. Housing Costs Increasing Despite Growth in Units," May 29, 1986.

As a direct result of rising housing costs, the homeownership rate is falling. The national percentage of homeowners rose to a peak of 65.8 percent in 1980 but had fallen to 63.5 percent by the end of 1985. The decline of 2.5 percentage points virtually erased the increase that had occurred over the previous 20 years. In 1986, prices for new homes and resales rose 10.4 percent to a national average of $117,400.

Housing affordability is emerging as a major issue for the 1980s and will likely continue to be so at least through the mid-1990s. Among the solutions used to maintain affordability will be increased residential densities. Higher land prices and labor costs can be directly amortized over a greater number of units through innovative designs for higher-density housing.

LAND COSTS

Soaring land costs in much of the nation are affecting greatly both product design and affordability. Average single-family lot prices increased 40 percent in 1985 in four of the five largest eastern markets; in the Boston area, land costs doubled in the two-year period between 1984 and 1986. These increases can be attributed to a variety of factors—heavier environmental regulation; increased exactions from local agencies; additional developer responsibilities for providing infrastructure and public services; and, growth moratoriums that are sweeping many of the nation's major metropolitan areas.

Higher land costs mean higher prices for new houses. As a rule, builders try to keep lot prices below 25 percent of the sales price but this ratio is becoming impossible to maintain in high-growth markets like Boston and southern California. Finished lots within 15 to 30 miles of Los Angeles now cost $50,000 to $70,000 while land for multiple-

family housing is selling for $200,000 to $300,000 per acre. In nearby Orange County, residential land is selling for up to $500,000 per acre. Clearly, the skyrocketing cost of land is forcing more creative, higher-density designs.

CHANGING LIFESTYLES AND BUYER PREFERENCES

Although buyer preferences for detached houses are not on the wane uniformly, affordability and maintenance-free living will continue to be major factors in the single-family versus multifamily choice. Further, an increased momentum for change and flexibility is being brought about by the information age. These factors suggest a growing demand for the convenience, location, and lifestyle typically inherent in higher-density products.

Housing options for the information society will focus more than

". . . Clearly, the skyrocketing cost of land is forcing more creative, higher-density designs."

ever on time and its effect on lifestyle. As the detached home must be located farther away from employment centers in order to maintain affordability, commuting time will become an increasingly major element in making decisions on location. Time savings versus space has already become a trading point at close-in sites near emerging suburban centers.

Today's homebuyers often are purchasing lifestyles more than they are houses. Convenience and opportunities to enjoy leisure time are of primary importance; therefore,

buyers increasingly are willing to trade private space in order to live in a quality community. They are in effect purchasing a community with the amenities and services that it offers.

The desire for increased leisure activities means that buyers are less interested in maintenance chores. Homeowners' associations are assuming a greater share of maintenance responsibilities, and homeowners have demonstrated a willingness to pay for services such as landscaping maintenance, snow removal, and exterior building repairs. The condominium form of ownership requires the least upkeep; thus, it offers the most freedom and remains popular with empty nesters, young professionals, and households with two working adults.

NEW HOUSING FORMS

The effect of demographics, affordability, and lifestyle preferences on housing is creating what some professionals have termed a "Europeanization" of residential standards—living with less but at a higher level of quality. Across the board, housing products will be geared toward higher densities. From single-family homes through high-rise towers, greater land yield will be expected. The challenge to housing professionals will be to satisfy this higher-density standard while maintaining quality design and desirable living environments.

A review of historical housing forms clearly demonstrates the inherent qualities of housing that can and should be preserved at higher densities. By studying classical American housing types, we can translate their essence into new products that respond to current market and demographic trends.

From Estate Homes to...

Perhaps the most dramatic example of increased density can be found in an American icon—the estate home. Owned by few but revered by many, the estate home was traditionally an exclusive multiacre compound affording extreme privacy yet providing reasonable access to the city. For the wealthy commuter of today, estate homes are shrinking to fit on quarter-acre lots and might be called "small-lot villas."

...SMALL-LOT VILLAS

Categorically, increased density can be resolved by creating images, in a sense, of the reality pursued. To market estate houses at higher densities, the image of luxury must be replicated at a smaller scale, particularly from the street.

In the small-lot villa prototype, the entry statement made by gates and a curved driveway to the portico can be reduced to fit on 50- to 70-foot-wide lots. Garage entrances are often perpendicular to the street or set back toward the interior of the lot in order not to detract from the elegance of the front door entrance. A two-story entrance

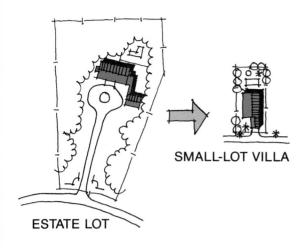

ESTATE LOT

SMALL-LOT VILLA

■ The image and quality found in historical estate houses can be replicated for today's wealthy buyers on lots less than 6,000 square feet.

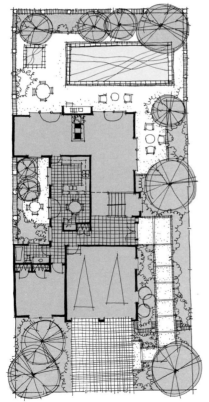

TYPICAL LOT PLAN

■ Intensive landscaping and amenities such as a pool, a hot tub, and patios make maximum use of these small lots.

facing the street will connote height, volume, and value. Symmetrical plans may be favored and high-quality veneer materials can be used for the curb side of the house.

In terms of site planning, small-lot villas require efficient use of every square inch of the lot. Rear yards may include a 20-foot-by-40-foot pool with surrounding deck. The lot should be carefully landscaped to give both shade and privacy without absorbing too much of the limited site area. Because most of the site will be developed, the small-lot villa prototype needs to be reviewed carefully for potential problems that might be caused by impervious surfaces. If there is no public storm sewer, on-site retention of stormwater may become a major problem.

Market emphasis on single-level living in small-lot villas affects both interior design and site planning considerations. The preferred placement of the master bedroom on the first level may crowd both the site and/or other room areas on the first floor. Designing a structure with a very large master bedroom suite on the upper level could supplant the single-level marketing feature and help free the limited ground plane.

The interior design requires special effects such as dramatic volume spaces, generous glazing providing views to exterior amenities and natural light, and large flexible rooms for entertaining. Because of space constraints, small-lot villas are more likely to consolidate programmed room areas such as living/dining or kitchen/family spaces, which are formally separated in a traditional estate home. The use of elegant materials on the exterior emphasizes the importance of quality rather than quantity in today's higher-density housing forms.

VILLA D'ESTE AT SWEETWATER
LONGWOOD, FLORIDA

Donald F. Evans

Located within the prestigious Sweetwater Oaks master-planned community in central Florida, Villa D'Este was designed to appeal to wealthy professionals wanting an estate or country club lifestyle without the burden of maintaining a large property. Because many product types are available within the 2,000-acre Sweetwater PUD, including other golf villas, single-family homes, and lux-

Donald F. Evans, AIA, is president and founder of the Evans Group, a full-service architectural and land planning firm. With offices in Orlando and Jacksonville, Florida, the group has earned approximately 200 design awards in 12 years. Evans is a member of the National AIA Housing Committee and a featured speaker at many housing industry events.

ury estates, Villa D'Este had to project a distinctive character to compete successfully with lower-density products.

The solution was to create a private enclave of 30 zero-lot-line golf villas reminiscent of an Old World Mediterranean village. Lush landscaping, private entry courtyards, ornate fountains, stamped concrete pavers, and Renaissance-style sculpture all convey the elegance and prestige necessary to attract affluent buyers to these small-lot villas.

DEVELOPMENT STRATEGY AND FINANCING

Styled after a very successful, similar project in Deerfield Beach, Florida, Villa D'Este was conceived to fill a gap in the Orlando housing market. The developer recognized

■ Stamped concrete paving and lush landscaping create a luxurious streetscape. Garage doors are set back 20 feet from the curb and are made of carved stained wood to give a positive visual effect.

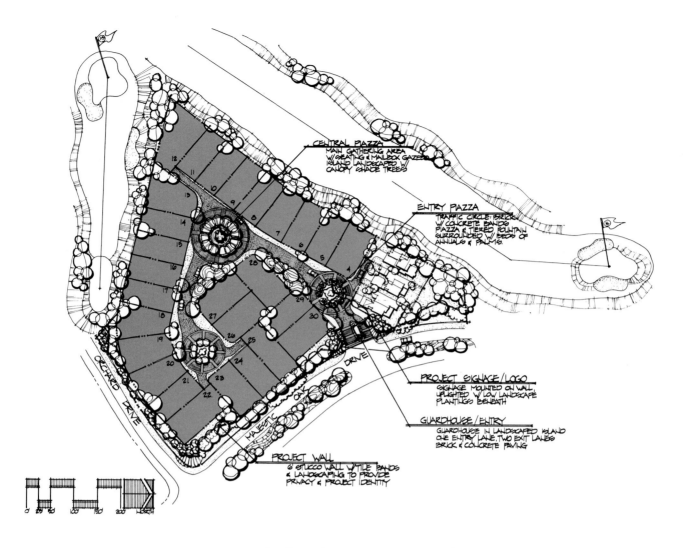

CENTRAL PLAZA
MAIN GATHERING AREA
W/SEATING & MAILBOX GAZEBO
ISLAND LANDSCAPED W/
CANOPY SHADE TREES.

ENTRY PLAZA
TRAFFIC CIRCLE: BRICK
W/CONCRETE BANDS
PLAZA & TIERED FOUNTAIN
SURROUNDED W/ BEDS OF
ANNUALS & PALMS.

PROJECT SIGNAGE/LOGO
SIGNAGE MOUNTED ON WALL,
UPLIGHTED W/ LOW LANDSCAPE
PLANTINGS BENEATH

GUARDHOUSE/ENTRY
GUARDHOUSE IN LANDSCAPED ISLAND
ONE ENTRY LANE, TWO EXIT LANES
BRICK & CONCRETE PAVING

PROJECT WALL
6' STUCCO WALL W/TILE BANDS
& LANDSCAPING TO PROVIDE
PRIVACY & PROJECT IDENTITY

■ **Located on a 6.8-acre site bounded on two sides by a golf course, Villa D'Este is a private enclave of 30 houses designed to appeal to upper-income buyers. The zero-lot-line design allows a density of 4.4 units per acre—substantially higher than buyers in this bracket typically have accepted. As a trade-off for higher density, homes offer elaborate design features, extensive use of quality materials, and the reassurance of privacy and security.**

that move-down buyers in central Florida had virtually no other small-lot luxury community to consider. He also saw the potential for sales to the second-home market segment.

Because of high land costs that amounted to $100,000 per unit, cre-

ative financing programs were used to lure potential buyers. One plan, for instance, called for no payments for two years if the buyer put down 20 percent of the sales price. All homes were sold on fee simple lots, with individual yard maintenance handled by a homeowners' association.

SITE PLANNING

Faced with the challenge of siting 30 luxury homes on a tight parcel of 6.8 acres, the land planning team oriented the rear of each lot toward the bordering golf course to provide premium views. Interior pools and gardens serve as focal points to expand the internal living space and to maximize individual unit privacy. These outdoor living environments also capitalize on central Florida's ideal weather conditions.

Thirty patio lots were arranged along the perimeter of the wedge-shaped site with a common, state-of-the-art security-controlled entrance, accessed from a small road within Sweetwater Oaks. Lot sizes were approximately 53 feet wide and 110 feet deep, allowing a density of 4.4 units per acre.

In keeping with the European design theme, the homes are clustered around three landscaped plazas with ornate fountains and special paving. These common grounds act as a focal point of the community and enliven the streetscape. Plant materials are formal and stately, highlighted by Canary Island date palms, manicured yew shrubs, and bright flower beds. A carefully detailed stucco wall surrounds the project to preserve privacy and security.

ARCHITECTURE

Stucco exteriors accented by tile band detailing, colored tile roofs, and arched entry gates carry through the Old World Mediterranean theme. The main entry courtyard for each home is tucked be-

hind a two-car garage for added privacy, and features an ornate fountain, stamped concrete pavers, and eight-foot, carved wood double doors opening into a ceramic tile foyer. A beveled glass fanlight above the doorway adds elegance and establishes the arched doorway design theme that is repeated throughout the villa.

Three floor plans were designed to meet the needs of the upscale buyer profile, including a 2,102-square-foot, two-bedroom plan; a 2,150-square-foot, two-bedroom plan with den; and a 3,280-square-foot, three-bedroom plan with library. The project architect specified volume ceilings wherever possible to enhance spaciousness in the plans. Flat trusses were used to retain a maximum ceiling height; although labor costs were slightly higher as a result, the increase in the perceived value of the villa justified the additional expense.

■ The entrance to each of the houses is identified easily from the street by a gated archway adjacent to the garage door. Behind the archway lies a private courtyard entrance with fountain and stamped concrete pavers. Inside the house, the tone of grandeur is sustained with double carved wood doors, tiled foyer, 20-foot ceilings, and beveled glass windows located above the doorway.

■ The smallest floor plan has 2,102 square feet; a master bedroom suite with his-and-hers walk-in closets; a guest bedroom; two and one-half baths; a living room; a library; and a breakfast room. With a single-level layout, the plan features extensive skylights and glazing.

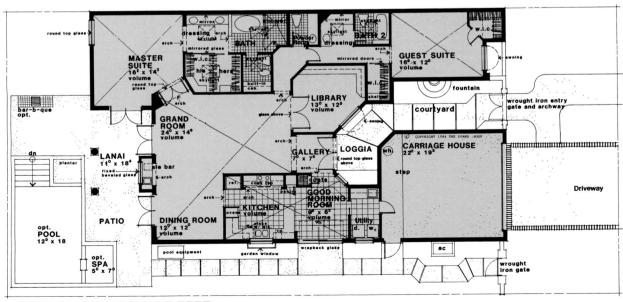

MODEL A—2,102 SQUARE FEET

■ **Interior features promote a sense of quality and luxury with extensive use of wood molding, high ceilings, and beveled and stained glass windows. All houses feature double French doors leading to rear yard patios that serve as an extension to the everyday living space in this temperate Florida setting.**

Many other luxury design features convey a feeling of grandeur. Double doors with arched transom glass lead to the master suite. Arches are repeated in recessed wet bars,

transitions from room to room, recessed shelving, and a recessed cooking wall in the kitchen. Overhead plant shelving embellishes high spaces and softens light from clerestories and skylights. Continuing the Mediterranean design theme, patios feature columned archways, fountains, and colored tile.

As large as 21 feet by 17 feet in one model, master suites appeal to the uncompromising standards of the high-end buyer. Double French doors lead to a lanai, adding to the open feeling of the room. Master baths feature imported ceramic tile, double vanities with a dressing area, oversized Roman tubs, separate glass-enclosed showers, and his-and-her walk-in closets with skylights.

■ **The largest floor plan, with 3,280 square feet, contains three bedrooms; three and one-half baths; a library; formal and informal living rooms; and a breakfast room. The two-story design keeps the master bedroom suite on the first floor, which is a strong market preference.**

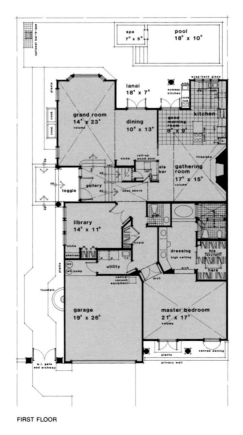

FIRST FLOOR

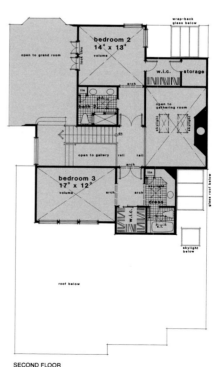

SECOND FLOOR

MODEL C—3,280 SQUARE FEET

Designed for people who entertain frequently, the kitchens are spacious and sophisticated, with wood cabinets and ceramic tile countertops. A large greenhouse solarium in the adjoining morning room and a greenhouse window over

■ Limited back yard space is used to the fullest: pool, spa, raised planter boxes, and extensive patio areas are common features. The emphasis on quality over quantity is exhibited in the use of expensive materials and attention to design details.

■ From the first point of entry, Villa D'Este conveys an image of luxury and quality. Privacy and security are ensured by the gated guardhouse.

the sink add natural light and make
the kitchens seem even larger.

Energy conservation features include bronze-tinted sliding glass
doors and windows, R-19 ceiling and
R-11 wall insulation, paddle fans,
and an air-conditioning system with
a heat exchanger for water heaters.

MARKETING

Although the developer initially
envisioned a second-home market
for the villas, the majority of buyers
have been dual-income professional
couples or move-down buyers. The
double garages, his-and-her walk-in
closets, and gourmet kitchens appeal to both categories of buyers.

Sales resulted from substantial
advertising in the local newspaper
and various magazines; recognition
as a national award recipient;
broker networking; and creative financing packages.

PROJECT DATA

LAND USE INFORMATION:
Site Area: 6.8 acres
Density: 4.4 units per acre
Parking Spaces: 120
Parking Index: 4 spaces per unit[1]
Total Units: 30

LAND USE PLAN:

	Acres	Percent of Site
Open Space	2.7	39%
Buildings	2.2	33
Roads/Parking Area	1.1	16
Amenities[2]	0.8	12

UNIT INFORMATION[3]:

Type	Square Feet	Garage	Sales Price
2-bdrm./2½-bath	2,102	2-car	$219,900
2-bdrm./2½-bath/den	2,150	2-car	$249,900
3-bdrm./3½-bath/library	3,280	2-car	$309,900

ECONOMIC INFORMATION:
Site Value: $3,000,000[4]
Site Improvement Costs: $1,200,000[5]
Construction Costs: $5,900,000
Amenities Costs: $250,000
Homeowner Fee: $200 per month

Notes:
[1]Two-car attached garage, plus driveways.
[2]Greenbelts, entry signage and security, and landscaped plazas.
[3]Homes are built upon purchase, so unit mix is not final.
[4]$100,000 per unit.
[5]$40,000 per unit.

DIRECTIONS:
From Orlando International Airport, take the Beeline Expressway west to Interstate 4
east. Exit Interstate 4 east at State Road 434 and go west to Wekiva Springs Road. Go
right on Wekiva Springs to Sweetwater Sales Center.

DEVELOPER:
Carl Trauger
Trendsetter Homes
551 Via Genova
Deerfield Beach, Florida 33441

ARCHITECT:
The Evans Group
518 South Magnolia Avenue
Orlando, Florida 32801

LAND PLANNER:
Enviroscape
The Evans Group
518 South Magnolia Avenue
Orlando, Florida 32801

AWARDS:
• Best in American Living Grand Award
• Grand Aurora Award
• Aurora Detached Home of the Year
• FAME Award (First Place)

"... bungalows had generous porch or deck areas extending off several elevations."

From Bungalows to...

The bungalow style evolved early in this century as a form of comfortable, affordable housing for the middle class. Often built in second-home or resort locations, bungalows had generous porch or deck areas extending off several elevations. Construction details reflected an unpretentious level of craftsmanship popular during the industrial era. Bungalows were most often single level in plan, with bedrooms or auxiliary spaces under dormer roofs on the second floor.

...PATIO HOMES

The traditional bungalow offers an affordable model of comfortable living for what today is commonly known as the patio home. Simply stated, the design objective then and now was and is to use the outside deck as an extension of the limited interior space.

Like the bungalow, the primary characteristics of the contemporary patio home include a strong single-level plan, easy access to outdoor areas, simplified construction, and affordability. Modern patio homes are often sited on irregular lots to concentrate decks at one area within the lot.

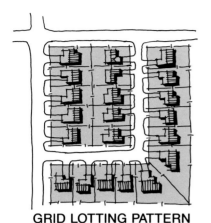

GRID LOTTING PATTERN

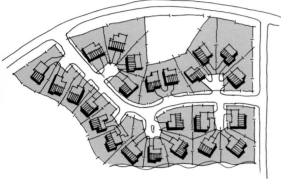

CLUSTER LOTTING PATTERN

■ Versatility in lot design is a popular feature of the patio home. The small, square-shaped houses can work equally well on grid, cluster, or irregularly shaped lots.

Patio units generally range from 900 to 2,000 square feet and can achieve densities of around six units per acre. Due to the popularity of double-car garages, wider lots with less depth are rapidly becoming more common. Interestingly, the wide lot was a salient characteristic of the traditional bungalow homesite.

In terms of entry elevations and curb views, patio homes typically are simply designed, using affordable regional materials with accents or details highlighting the fronts of the units. A covered entry porch is often provided as a hospitable gesture toward the street and sidewalk.

The porch dominated the traditional bungalow. In the patio home design, however, the entry porch has often been reduced or omitted in order to include a garage or a side entrance. Current design thought is reconsidering the "friendly community" impact that the porch projected.

As with most high-density housing products, site planning and interior layout must be strongly integrated. Major room areas adjacent to the outside should be carefully designated to include the rooms used most—living room, kitchen/breakfast room, family room, and master suite. Often, two or three extra deck areas may be provided or op-

■ Typically, the bungalow had a detached garage at the rear of the house, while today's patio home ties the garage into the front elevation. The extensive front porch found on the bungalow is reduced in the contemporary patio home.

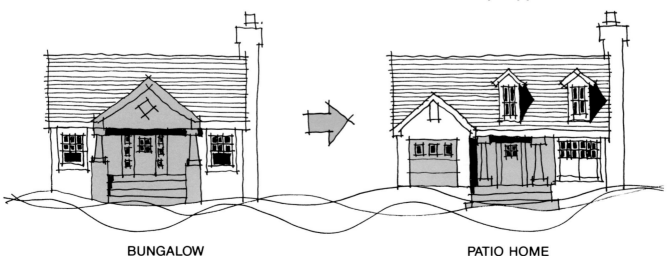

BUNGALOW **PATIO HOME**

tioned to allow a deck off the master suite or guest room/den in addition to the primary deck area.

Space flow between the rooms is again used as a technique to "expand" constrained interior square footage. Spacious ceilings can be used in lieu of extra windows or doors to deck areas. Skylights can increase the sunshine and natural light admitted to interior rooms.

...ATRIUM HOMES

A variation of the patio home that gained tremendous popularity in California during the 1950s was the "atrium home." Designed to have outdoor deck or patio access from most interior rooms, this housing type differed from the bungalow in that the exterior orientation was internalized within the lot.

The atrium home was often built on standard lots with two side yards. Open space was concentrated in a front or rear courtyard with interior rooms facing the courtyard and easily accessible through glass doors. The home thus assumed an L or H shape to expose more exterior wall to the courtyard.

Atrium homes were often sited at densities of four to seven units per acre, depending on the interior program. They were, with a few exceptions, built on one level so that all parts of the home were accessible to the outdoors. Stylistically, they were contemporary, reflecting the influence of simple oriental forms on architecture along the West Coast.

Although seldom built today, the atrium home exhibits design qualities and solutions relevant to current higher-density requirements. Efficient use of the land, an internalized design for maximum privacy, and plentiful access to light and air are elements that remain important both to developers and homebuyers.

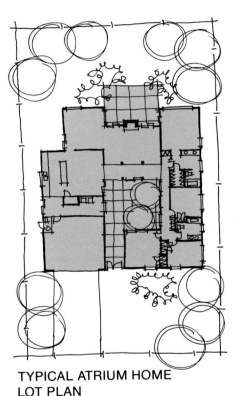

TYPICAL ATRIUM HOME
LOT PLAN

■ Atrium homes were sited on the lot so that the entire perimeter of the house had access to the outdoors. The central atrium became the archetype of the housing style.

FAIRWAY POINTE
MYRTLE BEACH, SOUTH CAROLINA

Victor L. Barr, Jr.

Fairway Pointe was developed in response to the growing need for primary housing in the Myrtle Beach/Grand Strand area. Sited within a larger master-planned golf community called Plantation Pointe, the 24 homes of Fairway Pointe were part of a wide variety of housing products offered within this planned community. Residents were attracted to the project because of its central location and easy access to major highways, as well as to the views and amenities of the Plantation Pointe community.

DEVELOPMENT STRATEGY

The Fairway Pointe site was purchased in early 1982 by the Landing Corporation from the master developer, the Myrtle Beach Farms Company. The overall land plan, architectural concept, and specific home designs were subject to design review by the Farms Company prior to construction.

The developer's objective was to create detached homes ranging from 1,500 to 2,200 square feet that would appeal to the middle-income and upper-end market—primarily young professionals in the move-up market. Three model units were constructed on sites adjacent to the primary entrance to Plantation Pointe to stimulate presales of the balance of the lots. This was the low-risk alternative that was considered preferable to building a large speculative inventory that would need to be carried through fluctuations in market demand and interest rates. After the models were completed, the remaining lots were presold with specific design revisions. Working with the architect's design concept drawings, the builder allowed extensive modifications according to buyer preference, while maintaining the original architectural style and consistent use of exterior materials and colors.

■ **The generous deck, porch, and patio areas typical at the rear of the houses provide ample outdoor space for enjoying views of the adjacent golf course.**

Victor L. Barr, Jr., AIA, is a principal at The Martin Organization, Architects and Land Planners. Based in Philadelphia with regional offices nationwide, the firm is the country's 24th largest planning and design firm. Barr specializes in low- and high-rise residential development, with projects ranging from high-density, first-time-buyer communities to destination resort facilities.

SITE

The 8.9-acre site is basically level and ideally suited for development. Existing trees were abundant enough to provide an attractive natural setting without constraining lot placement or generating controversial preservation issues. The parcel is bordered by the second fairway on the east and a small lake to the north, providing several lots with prime views. Access to the site is available from the other boundaries, with the primary entrance being off Arundel Drive to the south.

PLANNING

The site concept was to create irregularly shaped lots with the houses oriented off parking "courts." A private street connecting Arundel Drive to Fairway Drive permitted easy access through the site. Lots were platted based on standard footprints developed for the floor plans, and provided a varied street view of homes clustered near the parking courts.

The decision to provide grade-level parking instead of enclosed garages was based on several factors. One was the desire to reduce construction costs and, ultimately, sales prices. Although outdoor parking would not be feasible in harsher climates, the mild temperatures of South Carolina diminish market demand for the enclosed garage.

Second, no matter how artfully handled, garages have a negative effect on streetscapes, and driveways require additional paving throughout the site. Finally, the parking court solution allowed the architect to incorporate generous windows and decks for the entire perimeter of each home.

Although the garage is omitted, each floor plan has an exterior storage area that typically faces a side yard. In later stages of Fairway Pointe's development, sales contracts for some lots included permission to build with garages, but this option was not widely exercised.

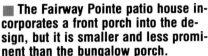 **The Fairway Pointe patio house incorporates a front porch into the design, but it is smaller and less prominent than the bungalow porch.**

ARCHITECTURE

The three models at Fairway Pointe have two or three bedrooms; all three have strong front/rear orientations for interior rooms, with two or sometimes three extensive decks provided. Large entry porches at the front of the houses face the street—a traditional feature found in cottages and bungalows throughout the "low country" of the Carolina coasts.

Units have low-pitched roofs with gables accenting the porch areas. The primary exterior material is stucco, with approved color gradations of light tones of buff, clay, and rose occurring between units to add

Some of the build-to-suit houses incorporated garages that effectively eliminated porches or deck areas at the front of the houses. Extensive rear or side yard decks were maintained throughout the building program.

MODEL A—1,500 SQUARE FEET

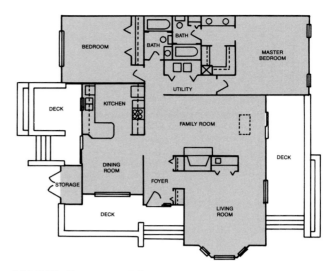

MODEL B—1,850 SQUARE FEET

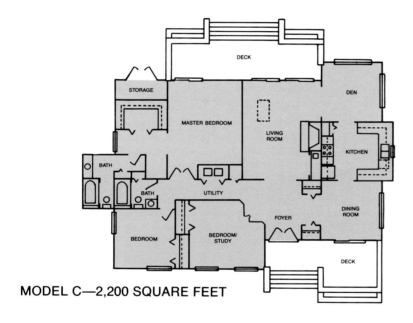

MODEL C—2,200 SQUARE FEET

■ **Ranging from 1,500 to 2,200 square feet, the three original models featured: all single-level plans, a covered front porch and extensive deck areas easily reached from inside the house; free-flowing rooms designed for informal living; skylights and extensive use of windows; and outdoor storage rooms to substitute for the lack of garage storage space. Fairway Pointe evolved into a build-to-suit program following construction of the first six houses but the qualities inherent in the patio home concept remained intact.**

variety to the street scene. Stucco is accented by wood trim and lattices stained with compatible colors. The objective was to evoke an informal architectural style with materials and detailing that are indigenous to the area.

Interiors are made more "expansive" through unrestricted circulation and informally defined living, dining, and kitchen areas. Volume ceilings reinforce the light, open quality of the interiors.

MARKETING STRATEGY

Fairway Pointe was conceived as primary housing developed for the local market. Thus, advertising was concentrated in the local newspaper and magazines, along with billboard advertisements near the site or gateway routes throughout the area. One of the three models was decorated and staffed for visitor traffic.

The advertising campaign stressed the lifestyle issues associated with the golf and country club image inherent at Plantation Pointe. Lots were priced according to the desirability of views, privacy, and access. Prices ranged from $34,500 to $59,900 for individual fee-simple lots. Agreements of sale carried the restriction that construction must begin within one year of purchase. This alleviated the problem of speculation, or holdouts that would stall buildout of the community.

Club privileges were not included in the sales price or homeowner fee; however, membership was available at the semiprivate course. Each owner is responsible for the maintenance and care of his or her individual grounds and structure, with the homeowner association responsible only for the common entrance area and roadways.

Sales began in late 1983 and lots were sold at an average rate of eight per year; buyers were all in the primary market.

■ **Located on irregularly shaped lots averaging over 12,000 square feet, the 24 houses of Fairway Pointe achieve a gross density of only 2.6 units per acre. When land costs dictate a higher yield, the patio home concept can provide densities of more than six units per acre. Fairway Pointe's use of "parking courts" instead of attached garages allowed windows and decks to be placed around the entire perimeter of the houses.**

PROJECT DATA

LAND USE INFORMATION:
Site Area: 8.9 acres
Total Units: 24
Gross Density: 2.6 units per acre
Parking Spaces: 48
Parking Index: 2 spaces per unit at grade

UNIT INFORMATION[1]:

Type	Original Program	Square Feet	Sales Price
A	2-bdrm./2-bath	1,500	$137,900
B	2-bdrm./2-bath/family	1,850	142,900
C	3-bdrm./2-bath/den	2,200	152,900

ECONOMIC INFORMATION:
Site Value: $624,000[2]
Site Improvement Costs: $168,000[3]
Construction Costs: Approximately $1,430,000[4]
Homeowner Fee: $170 per year
Amenities: A pool site has been reserved. It will be built if 75 percent of the homeowner membership votes to build it and assume its maintenance.

Notes:
[1]Unit information is for original sales program. The project evolved into a build-to-suit program after construction of the first six homes. All units in the original program are single-level with attached, exterior storage areas.
[2]$26,000 per unit.
[3]$7,000 per unit.
[4]$35 per heated square foot.

DIRECTIONS:
From the Myrtle Beach Jetport, take Route 17 Bypass north and continue for about eight miles to the Plantation Pointe community, which will be on the left. Turn left into Plantation Pointe and travel approximately .25 mile to Fairway Pointe entrance on the right.

DEVELOPER:
Landing Corporation
1107 48th Avenue North
Suite 110
Myrtle Beach, South Carolina 29577

ARCHITECT/PLANNER:
The Martin Organization
242 North 22nd Street
Philadelphia, Pennsylvania 19103

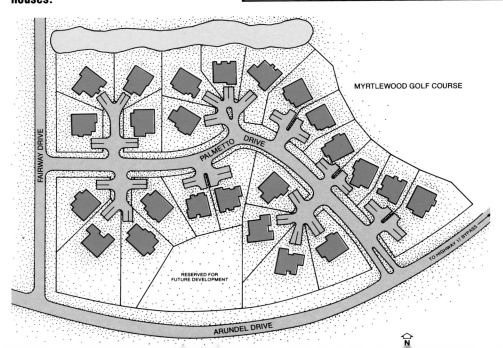

EICHLER HOMES
SAN FRANCISCO BAY, CALIFORNIA

Jack B. W. Ken

I n the postwar era of the 1940s, Joseph Eichler, a food broker turned real estate developer, was convinced that low-cost, mass-produced housing could be developed that would be different from the California styles prevailing at the time. In 1948, he saw the work of Anshen & Allen, Architects, and commissioned the firm to develop a new housing prototype to meet his

Jack B.W. Ken., *AIA, is a principal at Anshen + Allen Architects of San Francisco, California, where he serves as principal-in-charge of housing projects for the elderly. Ken is the 1988 vice chairman, and the 1989 chairman-elect, of the National AIA Housing Committee; a commissioner on the California State Board of Architectural Examiners; and, a representative on the ACSA/AIA Council on Architectural Research.*

objectives. Working with Eichler over a productive period that lasted 12 years, Anshen & Allen (and later the firms of Jones and Emmons, and Claude Oakland, FAIA) developed more than 1,000 design variations.

The basic design principles that led to the final central atrium concept for all prototype houses were as follows:

- Family-oriented living spaces.
- Private outdoor spaces off major rooms.
- Ease of access to outdoor patios or decks.
- Design for year-round climate and enjoyment of outdoors.
- Full use of the site through landscaped access.
- Natural wood finishes throughout the house, interior and exterior.
- On-grade radiant heat within the concrete floor slab.

Ernest Braun

■ **In the Eichler Homes prototype, generous use of glass walls and sliding doors "extends" the indoor living area into the private outdoor space. Four-foot roof overhangs provide shade for interiors. Rear yard areas emphasize privacy and landscape design; common yard features include raised planter boxes, barbecue pits, decorative ponds, and benches.**

Although initially a variety of house plans and exterior treatments was offered, eventually the basic features and prices became fairly uniform. All models offered three bedrooms and two baths, with a spacious open living/dining room and informal family room/kitchen area of exposed redwood construction. Also included were a two-car garage, brick fireplace, radiant heating, and a glass-walled living area that was oriented toward an internal courtyard. Houses averaged 1,200 square feet, exclusive of the garage, and sold for $11,950 to $13,000 in the mid-1950s.

Between 1947 and 1963, when Eichler Homes were being constructed, there was an abundance of low-cost agricultural land adjacent to neighboring cities. While the predominant subdivision layout was a gridiron pattern, Eichler's units were often planned on circular and curvilinear streets with different sizes and shapes of lots to create variety in the streetscape. With assistance from community authorities, vehicular traffic movement was slowed through the area.

The permitted density for each community varied, even within the same tract. The Eichler atrium house was designed typically to fit within a 7,000-square-foot lot, which yielded a density of five units per acre. A lot size of 5,000 square feet was also used (yielding eight units per acre) but required a different

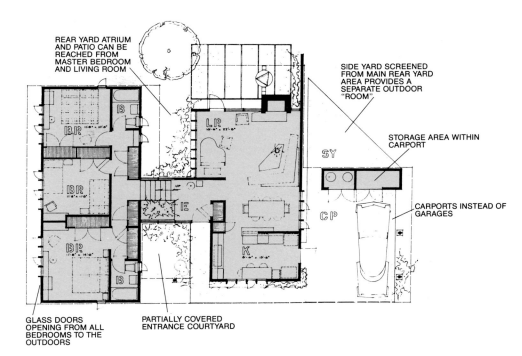

REAR YARD ATRIUM AND PATIO CAN BE REACHED FROM MASTER BEDROOM AND LIVING ROOM

SIDE YARD SCREENED FROM MAIN REAR YARD AREA PROVIDES A SEPARATE OUTDOOR "ROOM"

STORAGE AREA WITHIN CARPORT

CARPORTS INSTEAD OF GARAGES

GLASS DOORS OPENING FROM ALL BEDROOMS TO THE OUTDOORS

PARTIALLY COVERED ENTRANCE COURTYARD

■ **Early Eichler Homes featured a modified version of the central atrium with a deeply recessed entrance courtyard and private rear yard patio. In this model, the sleeping and living areas of the house are defined by the outdoor space and the split-level design.**

■ **Rooms within this inward-looking house share views to the central atrium. This larger floor plan features four bedrooms (rather than the typical three), two baths, and a large storage and laundry area next to the garage. The sleeping area is separated from the living quarters and the living room is located in a traffic-free corner of the house.**

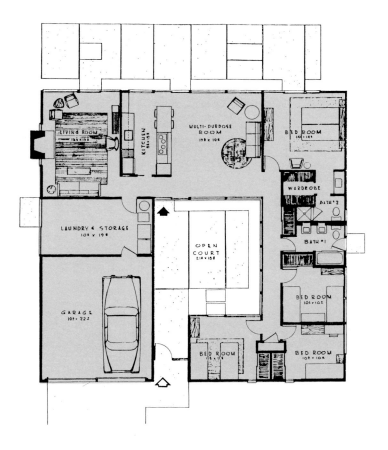

27

■ The glass walls and central atrium allow views through the house, creating a sense of spaciousness—even where space is limited. Typical floor plans average only 1,200 square feet and include three bedrooms and two baths.

shape for the house. With the abundance of available land, the zero-lot-line concept was not yet a viable (or needed) alternative during the postwar era.

Following the completion and occupancy of each tract, an evaluation questionnaire was sent to each new homeowner soliciting input so that the architect could improve the future design of the house. As a result of the information received from these questionnaires, further innovations were conceived: more patios; a mudroom entrance to the second bath; washer/dryer space in the sleeping area; compartmented baths; walk-in closets in the master bedroom; sliding glass doors to garden patios from any room; built-in, rotating, expandable kitchen tables; hobby rooms; and a combination garage and carport.

In 1956, the first Eichler central patio house was constructed in San Mateo, California. By combining all the previous design attributes of the patio home and by adding a central atrium, it became known as the "atrium house." The perfect response to the moderate climate of California, it offered outdoor living in a completely private interior patio fully enclosed by the house. Furthermore, it invited relaxed, outdoor dining and other activities even on the chilly, windy days that made unprotected patios unusable.

The design includes a front atrium, which acts as an entrance garden court and transition area

■ Rich interior features like ceramic or cork tile floors, mahogany paneling, and wood ceilings characterize the Eichler Home. Ten-foot ceilings are common, although some designs feature vaulted ceilings. In their design and decor, the houses stress simplicity, clean lines, and comfort.

from outdoors to indoors. A four-foot-deep overhang shelters the entry walk. A pushbutton release from the entrance hall in the center of the house unlocks the street door into the atrium. A minimum of three rooms open into the central atrium. With glass walls, each room shares the light, the air, and the garden view. This design continues throughout, permitting additional rooms to open onto other outdoor areas, thereby turning the entire lot into a livable, landscaped space accessible from every room.

All of the attributes and functions of the atrium houses are as applicable today as they were 30 years ago. The atrium home can be adapted to meet adult-oriented lifestyles. Children's bedrooms can be converted to library/dens, sewing rooms, or guest rooms, all with access to outdoor spaces. The atrium can become a vestibule-lobby for the new, more formal lifestyles of its occupants. The kitchen is as efficient as any present-day model, and the general ease of access protects older people as they move about.

The atrium house can grow with its occupants, unfold its benefits over time, and retain its integrity through its structure and well-studied layout. Although its original features may not address all the new demands of today's housing needs, they have the potential to be modified for current markets, while still retaining the unique qualities that define the atrium house.

EXTENSIVELY LANDSCAPED REAR YARD FOR MAXIMUM USE OF SPACE

5-FOOT SIDE YARD

CENTRAL ATRIUM SERVES AS AN ENTRANCE COURT AND IS VISIBLE FROM MOST INTERIOR ROOMS

8- TO 10-FOOT SIDE YARD

GARAGE IS PULLED INTO THE HOUSE STRUCTURE, MAKING IT LESS PROMINENT FROM THE STREET

GENEROUS LANDSCAPED FRONT YARD PROVIDES STREET APPEAL

STREET

PLOT PLAN

■ Typical lots averaged 7,000 square feet, but some houses were built on lots as small as 5,000 square feet. Although not appropriate for its time, the atrium home concept could have achieved a much higher density with a zero-side-yard approach and a reduced front yard setback. The placement of the garage reduced its visibility from the street.

Editors' Note: Unlike the other case study projects, the Eichler Homes are not being built in the 1980s but represent a popular regional housing form from the post–World War II era that is worthy of reconsideration today.

From Cottages to...

The small, detached home has always been a popular type of affordable housing. Testifying to this was the mail-order component housing produced by Sears and shipped by rail to sites throughout the country from 1908 to 1940. Mass-production techniques allowed custom detailing to be manufactured on a large scale at affordable prices.

The "cottage"-style house was affordable to middle-income buyers. Like the bungalow, it was pleasantly detailed; however, the architecture was more diverse. Victorian, Tudor, Italianate, or other ornamental styles were applied according to the region and the economics of construction. Although many cottages had single levels, full second floors were also common. In general, the cottage was designed for more diverse climates than the bungalow and therefore emphasized fewer outdoor porches and decks.

...SMALL-LOT SINGLES

The contemporary small-lot single retains the regional styling and craftsmanship of the cottage's exterior while the interior has been greatly modified. Small-lot singles are generally planned for 5,000- to 10,000-square-foot lots with frontages varying from 45 to 75 feet. Unit sizes range from 900 to 1,500 square feet and may include two-car garages. Generally, these homes have traditional front/rear orientations with two small side yards used primarily to admit light into secondary rooms.

From the curb view, elevations of small-lot singles are most affected by garage treatments. In a minority of wide-lot or corner-lot situations the garage may be entered from the side. The impact of a front-loaded garage must be mitigated architecturally; by pulling the garage into the lot away from the street, the streetscape is vastly improved. This may force some room areas to a second-level location over the garage, further softening the garage's effect on the street.

Entry doors in small-lot singles are most often in the true "front" of the house with symmetrical elevations common. In view of the typical front/rear orientation, the conflict between the entrance to the house and the garage can be resolved by ensuring that the home's front wall facing the street is flush with or in front of the garage. Porches are usually covered.

Two-story plans are more likely to be found in small single prototypes, where lot footprints are tight. In contrast to the single-level

■ **The small-lot single offers the affordability and architectural details found in the cottage. Second stories and garages on the front elevation are contemporary modifications to the cottage theme.**

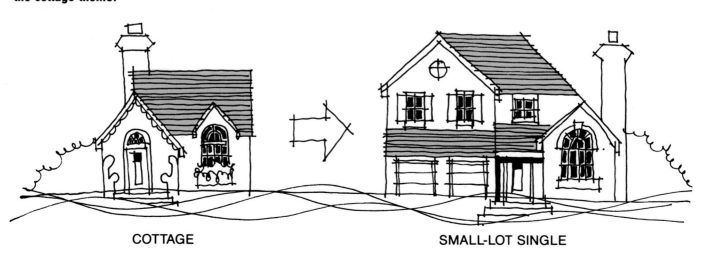

COTTAGE

SMALL-LOT SINGLE

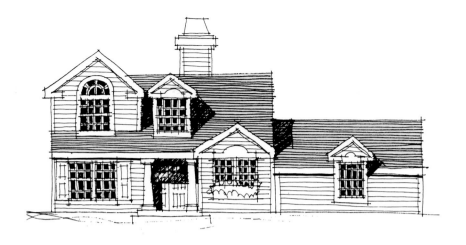

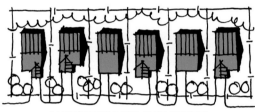

The front elevation of the small-lot single is often highly articulated to give a pleasant appearance from the street. Where the lot layout will permit, a side entrance to the garage can further enhance the streetscape.

NARROW-LOT CONCEPT

WIDE-LOT CONCEPT

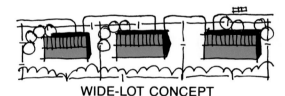

The wide-lot concept has been used to lessen the prominence of the garage and to improve the streetscape.

patio home, the small-lot single may be more internally focused, reflecting a less temperate climate. The small-lot single's bilevel design allows volume space to be integrated with upper-level rooms in the form of lofts, overlooks, and open balconies.

...WIDE-LOT SINGLES

Within the density range of small-lot singles, the current debate centers around the narrow-lot versus the wide-lot choice. With the popularity of narrow-lot homes increased by zero-lot designs, which call for less front footage and therefore lower land costs, major concerns have arisen over the impact these designs will have on the streetscape. While admittedly the wide-frontage/narrow-depth alternative loses some density and increases site improvement costs somewhat, the trade-off—an improved curb view of the home—may prove worth it. As a design choice, it is gaining momentum.

...CLUSTER HOMES

Cluster housing has emerged as a middle ground in the "lot size" debate by breaking the traditional street-to-house relationship. Organized around a court or cul-de-sac, detached homes can be spaced closely together while preserving unit individuality and privacy. Interior design of the units can be coordinated to alternate the orientations of units and thus maintain privacy of outdoor spaces regardless of their proximity.

CLUSTER-LOT CONCEPT

The cluster arrangement has emerged as a popular lotting choice for the small-lot single because of the privacy, density, and sensitive treatment of the site that can be achieved.

WESTGREEN
LEESBURG, VIRGINIA

Jeanne Whyte

L eesburg, Virginia, has honored
its architectural heritage of the
1700s with careful planning
and attention to its historical district. This district encompasses a
commercial area along the original
main street and a beautifully preserved residential area surrounding
the old downtown. By acquiring a
parcel integrated with such an
amenity, developer Brownell, Inc.,
had an excellent opportunity to
create an in-town, higher-density
residential community within convenient walking distance of the historical business district and professional locations.

*Jeanne Whyte, AIA, is president of Al-
ternative Building and Design, a de-
sign/build company based in Leesburg,
Virginia, specializing in custom home
design and construction. She is a member of the National AIA Housing
Committee.*

DEVELOPMENT STRATEGY AND APPROVALS

The zoning designation assigned
to the site when purchased was
suitable for planning 17 residential
R-1 lots, each with its own access to
the street. A plan conforming to this
arrangement was submitted immediately to the town for its review.
Subsequently, a more appropriate
plan, with only one street entrance
and common driveways, was submitted to the zoning board and highway
departments for comparison.

Although the zoning board and
neighboring residents objected
strongly to a high-density project of
any kind on the parcel, they found
the plan indicating one entranceway
superior to a plan that would inter-
rupt the already busy residential
streets bounding the property with
17 new curb cuts. However, the idea
of a denuded site with a collection

■ **Features such as front porches,
steep cedar shake roofs, clapboard
wood siding, and decorative window
treatments create the Victorian architectural character of the project.
Large, contiguous areas of open
space help to reduce the appearance
of density.**

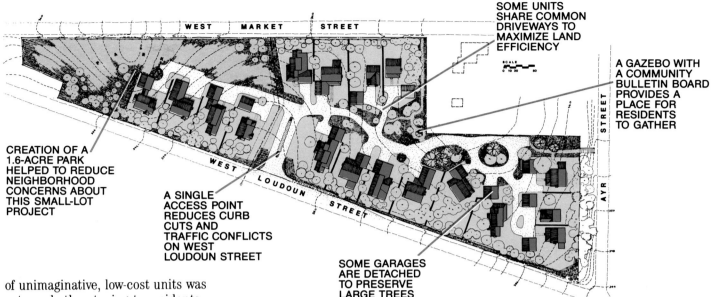

WEST MARKET STREET

SOME UNITS
SHARE COMMON
DRIVEWAYS TO
MAXIMIZE LAND
EFFICIENCY

A GAZEBO WITH
A COMMUNITY
BULLETIN BOARD
PROVIDES A
PLACE FOR
RESIDENTS
TO GATHER

CREATION OF A
1.6-ACRE PARK
HELPED TO REDUCE
NEIGHBORHOOD
CONCERNS ABOUT
THIS SMALL-LOT
PROJECT

A SINGLE
ACCESS POINT
REDUCES CURB
CUTS AND
TRAFFIC CONFLICTS
ON WEST
LOUDOUN STREET

WEST LOUDOUN STREET

AYR STREET

SOME GARAGES
ARE DETACHED
TO PRESERVE
LARGE TREES

of unimaginative, low-cost units was extremely threatening to residents after they had spent years protecting and preserving their valuable setting. Neighbors raised heated objections at each of several zoning board hearings, based upon fears of the impact of any development near their authentic, carefully maintained Victorian homes.

A series of town planning commission meetings eventually led to the Westgreen project's approval. The concerns of neighboring homeowners subsided when the developer agreed to erect a brick wall, similar to those on their own properties, as a buffer to seclude the small-lot development from the larger homes. The developer would also continue the town sidewalk along all property lines. As this spirit of cooperation grew, the project was gradually accepted.

SITE

The 4.07-acre, triangular site slopes down gently to the east, where a 10-foot grade change provides a natural buffer from the road. Natural landscaping includes many well-established, sizable trees. To maximize the potential of the existing vegetation and topography, the developer and the planner decided to site-locate all trees larger than

two inches in diameter, and plan development around them. This site-sensitive planning resulted in a single-family detached housing program, rather than townhouses, which the developer initially had planned.

Following the location of the trees, house and garage sites were selected within groves, and lot lines were planned schematically for presentation to the site engineers. The final site plan was developed within the same careful guidelines.

PLANNING

Much thoughtful planning and design followed in order to alleviate the concerns of residents in the immediate neighborhood. Lots were designed with more emphasis placed on individual lot characteristics and on preserving existing vegetation than on achieving a minimal size. Lot lines were created after, rather than before (as is customary), the homes were located. This resulted in slightly less common area, but allowed a generous amount of continuous green space that was well within the requirements of town ordinances. An economical density of more than six

■ Typical lots average 6,000 square feet—small by the standards of Leesburg, Virginia, the historic town in which the project is located. Neighborhood concerns about density were alleviated by the creation of a 1.6-acre park, construction of a brick wall surrounding the project, and the preservation of all mature trees on the site. Houses were located so that trees would not have to be removed, and lot lines were then platted.

dwelling units per acre (net) was achieved, and a common private drive was planned as a single entrance to the property, thus eliminating the 17 separate driveway cuts originally allowed in the town plan.

Pathways were designed to provide convenient access points to town sidewalks, and a gazebo was located where neighbors could check the community bulletin board or meet before walking downtown. A combination of split-rail fencing and a brick wall surrounding the perim-

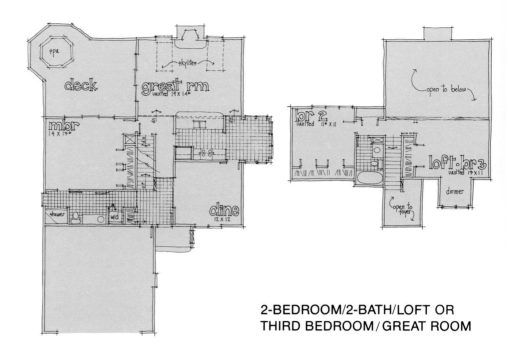

2-BEDROOM/2-BATH/LOFT OR
THIRD BEDROOM/GREAT ROOM

3-BEDROOM/2-BATH

■ **Houses in Westgreen range from 1,100 square feet to 1,400 square feet (without basements) and were targeted for both the young professional and empty-nester markets. Buyers could personalize their houses by selecting from several floor plans; for example, one buyer might select a great room while another might choose a more traditional formal living and dining room. Participation in choosing floor plans and exterior architectural treatments contributed to a high level of buyer satisfaction.**

eter of the site defined the neighborhood and created a sense of privacy. At the western portion of the site, a 1.6-acre park of existing trees and grass was designated for the use of both Westgreen and Leesburg residents.

ARCHITECTURE

The desired unit mix was a combination of one- and two-story houses, with 1,100 to 1,400 square feet of living space. One- and two-car garages were offered as either attached or detached; rear screened porches and wood decks were upgrade options. To blend with the historical setting, a Victorian character was sought. This was achieved through the use of generous front

porches with railings, clapboard wood siding with contrasting trim, double hung and decorative windows, and the integration of gables and dormers in the steep roofs. Cedar shake roofs enhance the project's look of quality and endurance.

While the exterior appearance is traditional, contemporary openness and versatility characterize interiors of the three-bedroom, two-bath houses. Efficient working kitchens containing eating nooks are provided, and buyers may choose be-

tween a formal living room/dining room, or a combination of these in a great room. Also optional are vaulted ceilings with "look-over" lofts. Two plans cater to mature homeowners with master suites and laundry facilities on the first floor. Careful siting of the houses works with the architecture to promote indoor/outdoor integration and thus extend the "living" space.

As each lot was reserved and a plan chosen, homeowners were encouraged to participate in the final design by tailoring plans to their individual needs. Although a specific palette of approved exterior colors was offered, owners could select colors and finishes according to their own tastes. Thus, each dwelling has its own distinct personality. The builder's foresight in permitting such diversity proved a key factor in achieving a genuine Victorian flavor. And by being involved in the design process, homeowners gained a sense of pride.

MARKETING

Working professionals, retirees, and empty nesters who want to live in a secure and exclusive neighborhood were the target market. Leesburg itself attracts this population, and Westgreen's proximity to this historic town added to the project's appeal.

To mitigate financing, cash flow, and delivery commitment problems, the development plan was structured in two phases. Every lot in the first phase was sold during the first weekend of the offering. Phase II sold out during the second year with very minimal advertising, in spite of price increases ranging from $15,000 to $25,000 per unit.

The Westgreen community demonstrates the successful adaptation of a high-density, small detached home development to an early American setting. Careful design and planning and responsiveness to community concerns effectively allayed the fears of Leesburg's history-sensitive population.

■ **Although houses are sometimes spaced closely, Westgreen achieves the traditional style popular in this historic Virginia town. The preservation of mature trees and the limited use of concrete curbing give the project an established, rural look.**

PROJECT DATA

LAND USE INFORMATION:
Site Area: 4.07 acres[1]
Net Lot Area: 2.47 acres
Total Units: 17
Density: 4.2 units per acre (gross)
　　　　6.9 units per acre (net)
Parking Index: garage plus 2 spaces per unit
Unit Types: 3-bedroom/2-bath

UNIT INFORMATION:

Square Feet[2]	Number Built[3]	Base Price
1,100	5	$108,500
1,100	2	$119,500
1,400	6	$122,500
1,100	2	$119,500

ECONOMIC INFORMATION:
Land Cost: $200,000
Site Improvement Cost: $72,500
Construction Cost: $70 per square foot
Homeowner Fee: $20 per month

Notes:
[1]Includes 1.6 acres of green space and park.
[2]Excludes finished basements.
[3]Two additional custom homes were built.

DIRECTIONS:
From Dulles International Airport, travel north on Route 28, then west on Route 7 to Leesburg. Bear left on Loudoun Street and continue to Westgreen, which will be on the right.

DEVELOPER:
Brownell, Inc.
203-R Harrison Street, S.E.
Leesburg, Virginia 22075

BUILDER:
Brownell, Inc., and
Alternative Building and Design, Inc.
P.O. Box 1351
Leesburg, Virginia 22075

ARCHITECTS/PLANNERS:
Kevin Reudisueli, AIA, and
Jeanne Whyte, AIA
Alternative Building and Design, Inc.
16 West Market Street
Leesburg, Virginia 22075

John Bare

BARCELONA IN WESTPARK
IRVINE, CALIFORNIA

Arthur C. Danielian

The wide-and-shallow-lot configuration is a recent variation of the zero-lot-line concept. Wide-lot homes actually are modern versions—set on smaller lots—of the single-family housing that was developed throughout the United States shortly after World War II.

The "wide-lot single" provides a viable solution to the problem of detached housing that is affordable, especially for young families in areas where high land costs prevail. These homes offer the conventional single-family style desired by so many Americans, with higher densities made more acceptable through innovative planning that provides more usable yard space and increased privacy on a smaller lot.

The wide-lot concept calls for frontages ranging from 60 to 70 feet, with depths from 55 to 80 feet. Density yields generally range from six to eight units per acre. In contrast to the more frequently used zero-lot-line homes on narrow, deep lots, the wide-lot concept provides a more impressive and attractive appearance from the street at approximately the same density. This was a primary objective in developing the Barcelona project in Westpark, one of the first wide-lot projects in the United States.

DEVELOPMENT STRATEGY

Barcelona in Westpark is an integral component of the master-planned community (or "village") of Westpark, located in the city of Irvine. Westpark includes 833 acres,

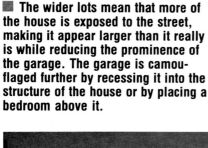

The wider lots mean that more of the house is exposed to the street, making it appear larger than it really is while reducing the prominence of the garage. The garage is camouflaged further by recessing it into the structure of the house or by placing a bedroom above it.

Arthur C. Danielian, FAIA, is president of Danielian Associates, an architectural and planning firm in Irvine, California, that has been active in a wide range of projects with major emphasis on residential designs and land planning services. The firm has received numerous design awards. Danielian is past chairman of the National AIA Housing Committee and serves on a Residential Development Council of the Urban Land Institute.

John Bare

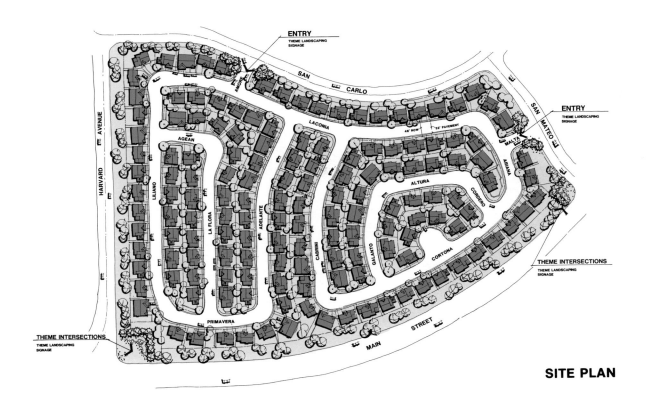

SITE PLAN

LOT DIAGRAM

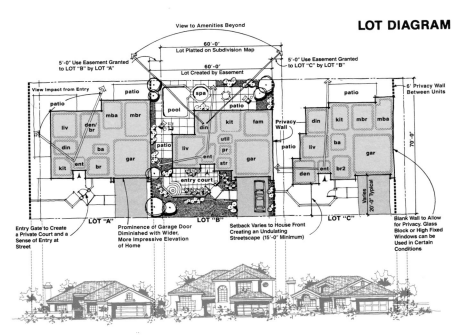

High land costs in Irvine's newest village of Westpark, combined with a strong market demand for detached houses, led to this wide-lot concept that attained 7.8 units per acre on a 19.3-acre site. Although lots generally are 57 feet wide by 55 feet deep and total just over 3,100 square feet, the street view suggests that both the house and lot are larger. The wider lot makes the garage less prominent than it would be with the typical 45-foot-wide zero-lot-line house, and it allows for a stronger, more traditional street elevation. The trade-off is a shallow back yard (only 30 feet between some back-to-back units) and slightly increased infrastructure costs that added about $1,500 to the cost of each house in the Barcelona project.

with more than 4,300 residential units in approximately 12 product types. When completed in 1992, the project is anticipated to have 12,000 residents.

With raw land costs approaching $500,000 per acre, density yield became an important factor in planning and determining the product for Westpark. The wide-lot concept

at Barcelona allowed increased densities with lots that were substantially wider (57 feet, as opposed to 40 to 50 feet) than those of competing detached housing programs in Westpark. The resulting increase in aesthetic appeal significantly boosted the marketing advantages for Barcelona's developer, the Bren Company.

A comprehensive community design guideline provided by the Irvine Company (Westpark's developer) also affected development plans. It established the contemporary Mediterranean motif, as well as the overall landscape and signage themes.

■ Generous windows, high ceilings, light colors, and rounded corners on drywall are interior features that give the houses a more spacious look.

SITE AND PLANNING

The Barcelona site covers 19.3 level acres and is served by two entranceways. Its enhanced landscape and signage treatment is consistent with entrance treatments throughout Westpark.

The site plan yields a net density of 7.8 units per acre, based on a minimum lot size of 57 feet by 55 feet (or 3,135 square feet). All roads within the property are dedicated—with a standard paved width of 32 feet—are double-loaded (that is, houses front on both sides of the streets), and allow parking on both sides.

The wide-lot concept diminishes the exposure of garages to the streetscape. On a typical narrow lot (40 feet wide with a 30-foot-wide house), the garage accounts for approximately 66 percent of the architectural exposure. On a Barcelona lot (57 feet wide with a 47-foot-wide house), the garage accounts for only 42 percent of the architectural exposure. Thus, the house itself is emphasized, making a more desirable architectural statement from the street.

This benefit is not without cost. The wider lot requires that the infrastructure for each lot be 30 percent longer, which adds approximately $1,500 to the base price of the unit. But the developer can compensate for this increase through increased absorption rates and the buyer's willingness to pay more for these houses than for typical narrow zero-lot-line homes of comparable square footage.

The wide-and-shallow lot brings other benefits. A lot deeper than 75 feet allows parking for up to six cars per unit—two in the garage, two in the driveway, and, in most cases, two in the street. Combined with the double-loading of the 32-foot-wide street at Barcelona, the wide-lot concept greatly alleviates parking and traffic flow problems experi-

Eric Figge

enced with plans that rely on narrow lots and streets.

On each lot, usable outdoor space is concentrated in both the rear yard and the 10-foot-wide side yard. A blank or windowless side wall from the neighboring unit safeguards privacy. With the shallower rear yards and homes that are back-to-back, less distance exists between units—in some cases, only 30 feet. To alleviate privacy problems, the number of second-story windows facing the rear is minimized in favor of side- or street-facing exposures. Windows in baths are designed with high sills to ensure privacy. Special treatments or options, such as awnings or sloped Bermuda louvers, further protect privacy.

Wide-lot programs should include prominently landscaped front yards—another important design benefit. The 10- to 20-foot front setback is landscaped imaginatively to enhance the curb view. Builders contemplating this type of design plan are advised to include a complete landscape package for front yards as part of the sales price. Maintenance can be transferred to the homebuyers after they move in.

ARCHITECTURE

The Barcelona models were targeted primarily to young couples and families. Four floor plans were offered, ranging from 1,253 to 1,880 square feet. Only the smallest plan is one story, and all plans include three bedrooms and two and one-half baths; the third bedroom is designed to convert to a den. Larger plans feature family rooms on the first level; all bedrooms are located on the second level.

At the entry, initial views travel diagonal sight lines through the home and out to the rear and/or to the side yard, creating a feeling of expansiveness that is complemented with: high ceilings created by scissor trusses; higher than normal plates; and eight-foot-high sliding doors. A fluid circulation pattern, light colors, and an abundance of light introduced through generous windows combine to make the house seem larger and more luxurious. Distinctive details, such as plant niches and rounded corners on drywall, infuse these modestly priced homes with a tone of superior quality.

Articulated stucco exteriors with barrel roof tiles project the image of California architecture, taking on color and animation from the generous use of decorative glazing. Exterior colors are in pastel shades, accented with deeper tones in selected recessed areas.

MARKETING

Proper presentation of models of the wide-and-shallow-lot house is an important factor in its sales success. Innovative landscaping is particularly important, especially for the shallow rear yards. Lap pools, rather than standard pools; raised planters; and trellises and mature trees that offer shade and privacy are typical features that can be used

John Bare

■ **The wide-lot program requires shallow back yards if a density of nearly eight units per acre is achieved. Still, these wide yards leave room for a spa, patio, and landscaping. Special care must be taken during design to ensure privacy between back-to-back units.**

SECOND FLOOR

■ **All floor plans are designed for the primary market—young professionals, young married couples, and growing families.**

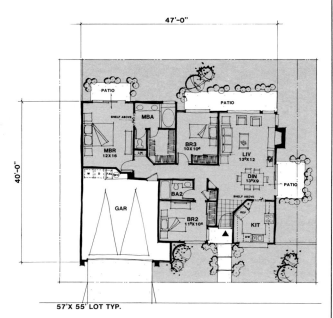

57'X 55' LOT TYP.

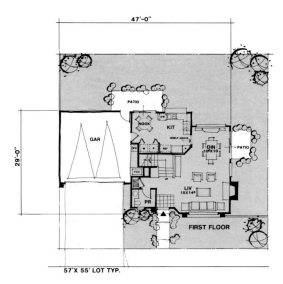

FIRST FLOOR

57'X 55' LOT TYP.

PLAN 1—1,253 SQUARE FEET
3-BEDROOM/2-BATH/SINGLE LEVEL

PLAN 2—1,514 SQUARE FEET
3-BEDROOM/2½-BATH/BREAKFAST NOOK

PLAN 3—1,779 SQUARE FEET
3-BEDROOM/2½-BATH/FAMILY ROOM

PLAN 4—1,880 SQUARE FEET
3-BEDROOM/2½-BATH/BREAKFAST NOOK/FAMILY ROOM

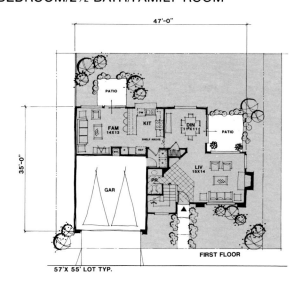

FIRST FLOOR

57'X 55' LOT TYP.

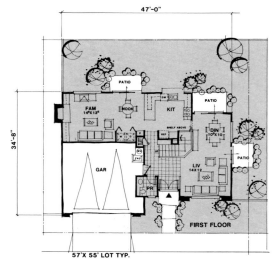

FIRST FLOOR

57'X 55' LOT TYP.

SECOND FLOOR

SECOND FLOOR

to show buyers that their investment in wide-lot housing is a wise one.

The small rear yards at Barcelona were accepted as a palatable trade-off for the many positive aspects of the architectural design, planning, and close location to work centers. Prospective buyers were very favorably impressed by the streetscape view of the Barcelona homes; nearly all visitors registered surprise at the modesty of the actual square footages, and all were pleased with the large and substantial appearance achieved by the architect/planner.

All floor plans received high marks for being both aesthetically pleasing and extremely workable. The only negative comment concerned the absence of a family room in the 1,514-square-foot plan, which buyers in the target market would have preferred.

Marketing efforts were formulated by a project team that included professional consultants in architecture, planning, interior design, landscape architecture, and sales office design, as well as in marketing. Buyer response was immediately favorable, and Barcelona quickly became one of the fastest-selling projects in Irvine. This success has been sustained through the project's succession of construction phases.

PROJECT DATA

LAND USE INFORMATION:
Site Area: 19.3 acres
Total Units: 150
Density: 7.8 units per acre
Parking Spaces: 300
Parking Index: up to 6 spaces per unit

UNIT INFORMATION[1]:

Types	Square Feet	Number	Base Prices
3-bdrm./2-bath	1,253	18	$162,990
3-bdrm./2½-bath	1,514	43	$194,990
3-bdrm./2½-bath	1,779	42	$203,990
3-bdrm./2½-bath	1,880	47	$218,990

ECONOMIC INFORMATION:
Land Cost: $10,950,000[2]
Site Improvement Costs: $3,600,000[3]
Construction Costs: $39 per square foot
Average Home Sales Value: $183,000
Homeowner Fee: $42.50 per month

Notes:
[1] Each unit has attached, two-car garage.
[2] This figure is based on the architect's estimate of $73,000 per lot.
[3] Based on the developer's figure of $24,000 per unit.

DIRECTIONS:
From John Wayne Airport (Orange County), turn left on MacArthur, follow to Main and turn right. From Main, take a left at Harvard, follow to San Carlos, turn right on San Carlos and right again on Laconia. Follow to 15 Laconia, turn right and follow to the Barcelona Project.

DEVELOPER:
The Bren Company
5 Civic Center Plaza, Suite 100
Newport Beach, California 92660

LANDSCAPE ARCHITECT:
Hogan, Roy, Partners
3242 South Halladay, Suite 203
Santa Ana, California 92705

ARCHITECT/PLANNER:
Danielian Associates
60 Corporate Park
Irvine, California 92714

INTERIOR DESIGNER:
Design Tec
151 Kalmus
Costa Mesa, California 92626

Chris Eden

SPINNAKER RIDGE
GIG HARBOR, WASHINGTON

Bill Kreager

Gig Harbor, Washington, a 20-minute drive across the Narrows Bridge from neighboring Tacoma and 70 minutes from downtown Seattle, was once a fishing village and still retains the charm of its small town origin. Visitors find appealing boutiques, art galleries, and antique stores along its main street, but its spectacular natural setting makes the most lasting impression. Against a backdrop of the distant, snow-covered Cascade Mountains, the sailboats, freighters, and ferries of Puget Sound reinforce a dramatic sense of place for residents and visitors alike.

Bill Kreager, AIA, is a principal and the director of residential design at Mithun Partners of Bellevue, Washington. His residential projects have achieved national recognition for environmentally sensitive master site planning and innovative architectural designs. Kreager is a frequent lecturer on housing issues.

■ **Over 80 percent of the houses are single story, conforming to the strong preference of the empty-nester market.**

The Gig Harbor area provides the slow pace typical of small towns, and appeals to those seeking an active lifestyle in a relaxed setting. The developer of Spinnaker Ridge made use of this environment in designing a cluster housing community targeted primarily to affluent empty nesters—middle-aged or retired couples whose children have grown up and left the "nest."

DEVELOPMENT STRATEGY

Exhaustive market research was a key component of the development strategy. The research identified who the potential buyers were; what they wanted in a community; the anticipated market absorption rate; appropriate prices; the features, sizes, and other product preferences; and ways in which to reach the buyers, attract them to the site, and motivate them to purchase Spinnaker Ridge homes.

Chris Eden

The market—identified as empty nesters and active older families with children nearing adulthood—called for predominantly one-story homes (81 percent) to minimize level changes. Units were to be spacious enough to accommodate large-scale furniture and lifestyles that focused on social gatherings. Views were important—from as many primary rooms as possible.

Because a community association would maintain yards and exteriors, lots should be small. While houses would be detached to promote a sense of independence, clustering them would provide security and a sense of community. Each house was to project its own identity; each was to have an attached, two-car garage and a single-family street address.

The development strategy also involved a commitment to a site plan that would play an essential role in marketing efforts. Working from the philosophy that an exceptionally appealing site plan can sell even "plain vanilla" architecture, planners incorporated market research with development strategy to determine site solutions for Spinnaker Ridge.

SITE AND PLANNING

Planning for the 16.2-acre site was complicated both by the restrictive tree preservation requirements of the city of Gig Harbor and by a significant site slope. The desire to protect the forested property, together with the empty-nester market preference for detached homes, led to a village design of clustered 45-foot-wide lots with each home angled at 45 degrees toward the principal views. The units are clustered around cul-de-sacs in six distinct villages of four to 13 houses, creating a sense of privacy and exclusivity within the project as a whole.

■ **Architecture appeals both to contemporary and traditional tastes. The painted wood siding and the heavy shake roofs blend well with the wooded site.**

This planning solution also set aside 45 percent of the site as a naturally landscaped reserve, in which a forested "vestibule" serves as an area of transition from the busy thoroughfare at the entrance to the interior of the property.

Surrounded by a natural reserve, each village steps down the hillside, providing most homes with spectacular views—over the homes or villages below—of the Sound and Point Defiance. The angled lots maximize both the street elevation

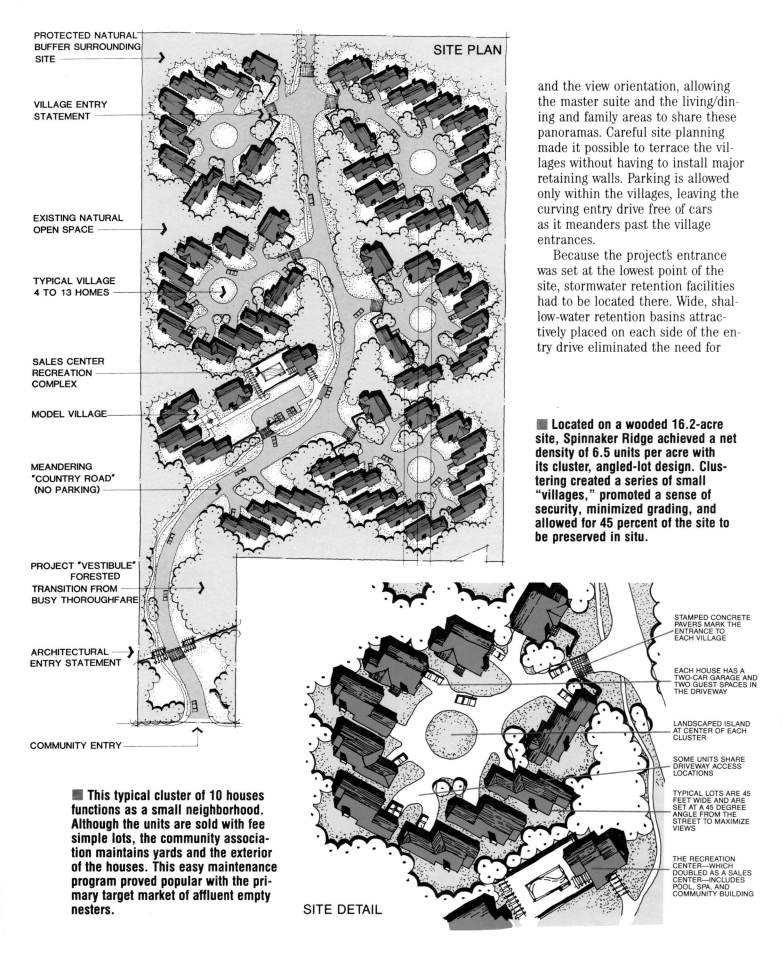

PROTECTED NATURAL
BUFFER SURROUNDING
SITE

VILLAGE ENTRY
STATEMENT

EXISTING NATURAL
OPEN SPACE

TYPICAL VILLAGE
4 TO 13 HOMES

SALES CENTER
RECREATION
COMPLEX

MODEL VILLAGE

MEANDERING
"COUNTRY ROAD"
(NO PARKING)

PROJECT "VESTIBULE"
FORESTED
TRANSITION FROM
BUSY THOROUGHFARE

ARCHITECTURAL
ENTRY STATEMENT

COMMUNITY ENTRY

SITE PLAN

and the view orientation, allowing the master suite and the living/dining and family areas to share these panoramas. Careful site planning made it possible to terrace the villages without having to install major retaining walls. Parking is allowed only within the villages, leaving the curving entry drive free of cars as it meanders past the village entrances.

Because the project's entrance was set at the lowest point of the site, stormwater retention facilities had to be located there. Wide, shallow-water retention basins attractively placed on each side of the entry drive eliminated the need for

■ Located on a wooded 16.2-acre site, Spinnaker Ridge achieved a net density of 6.5 units per acre with its cluster, angled-lot design. Clustering created a series of small "villages," promoted a sense of security, minimized grading, and allowed for 45 percent of the site to be preserved in situ.

■ This typical cluster of 10 houses functions as a small neighborhood. Although the units are sold with fee simple lots, the community association maintains yards and the exterior of the houses. This easy maintenance program proved popular with the primary target market of affluent empty nesters.

SITE DETAIL

STAMPED CONCRETE PAVERS MARK THE ENTRANCE TO EACH VILLAGE

EACH HOUSE HAS A TWO-CAR GARAGE AND TWO GUEST SPACES IN THE DRIVEWAY

LANDSCAPED ISLAND AT CENTER OF EACH CLUSTER

SOME UNITS SHARE DRIVEWAY ACCESS LOCATIONS

TYPICAL LOTS ARE 45 FEET WIDE AND ARE SET AT A 45 DEGREE ANGLE FROM THE STREET TO MAXIMIZE VIEWS

THE RECREATION CENTER—WHICH DOUBLED AS A SALES CENTER—INCLUDES POOL, SPA, AND COMMUNITY BUILDING

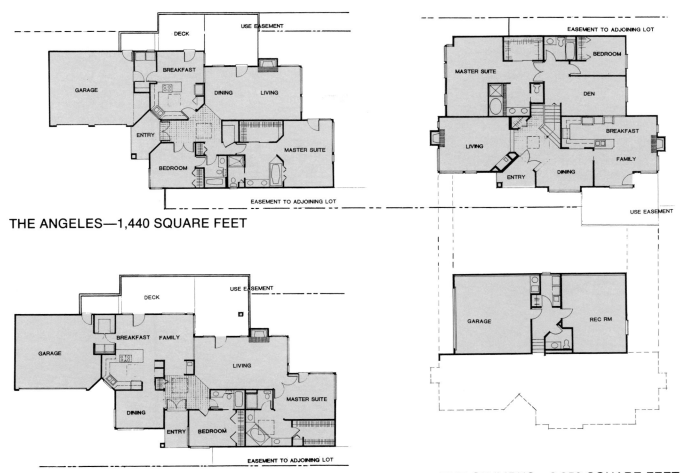

THE ANGELES—1,440 SQUARE FEET

THE TOWNSEND—1,650 SQUARE FEET

THE OLYMPUS—2,350 SQUARE FEET

protective fencing. This solution, combined with careful and abundant landscaping, converted a potential eyesore into a lush and inviting entrance.

ARCHITECTURE

In response to market preferences, the architecture of Spinnaker Ridge had to appeal to both traditional and contemporary tastes. White trim and detailing add distinction to the natural gray tones of the exterior. A white arbor, brick pavers, and accent entry doors complete the exterior image.

To broaden market appeal, a flexible floor plan with a double "swing room" concept was used, allowing rooms to change purposes without changing the structure or exterior design. The Townsend model, which became the most popular of the three plans offered, could therefore be marketed with three different floor plans:

- Two bedrooms with formal living room, formal dining room, and family room with breakfast area.
- Two bedrooms with formal living room, formal dining room, den, and breakfast area.
- Three bedrooms with informal living/dining room, and family room with breakfast area.

The interiors of all three models emphasize natural light, space, and volume, with views from within the home extending as far as 48 to 60 feet, providing a sense of expanding space usually found only in much larger houses. Plant shelves and skylights dramatize the spaces. Warm, light colors were specified

The three floor plans range in size from 1,440 to 2,350 square feet and emphasize natural light, large flowing spaces, and flexibility. The popular Townsend model is designed to allow rooms to change purposes without changing the unit's structural design. In one concept the family room (shown above) can be converted to a den. In another option the formal dining room can convert to a third bedroom.

throughout to complement these design elements.

A community center completes Spinnaker Ridge, and provides generous entertainment spaces, a kitchen, and a swimming pool and Jacuzzi.

■ The contemporary interiors are oriented to views of the outdoors. The free-flowing rooms give the feeling of spaciousness and can accommodate large social gatherings—features popular with the area's empty-nester market.

also how they lived, where they lived, and their expected means of financing. Public hearings were well attended, and appropriate community comments were incorporated into the project design.

The entire process took only four months. The ultimate success of the planning approval process was a credit to the city's planning staff, the efforts of the developer and planners, and the recognized goals and concerns of the community.

APPROVALS

Gig Harbor strongly identifies with its natural, rural environment, and is committed to protecting it. To ensure an orderly hearing process with the design commission and city council, the developer and architect took special care to establish communications early with the city staff. The effort to create a master site plan that met all market expectations and dealt with sensitive community and environmental issues was rewarded with first-round approval of each submittal. Spinnaker Ridge was the first project approved under Gig Harbor's new PUD ordinance.

Public comment was solicited at many stages of planning. Initial market research requested the public's response to the type of residential project preferred—its architectural character, pricing, and amenities. This research identified not only who the buyers were, but

MARKETING

The marketing campaign was designed as a package to appeal to the tastes and interests of the empty nester. All efforts, from selection of sales staff and interior merchandising appointments, through radio and newspaper campaigns, were carefully directed toward this market. The accuracy of this campaign has been proved by sales to date, which have been entirely within this group.

The empty-nester buyers were attracted to the security provided by the cluster planning, and were happily surprised with the degree of privacy achieved, despite the clustering. The open space reserve also served to mitigate their initial concerns about the program.

OPERATIONS AND MANAGEMENT

Typical homeowners at Spinnaker Ridge have left large homes that required extensive maintenance. They have chosen new, less restrictive lifestyles that allow for extended travel and other leisure pursuits. They have little desire to assume responsibility for the exterior maintenance of their new environments.

Respecting these preferences, the developer created a community association management plan to maintain public areas, exteriors of all homes, and recreational facilities. Landscape maintenance includes common open space and all front yards, with individual back yards optional. A monthly fee covers the cost of this upkeep.

To ensure that initial maintenance problems are resolved and that quality service continues through sellout, the developer acts as the first-phase management company. Later, the association's elected homeowner officers will probably employ a management company to provide future services.

■ The narrow, angled lots resulted in a side entrance design for most of the houses. The clustered arrangement of houses strengthens security and permits views from within the house to the street and to most of the houses located on the cul-de-sac.

Chris Eden

PROJECT DATA

LAND USE INFORMATION:
Site Area: 16.2 acres
Open Space: 7.3 acres
Total Units: 58 units
Density: 6.5 units per acre of developed site
Parking Spaces: 232[1]

LAND USE PLAN:

	Acres	Percent of Site
Open Space	7.30	45%
Lot Area	6.46	40
Roads/Parking Area	1.64	10
Amenities	0.80	5

UNIT INFORMATION:

Program	Type	Number	Square Feet	Price
Angeles	2-bdrm./2-bath	15	1,440	$122,000
Townsend	2-bdrm./den/2-bath	28	1,650	133,000
Olympus	3-bdrm./2½-bath	15	2,350	153,000

ECONOMIC INFORMATION:
Site Value: $1,500,000[2]
Site Improvement Costs:

Excavation/Grading	$123,000
Sewer/Water	195,000
Paving	57,000
Curbs/Sidewalks	18,000
Landscaping	35,000
Demolition	20,000
Storm Sewer/Power/Fencing	162,000
Total	$610,000

Average Construction Costs per Unit[3]:

Structural/Carpentry	$18,000
Electrical	2,500
Plumbing	4,000
HVAC	2,400
Materials/Finishes/Etc.	69,800
Total	$96,700

Amenities: $160,000
Homeowner Fee: $90 per month

Notes:
[1]Four spaces per unit (two-car garage and two driveway spaces).
[2]$26,000 per lot.
[3]$42 per square foot.

DIRECTIONS:
From Seatac Airport, take I-5 south to Gig Harbor/Bremerton exit (Highway 16). Travel west on Highway 16 to first exit, the Gig Harbor exit, and follow to Soundview Drive. Follow Soundview Drive approximately .75 mile to Spinnaker Ridge, on left.

DEVELOPER/CONTRACTOR:
Nu Dawn Homes
32700 Pacific Highway South, #14
Federal Way, Washington 98003

LANDSCAPE ARCHITECT:
Tom Rengstorf
911 Western
Seattle, Washington 98104

ARCHITECT/PLANNER:
Mithun Partners, Inc.
2000-112th Avenue, N.E.
Bellevue, Washington 98004

CIVIL ENGINEER:
ESM, Inc.
941 Powell, S.W., Suite 100
Renton, Washington 98055

AWARDS:
• Grand Award: Best Single-Family Detached, Gold Nugget Awards, PCBC, 1986
• Grand Award: Best Low-Density Residential Community, Gold Nugget Awards, PCBC, 1986
• Best Community Land Use Plan, MAME Awards, Seattle Master Builders Association, 1986

From Duplexes to...

Twin houses, or duplexes, generally were mirror images of each other with a common structural wall. Connecting two homes both economized on the cost of construction and increased the neighborhood density. Duplexes still can be found in various forms and sizes, from rural farmhouses to fashionable streetcar subdivisions. Most often they were used as a type of affordable housing.

...ZERO-LOT-LINES

The twin home with its common party wall may well have inspired today's zero-lot-line housing. For the cost of one additional blank wall, these units assume the status of detached housing, which capitalizes on a private side yard orientation.

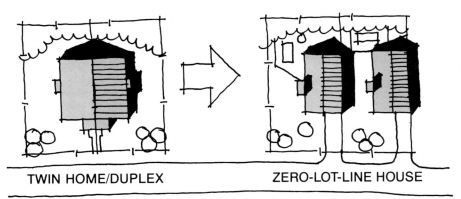

TWIN HOME/DUPLEX   ZERO-LOT-LINE HOUSE

At comparable densities, the zero-lot-line house is a popular alternative to twin homes when a strong demand for detached houses exists, along with high land costs.

Like the duplex, zero-lot-line homes can achieve densities of seven to 10 units per acre, with unit sizes that typically run from 1,000 to 2,000 square feet. Narrow lots, customarily 40 to 50 feet in width, achieve the original objective of cutting frontage costs per lot. Lot depth varies with overall density.

In light of some typical constraints, the entrance to a zero-lot-line home is a design challenge. Unlike the duplex, a contemporary zero-lot-line plan generally pulls the garage to the front of the home. Also, the narrow lot concept favors a linear plan that often requires a side entrance to the house. Resolving the garage-to-house ratio on the street level and providing a visible entrance to the house can be difficult.

As with other high-density prototypes, pulling the garage into the building footprint will help mitigate its visual impact. Locating second-floor bedrooms over the garage can further "camouflage," or soften, its presence. If the side entrance design is used, a combination of landscape elements such as garden walls, entry gates, or other architectural features may help direct visitors to the front door. Care must be taken to avoid a streetscape of solid garages.

The interiors of zero-lot units tend to resemble patio homes: extensive use of windows and other glazing make the outdoors accessible to the indoors. The units are appropriate for both affordable and luxury housing projects and are flexible in terms of geography and climate. For this reason, the zero-lot design has been popular throughout the country.

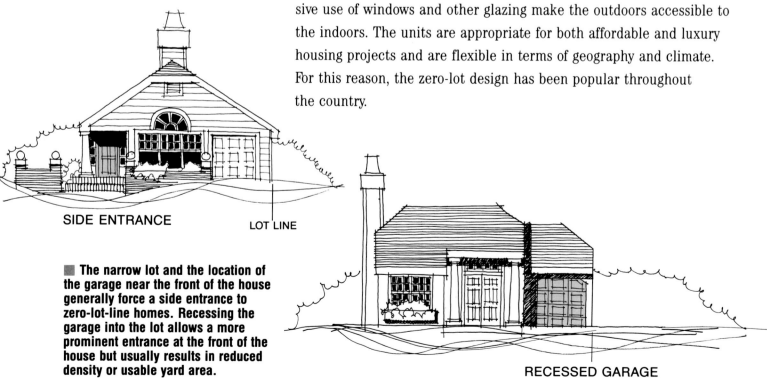

SIDE ENTRANCE   LOT LINE

■ The narrow lot and the location of the garage near the front of the house generally force a side entrance to zero-lot-line homes. Recessing the garage into the lot allows a more prominent entrance at the front of the house but usually results in reduced density or usable yard area.

RECESSED GARAGE

...ANGLED Z-LOTS

With the increasing popularity of narrow zero-lot homes, the angled Z-lot concept evolved to lessen the impact of closely spaced homes on the street. Of particular concern was the eyesore produced by two-car garages on 50-foot-wide lots dominating the street scene. The Z-lot concept rotates the home 45 degrees from its traditional perpendicular relationship to the street and jogs the lot lines to suggest a Z configuration.

The Z-lot is being used to achieve densities of seven to 10 units per acre, similar to standard zero-lot-line homes. The primary design principle behind rotating the house is that the garage can be alternated for visual appeal and variety. Other benefits can include a reduction in the length of windowless walls, an increased perception of rear yard width, and an extended site distance line (through the house and into the rear yard) upon entering the front door.

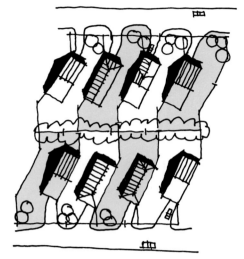

■ The Z-lot variation of the zero-lot-line concept is intended to reduce the negative visual effect of garage doors, thus enhancing the street appeal.

...ZIPPER LOTS

Another recent variation of the zero-lot-line home is the zipper lot. In this lotting approach, the rear lot line jogs back and forth to vary the depth of the rear yard and to concentrate usable open space on the side of the lot. The other side of the lot is shallow and is located against the blank wall (usually a garage wall) of an adjacent house. With lot widths around 60 feet on the street frontage, zipper lots can make the houses look larger than they actually are, and can minimize the visual impact of the garage on the streetscape. But because the lot pinches in at the rear and is fairly shallow, lot sizes can be kept to 3,000 square feet. Densities approaching 10 units per acre are possible.

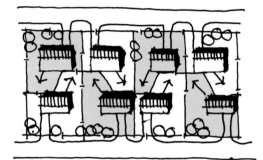

■ Zipper-lot houses are placed on wider lots. Typically, only garages are located on lot lines.

...ALTERNATE-WIDTH LOTS

With alternate-width lots, narrow and wide lots are combined along a curvilinear street to offer a varied streetscape. An almost countless number of combinations of unit plans and lot shapes and sizes can be created. The assortment of lot sizes also permits houses to be turned on the lots and thus can further vary the streetscape. As with most

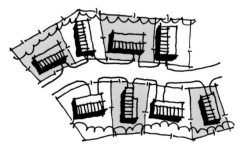

■ The alternate-width lot allows variety in the streetscape and in unit plans.

other small-lot, single-family detached programs, alternate-width lots depend on site plans being highly integrated with unit floor plans.

…MANOR HOMES

Another descendant of the side-by-side twin or duplex currently gaining favor may be called the "disguised twin," or manor home, which purposely assumes characteristics to negate a mirror image and to appear instead as a larger single-family home. To accomplish this, several techniques are being pursued, including stacking units vertically, horizontally, back-to-back, and side-by-side. One primary goal is to allow for the popular single-level floor plan.

Manor homes typically are designed with two to four units per building and afford densities of around eight units per acre. A unit generally contains 800 to 1,600 square feet. Special care is needed to resolve the entry elevation, garage elements, and exterior deck/patio orientation.

Manor home garages may be separated or pulled apart to avoid a wall of doors. If double garages are used, one pair can be rotated 90 degrees toward the other to form an entrance court. Direct access from the garage to the entry foyer is appropriate from a marketing standpoint. Front door entrances can also be separated and placed at alternate front/side elevations for privacy and individuality. The curb view, however, should present a grand unified appearance of single-family residences.

With interior spaces, the upper/lower unit differential needs to be addressed. Appropriate for certain markets may be a nine- or 10-foot ceiling at the lower level with volume ceilings or lofts on the second level. Stepping the building envelope back vertically may also open up some lower-level rooms, allowing them to have volume space or skylights. Properly designed, both upper and lower units will appeal to different markets and help to balance demand.

While the typical twin home featured side-by-side entries, front doors are separated in contemporary manor homes to individualize units.

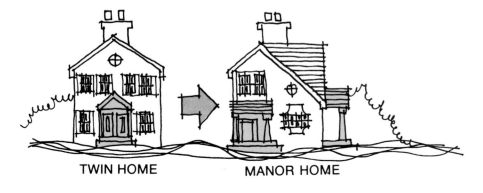

TWIN HOME   MANOR HOME

ARBOR CREEK
GARLAND, TEXAS

J. Robert Welty and Ed Rawls

Over the past several decades, urban sprawl has brought major changes to a Texas housing industry long rooted in the tradition of low density. In the late 1970s, the city of Dallas began its rapid growth as the center of commerce in the Southwest. Land that was once plentiful and inexpensive was being absorbed by developments, resulting in major changes in the local housing market.

The first noticeable change due to the shrinking land supply: developers began building traditional single-family homes on smaller lots. Later, builders attempted to construct northeastern-style townhouses in buildings of four to eight units and at densities of up to 12 units per acre. But, by the mid-1970s, the buying public's demand for outside living space, along with a growing resistance to attached housing from city councils around the metropolitan area, had worked against the townhouse concept. By the late 1970s, the zero-lot-line product seemed to be a viable solution to both the drive for higher density and the market demand for detached single-family homes.

DEVELOPMENT STRATEGY/SITE

In 1981, LSB Development commissioned architects Rawls-Welty, Inc., to design a project on a site in Garland, a suburban community northeast of Dallas. The site was a triangular parcel of 8.37 acres bounded by a creek, open land, and a major thoroughfare.

Across the creek was a single-family subdivision of homes valued from $60,000 to $80,000 and ranging around 2,000 square feet in size. Residents had organized the previous year to block an attempted

J. Robert Welty, AIA, and Ed Rawls, AIA, are principals of Rawls-Welty, Inc., based in Dallas, Texas. Formed in 1976, the firm specializes in housing design with projects ranging from single-family homes to high-rise condominiums. Welty is a member of the AIA Housing Committee.

■ On these narrow 40-foot lots, the visual impact of garages was minimized with generous front setbacks, extensive landscaping, and placement of garage doors so they are even with the house fronts.

zoning change for an 80-unit town-house project on the same site. Zoning across the thoroughfare had already been classified multifamily, leaving the site as an obvious transition between traditional single-family houses across the creek and apartments across the street.

The Rawls-Welty design strategy was to create a distinctive community at about six units per acre that would still be recognizable as single-family detached houses. In a joint meeting with city zoning officials and neighbors, the development team succeeded in introducing a zero-lot-line concept for consideration.

APPROVALS

As is often the case with new planning concepts, no zoning classification existed for a zero-lot-line product, and the city was unclear whether single-family or multifamily criteria should apply. Although it became critical that this project should have the image of single-family homes rather than town-houses, the density and construction type required attention to visual, noise, and fire concerns more commonly associated with multi-family housing. The project was filed as a planned unit development following single-family guidelines, with exceptions. This allowed the city to work with the development individually as an experiment in zoning use, and saved an estimated minimum of six months' approval time.

MARKET STRATEGY

A current market survey identified the optimum price range for units as $70,000 to $125,000, with 75 percent of the homes priced under $110,000. A unit in this range would attract a small percentage of buyers with school-age children, while opening an entirely new market for single professionals, young married couples without children, and empty nesters. Prices were set at $70,000 to $105,000, and units would be designed to appeal to younger age groups; thus, they would have larger entertainment spaces, glamorous kitchens and master baths, and fewer bedrooms. To capture the empty-nester market, one single-story, two-bedroom model was planned. The balance of the mix was unrestricted and, in fact, master bedrooms on the second floor were preferred.

SITE AND PLANNING

The developer needed to achieve a density of six units per acre, or a total of 50 units, to have an economically feasible project. Lots were approximately 40 feet wide and 85 feet

long. Frontage on dedicated streets with 30-foot rights-of-way was needed, since nearly 1.5 acres lay in the nondevelopable floodplain of the creek. A natural outcropping of rock near the center of the creek boundary was an appropriate location for an amenity package consisting of a club building, a large swimming pool and spa, and a tennis court.

The site plan was designed to take advantage of the creek's green-belt effect by maximizing lots along its length. The irregular shape also lent itself to short roadway lengths and some unusually shaped lots and varied setbacks, reinforcing the individuality of many units. The front wall and entrances were abundantly landscaped to enhance the overall quality of the community.

ARCHITECTURE

Four floor plans ranged from a one-bedroom, two-bath unit with study (1,694 square feet) to a three-bedroom, three-bath unit with game room (2,333 square feet). In addition, three prime lots were designated for homes specifically designed and constructed for individual owners. Although minor modifications to the standard units were allowed to encourage the more sophisticated buyers, such changes were requested on only two occasions. All units feature substantial amenities—vaulted ceilings in living rooms and master bedrooms, Jacuzzi tubs, separate glass-enclosed showers, skylights, wet bars, and attached garages. Whenever possible, small touches like window seats and extra built-ins are provided to give each unit a customized quality.

The zero-lot-line design calls for three walls with windows, and one blank wall along the property line. Large areas of glass in the windowed walls combine with vaulted ceilings to give the units a spacious, well-lit air. Interior space is "expanded" with diagonal entrances to rooms and corner glass opposite them; mirrors, vaulted ceilings, and half walls reinforce this perception.

The exterior design is a modified Victorian style. Each front facade incorporates one feature characteristic of Victorian architecture, such as wood corbels or a fan window, a window box or a stained glass window. The fronts of units are treated consistently, with blended brick and wood siding painted soft gray with white trim. Front doors differ from each other in style, but all are made of carved oak with stained glass inserts and side panels. The energy package consists of a trellis, glass-covered patios, double-insulated windows and patio doors, R-19 walls and R-30 attics, and a high efficiency heat pump.

MARKETING

The marketing strategy included use of a model complex of three units, local advertising, and 10-unit construction phases. However, market response exceeded all expectations and it quickly became obvious that phasing would not be necessary. The project was built and sold within 18 months.

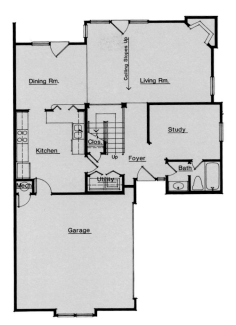

FIRST FLOOR
PLAN C—2,282 SQUARE FEET

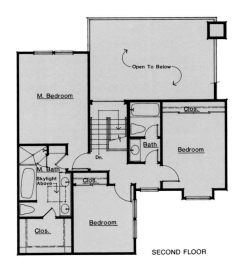

SECOND FLOOR

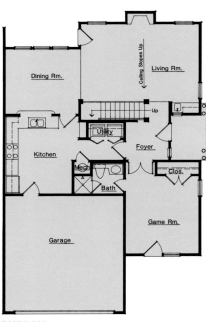

FIRST FLOOR
PLAN D—2,333 SQUARE FEET

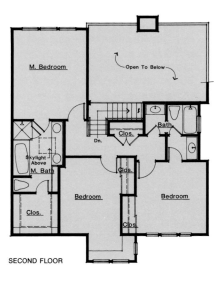

SECOND FLOOR

■ **With over 75 percent of the houses priced below $125,000, four floor plans were designed to appeal to empty nesters, young professionals, and young families. One single-level plan (not shown) was designed specifically for the empty-nester market. Among the remaining buyer groups, studies showed a strong preference for second-level master suites—a preference typical in the Dallas area but not nationally. All units feature vaulted ceilings in the living rooms and master bedrooms, fireplaces, Jacuzzi tubs, skylights, and wet bars.**

■ Zero-lot-line houses typically have side entrances because of the narrow lots on which they frequently are built. When the front door is not visible from the street, creating an identifiable entrance to the house always presents a design challenge.

■ This 8.37-acre site in Garland, Texas, lies between multifamily property to the north and an established detached community to the south. The zero-lot-line concept was perceived as a way to achieve a transition between these two off-site influences and alleviate city and neighborhood concerns about high density, townhouse development (as initially proposed). The project yields six units per acre and maintains a strong single-family image. A typical lot is 40 feet wide by 85 feet deep and totals 3,400 square feet.

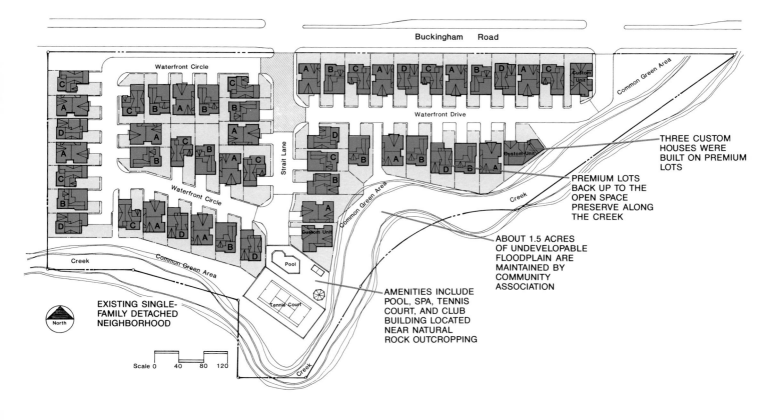

Buckingham Road

Waterfront Circle

Waterfront Drive

Strait Lane

Waterfront Circle

Creek

Common Green Area

Common Green Area

Common Green Area

Creek

Creek

Pool

Tennis Court

Custom Unit

Custom Unit

Custom Unit

North

Scale 0 40 80 120

THREE CUSTOM HOUSES WERE BUILT ON PREMIUM LOTS

PREMIUM LOTS BACK UP TO THE OPEN SPACE PRESERVE ALONG THE CREEK

ABOUT 1.5 ACRES OF UNDEVELOPABLE FLOODPLAIN ARE MAINTAINED BY COMMUNITY ASSOCIATION

AMENITIES INCLUDE POOL, SPA, TENNIS COURT, AND CLUB BUILDING LOCATED NEAR NATURAL ROCK OUTCROPPING

EXISTING SINGLE-FAMILY DETACHED NEIGHBORHOOD

58

PROJECT DATA

LAND USE INFORMATION:
Site Area: 8.37 acres
Total Units: 50
Density: 5.97 units per acre
Parking Spaces: 189
Parking Index: 3.8 spaces per unit

LAND USE PLAN:

	Acres	Percent of Site
Open Space	4.77	57%
Buildings	2.10	25
Roads/Parking Area	1.50	18

UNIT INFORMATION:

Type	Square Feet	Number	Garage[1]	Sales Price
1-bdrm./study/2-bath	1,694	15	1-car	$ 95,000
2-bdrm./study/2-bath	2,121	13	2-car	$115,000
3-bdrm./study/3-bath	2,282	11	2-car	$125,000
3-bdrm./game room/3-bath	2,333	8	2-car	$130,000
custom	2,200	3	2-car	$140,000 (average)

ECONOMIC INFORMATION:
Site Value: $455,000[2]
Site Improvement Costs: $125,000
Construction Costs: $3,000,000[3]
Amenities Costs: $75,000[4]
Homeowner Fee: $60 per month
Total Hard and Soft Costs: $3,780,000
Average Cost per Unit: $75,600

Notes:
[1] All garages are attached.
[2] $9,100 per unit; $54,000 per acre.
[3] $29 per square foot.
[4] Pool, $35,000; tennis courts, $30,000; other, $10,000.

DIRECTIONS:
From Dallas/Fort Worth International Airport, take north airport exit to LBJ Freeway (Interstate 635). Go east on LBJ Freeway to Plano Road exit, then north on Plano Road to Buckingham Road and east on Buckingham Road to project.

DEVELOPER:
LSB Corporation
Dallas, Texas

ARCHITECT:
Rawls-Welty, Inc.
14001 Dallas Parkway
Suite 1100
Dallas, Texas 75240

CASA DEL CIELO
SCOTTSDALE, ARIZONA

Walter J. Richardson

Casa del Cielo in Scottsdale Ranch, Scottsdale, Arizona, was among the first housing communities in the United States to experiment with the diagonal Z-lot concept. In 1983, Markland Development Company, one of the developers of the Scottsdale Ranch community, engaged the architectural firm of Richardson, Nagy, Martin to begin prototype housing designs for some of the narrow-lot homes included in the Scottsdale Ranch master plan.

Although marketing information provided by Markland favored a zero-lot-line concept, numerous objections arose. Among them: the design lacks usable yard areas next to garage entrances, and the long windowless walls at the property lines make for poor cross ventilation. The standard zero-lot-line plan also inhibits the architect's ability to design for maximum outdoor views.

These negative aspects can be reduced in the diagonal or angled Z-lot plan—a concept that was applied at Casa del Cielo.

Walter J. Richardson, FAIA, is president of Richardson Nagy Martin, which has offices in Newport Beach, California, and Deerfield Beach, Florida. The firm specializes in master planning, and in residential, commercial, recreational, and community designs. Richardson is a member and past chairman of the National AIA Housing Committee and the author of several industry-related publications. He is a frequent speaker on housing issues.

■ **The houses feature extensive use of windows and glass doors that open out to private rear yard patios.**

■ The Z-lot was designed to overcome some of the limitations commonly associated with conventional zero-lot-line houses. Intended benefits include improved streetscape, increased usable yard areas, and decreased length of windowless walls. The angled placement of the house increases site distance from inside, making the lot seem larger than it actually is.

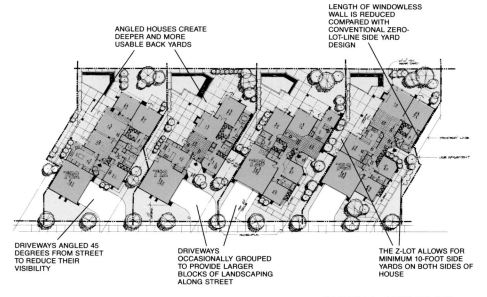

ANGLED HOUSES CREATE DEEPER AND MORE USABLE BACK YARDS

LENGTH OF WINDOWLESS WALL IS REDUCED COMPARED WITH CONVENTIONAL ZERO-LOT-LINE SIDE YARD DESIGN

DRIVEWAYS ANGLED 45 DEGREES FROM STREET TO REDUCE THEIR VISIBILITY

DRIVEWAYS OCCASIONALLY GROUPED TO PROVIDE LARGER BLOCKS OF LANDSCAPING ALONG STREET

THE Z-LOT ALLOWS FOR MINIMUM 10-FOOT SIDE YARDS ON BOTH SIDES OF HOUSE

PARTIAL SITE PLAN

DEVELOPMENT STRATEGY

The development company of J.M. Martin was launched in late 1984 with Casa del Cielo as its first project. Because competing builders were already successfully selling standard zero-lot-line homes in the area, the angled Z-lot concept became even more attractive. Its design and planning virtues added a marketing edge. For this reason, J.M. Martin committed to the angled Z-lot, and marketed it as a significantly improved version of the zero-lot-line home.

SITE

Casa del Cielo is located near the center of Scottsdale Ranch, a master-planned community of 1,100 acres in Scottsdale. Twenty-four different housing products are included in the master plan, along with parks and recreational facilities, shops, services, and a 42-acre lake. The community has an anticipated build-out of 4,004 units, with all units sold by 1991.

The Casa del Cielo site is a 28-acre parcel that is shaped like a horseshoe, with access at two collector roads. On alternate sides, it is bordered by higher-density housing or single-family homes. Although the Z-lot design does not work well on sloping sites, the basically level topography presented no problems. The master plan specified a total of 150 units, which yielded a gross density of 5.35 units per acre.

PLANNING

In Z-lot planning, the standard zero-lot-line plotting is modified to create a Z shape, which allows each unit to have a minimum 10-foot-wide side yard on alternating sides. Past the point of entry, the side yard is reversed and is placed on the opposite side of the unit. Because windows can then be located on all four sides, the windowless wall of typical

■ The interior site line begins at the angled front door and extends diagonally through the house and into the back yard. High ceilings, clerestory windows, skylights, and plant shelves add to the interior drama of the houses.

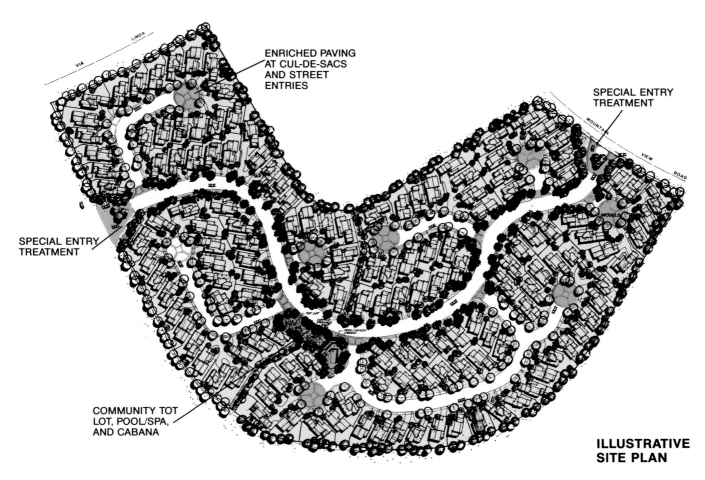

ENRICHED PAVING
AT CUL-DE-SACS
AND STREET
ENTRIES

SPECIAL ENTRY
TREATMENT

SPECIAL ENTRY
TREATMENT

COMMUNITY TOT
LOT, POOL/SPA,
AND CABANA

**ILLUSTRATIVE
SITE PLAN**

■ **Located on 28 acres in the resort setting of Scottsdale Ranch outside Phoenix, Arizona, the 150-unit Casa del Cielo community achieves a density of 5.35 units per acre. The Z-lots proved to work best on flat terrain and straight streets. Variations of the typical Z-lot were used around cul-de-sacs.**

zero-lot-line homes is eliminated, and the unit receives ample fresh air and natural light. The unit offers long, diagonal views from the entry to the outside, making it seem much larger. Private patios are located on both side and rear yards and can be seen from the living room, dining room, and master suites. This strengthens the indoor/outdoor relationship and creates ideal spaces for entertaining. The

major view each unit has is toward more of the larger yard spaces, rather than toward the narrow strip of side yard.

This unusual plotting also creates a lively and varied street scene, allowing front and side entry garages to be alternated. In this manner, large areas of open space are created along the street. Extended driveways at the end of each cul-de-sac feature several exclusive lots, each with more private access than other units. For all units, side yards at street fronts are designed as private entrance courts.

Each residential cul-de-sac is reached by the winding collector street, which links the neighborhood entries at each end of the site and accommodates minimal parking on both sides. With a consistent landscape theme, this circulation pattern integrates the entire neighborhood, while reinforcing the distinctive identity of the planned community.

Seen from the unfailingly accurate perspective of hindsight, the developer acknowledges two negative aspects: 1) the move-down market segment would have responded more quickly to the project if it had included a guarded gatehouse; and 2) the model complex should have been located on the most typical lots, rather than on cul-de-sacs. The move-down market is highly discretionary, and the buyers were unwilling to commit to sales without understanding completely the property lines and planning techniques. The cul-de-sac lots varied enough from the typical lots to cause some confusion.

ARCHITECTURE

Three floor plans were developed for Casa del Cielo, all in a single-level configuration. Basic lot dimensions were 48 feet by 110 feet, or 5,280 square feet. Plans ranged from a 1,382-square-foot, two-bedroom home to a 1,825-square-foot home with three bedrooms and a family room.

Each of the houses features corner windows and sliding glass doors leading to a covered patio; thus, the patio becomes an outdoor extension of the living area and accommodates a variety of social functions. Clerestory windows and skylights are used in conjunction with high gables and flat roofs to animate the building mass. Because of the climate, all windows are recessed; metal garage doors resist warping caused by the extreme heat of the desert.

Contemporary southwestern-style architecture relies on simple stucco forms in a range of mild desert hues accented with deep blue tile, red clay roofs, exterior plant pot shelves and arched windows. Colorful ceramic tile around windows enlivens the streetscape.

MARKETING

Characteristic of larger planned communities, a strong marketing program was established before development began in order to promote the lifestyle offered by the setting and the significant common amenities. Geared for market segments that included empty nesters from the local area (40 percent), second-home buyers from outside the area (40 percent), and young professionals in the vicinity (20 percent), units ranged in price from

■ **All three floor plans are of single-level design. Priced from $118,900 to $135,900, the houses are designed to appeal to empty nesters, second-home buyers, and young professionals. The houses feature a southwestern motif with luxurious interior touches, volume ceilings, and abundant access to side and rear yards.**

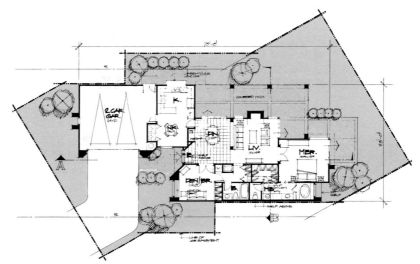

PLAN 1—1,382 SQUARE FEET
1-BEDROOM PLUS FAMILY ROOM (OR SECOND BEDROOM)/ 2-BATH

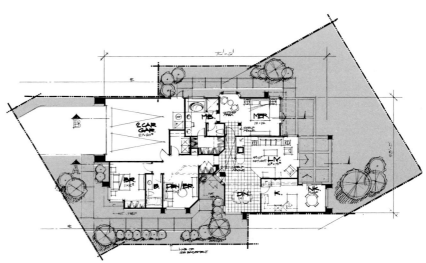

PLAN 2—1,630 SQUARE FEET
2-BEDROOM PLUS FAMILY ROOM (OR THIRD BEDROOM)/2-BATH

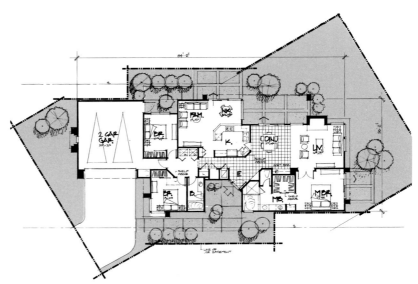

PLAN 3—1,825 SQUARE FEET
3-BEDROOM/FAMILY ROOM/2-BATH

■ Garage fronts are set at 45 degree angles to the street to minimize their visibility and create a pleasant streetscape.

$118,900 to $135,900. These prices were comparable to those for similar units in the area.

J.M. Martin devoted a full page in its Casa del Cielo sales brochure to explain the Z-lot as a new patio home concept. The brochure also compared the advantages of Z-lot diagrams with diagrams of traditional zero-lot-line housing. Buyers responded favorably, and all 150 units were sold in approximately two years.

Advantages of the Z-lot that were most often reported by buyers of Casa del Cielo homes included the number of rooms that face the rear yards, the generous size of these yards, and the direct access from garages to rear yards. The common area landscaping, which includes frontages of each individual lot, created an instant landscape theme that buyers also liked.

PROJECT DATA

LAND USE INFORMATION:
Site Area: 28 acres
Total Units: 150
Density: 5.35 units per acre
Typical Lot Size: 5,280 square feet
Parking Spaces: 600
Parking Index: 4 spaces per unit

ECONOMIC INFORMATION:
Site Value: $3 million[1]
Site Improvement Costs: $1.5 million[2]
Construction Costs: $9 million[3]
Amenities Costs: $100,000[4]
Homeowner Fee: $58 per month per unit
Average Finished Lot Cost: $32,000

LAND USE PLAN:

	Acres	Percent of Site
Open Space	14.8	53%
Buildings	7.2	26
Roads/Parking Area	6.0	21

UNIT INFORMATION:

Type	Number	Square Feet	Garage	Sales Price
2-bdrm./2-bath	47	1,382	2-car	$118,900
2-bdrm./2-bath/family room	53	1,630	2-car	$128,900
3-bdrm./2-bath/family room	50	1,825	2-car	$135,900

Notes:
[1]$20,000 average per unit.
[2]$10,000 per lot for off-site fees, drainage, and storm sewers.
[3]Building cost $34 per square foot.
[4]Includes pool, spa, sundeck, restrooms, and park area.

DIRECTIONS:
From Sky Harbor International Airport/Phoenix, take 44th Street north from the airport to Camelback Road. Turn right on Camelback and follow to Scottsdale Road. Turn right on Shea Boulevard, which leads to Scottsdale Ranch entrance. Follow directions from project signs at entrance to Scottsdale Ranch.

DEVELOPER:
J. M. Martin Development
3919 Westerly Place, Suite 100
Newport Beach, California 92660

ARCHITECT/PLANNER:
Richardson, Nagy, Martin
4611 Teller Avenue
Newport Beach, California 92660

AWARDS:
• Gold Nugget Merit Award, 1985; Single-Family Detached
• Gold Nugget Merit Award, 1984; Site Plan
• Award of Merit for Best Residential Site Plan (25 to 125 acres), Pacific Coast Builders Conference, 1984

CALIFORNIA MEADOWS
FREMONT, CALIFORNIA

Lloyd W. Bookout

Finding a successful compromise between market demand and economic reality is no easy task for today's homebuilder. Such compromises are particularly difficult in California, where the residential traditions of privacy and outdoor living are in almost constant conflict with rising land costs. One developer, however, has achieved at least a temporary solution and has been applying it with considerable success in both the northern and southern California markets.

Using a copyrighted "interlocking" lot design plan, the development company of Kaufman and Broad has developed in Fremont,

---

Lloyd W. Bookout is a senior associate in Housing and Community Development Research at the Urban Land Institute in Washington, D.C. He is the editor of ULI's Project Reference File, *the producer of several ULI videos, and the primary author of the second revised* Residential Development Handbook.

California, a 205-unit, single-family project with an overall density of 8.7 units per acre. Moreover, the project maintains the primary residential attributes characteristic of the California lifestyle: privacy, unit identity, outdoor living space, and an attached two-car garage.

Since California Meadows opened in November 1986, sales have averaged about six per week. The project was expected to sell out well within one year of opening, prompting the builder to undertake an additional 262 units on adjacent parcels. The success of California Meadows can be attributed largely to the right combination of innovative land planning and product design.

The interlocking lot design—sometimes called "zipper," "keyed," or "puzzle" lots—allows densities higher than most other detached products. Because only the garages are located on property lines, the sense of unit privacy is reinforced.

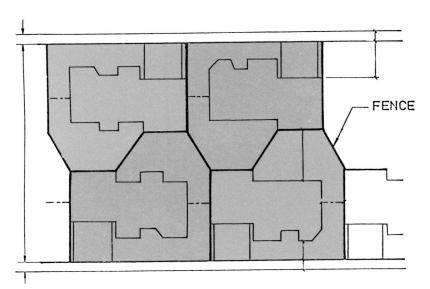

TYPICAL LOT CONFIGURATION

FENCE

■ **The rear lot line of zipper lots jogs back and forth, concentrating usable open space on one side of the lot. This design makes possible wider lots with only the garages located on property lines. The short back-to-back distance between houses requires special design attention.**

Another important feature is that private open space is concentrated for maximum use on one side of the house. And because the lots are relatively wide, they lend themselves to more traditional housing types.

To complement the lot concept, the builder selected units from its "California Series" line and made minor adjustments to floor plans and architecture to suit local market conditions. These products had the flexibility to work well with either the interlocking or the more traditional lots. However, the interlocking lots were used as much as possible to maintain the density and reduce the average land cost per unit.

THE SITE

California Meadows is located within the rapidly growing planned community of Ardenwood Forest. When completed, the 880-acre Ardenwood Forest community will provide a mix of up to 4,000 residential units, a commercial town center, a high-technology industrial park, and supporting parks, schools, and public service land uses. The developer, Ardenwood Development Associates, constructs major streets and provides to individual builders mass-graded sites with connections to public service utilities.

Ardenwood Forest is located roughly midway between major employment centers in San Jose and Oakland; commuting time is about

30 to 45 minutes to each center. The Dumbarton Bridge, about five miles west, provides convenient access to the southern San Francisco Bay peninsula. San Francisco and the larger East Bay Area are also accessible via Bay Area Rapid Transit (BART) service, with the nearest station four miles north. The community's location thus places its residents within 45 minutes of the Bay Area's most rapidly developing employment centers.

Another advantage of the Ardenwood Forest site is its proximity to regional and local recreational facilities. Those located within a few miles of the community include Ardenwood Park and Farm, Lake Elizabeth, and Coyote Hills Regional Park. The Ardenwood Forest developer also is putting in neighborhood parks and a large tennis facility near California Meadows. Because

of the location and nature of the recreational facilities available to California Meadows, the developer found it unnecessary to provide amenities on site. This not only kept down the project costs, but also maximized residential use of the site and increased the overall project density.

PLANNING AND DESIGN

The interlocking lot design was developed first by Peter Laden, an architect on staff with Kaufman and Broad in southern California. The concept was used on an infill site in Santa Ana and later successfully employed on sites in Mission Viejo and Paramount, all in southern California. In each case, as with California Meadows, the lot concept proved popular with both builder and buyers.

Because of the interlocking concept's popularity and uniqueness, Kaufman and Broad had the idea copyrighted. Floor plans developed by builders routinely are copyrighted; thus, it seemed appropriate to

■ **High land costs in the San Francisco Bay Area have made providing detached houses even to middle-income buyers a challenge. The developer of California Meadows was able to achieve a density of 8.7 units per acre on this project in Fremont, California, by using a copyrighted zipper-lot program. Typical lots encompass 3,000 square feet, and only the garage is located on a property line.**

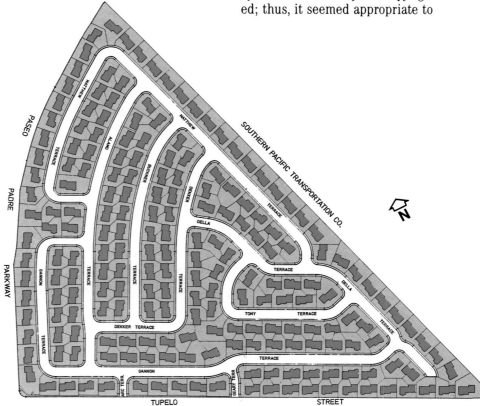

protect equally an innovative lot design. The builder hopes that the copyright will give it an edge in the small-lot, single-family market.

But California Meadows does not use the interlocking design exclusively. Although the typical lot is 3,000 square feet, larger, more traditionally configured lots stand at the project's periphery and wherever a substantial curve in a street occurs. The interlocking concept proves useful only when lots are back-to-back, and works best when streets are relatively straight and when grades vary little between lots. Because of these limitations, a mix of interlocking and conventional lots almost always is necessary.

The lot design approach calls for two walls of the garage to be placed on separate property lines. This technique eliminates the need to place any exterior walls of the house on a property line. The builder considers this feature to be a major advantage over more common, zero-lot-line side yard designs. Like the zero side yard approach, interlocking lots concentrate the limited back yard space into a more usable configuration and maximize use of the single side yard. The zigzag lot pattern minimizes direct views between rear-facing windows of back-to-back homes.

Another perceived advantage of the zigzag lot is its wider, shallower shape. The wider lot minimizes the garage's impact on the street-scape—a common concern in higher-density, single-family subdivisions. The design team further reduced the visual effect of the garage in California Meadows by setting it back eight feet from the building plane of the main portion of the house. This strategy increases the prominence of the houses from the street, and generally makes them appear larger than they actually are.

The streetscape was enhanced further through architectural and landscaping treatments. The archi-

tecture, termed "contemporary California with elements of Tudor," offers substantial detailing and color variation. Bay windows and distinctive entrances individualize the units and make them seem more spacious. The architecture combines stucco, masonite siding, detailed wood trim, and concrete roof tiles to promote a stately and traditional image.

Each unit's front yard is landscaped to accentuate the architecture and to establish consistency along the streetscape. Early market studies indicated that while buyers strongly preferred detached houses, they did not want to install and maintain landscaping. Providing

■ As seen during construction, the lotting program requires short back-to-back distances between houses— in most cases, just over 20 feet. From the front, however, the program offers a pleasant streetscape that is not dominated by garage doors.

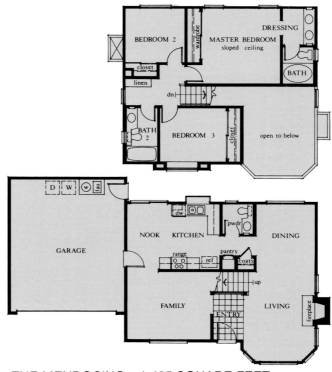

THE CARMEL—1,685 SQUARE FEET
4-BEDROOM/2½-BATH

THE MENDOCINO—1,405 SQUARE FEET
3-BEDROOM/2½-BATH

landscaping in front yards gave the houses an instantly finished look and ensured compatible landscape design.

A homeowners' association assesses each unit a $65-per-month fee, which is used primarily to maintain common areas, front yards, and private streets. All streets within the project are private, with a 32-foot cross section; parking is permitted on one side.

APPROVALS

The approval process for California Meadows was minimized because of Fremont's previous review and approval of the Ardenwood Forest community. Ardenwood Forest received a planned development (PD) permit, which established the general permitted land uses, development standards, and subsequent processing requirements. An en-

vironmental impact report was prepared for the overall community, thereby minimizing future environmental reviews for individual builders.

Given the standing approvals for Ardenwood Forest, the builder needed to secure only a tentative tract map and a precise plan (basically a site plan). The precise plan was reviewed and approved at a municipal staff level because the project was

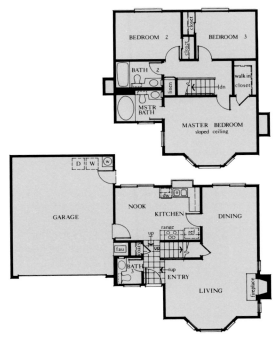

THE TAHOE—1,245 SQUARE FEET
3-BEDROOM/2½-BATH

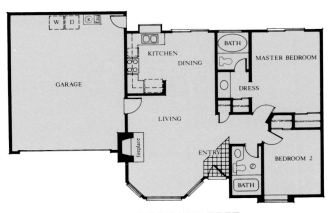

THE YOSEMITE—850 SQUARE FEET
2-BEDROOM/2-BATH

■ With sizes ranging from 850 to 1,685 square feet, the houses appeal to a highly varied market. Each unit type was designed for a specific target market.

determined to be within the standards established by the community PD permit. The builder's discretionary approval process was completed within three months—timely by California standards.

MARKETING

Before selecting the product type and mix, the developer prepared a marketing study to determine both the general market trend and a specific target market for each housing type. The study indicated a strong local market of married couples in their mid-30s with one or two children. Although many of the couples would be first-time buyers, a market also existed for first-time, trade-up families, especially those moving out of older homes and condominiums. These buyers were willing to commute up to 45 minutes, and 80 to 90 percent of them strongly preferred single-family detached houses. The "California Series" product, combined with the interlocking lot design, offered a successful compromise between the market research findings and the need for affordability despite high land costs.

The builder next prepared a specific target market plan for each of the four housing types. For example, the smaller, 850-square-foot unit was targeted for single-parent households and young, childless couples. This product type originally had only one bathroom, but market demand required that the unit be modified to include two full bathrooms.

Marketing studies also revealed that buyers were concerned with quality and finishing details. The first-time, trade-up market was especially concerned with product features, because, by and large, they were moving from older homes without modern features. To satisfy this demand, all homes are offered with bay and greenhouse windows, vaulted ceilings, fireplaces, ceramic tile counter tops and entrance floors, and automatic roll-up garage doors. These features, often found only in larger, more expensive homes, strengthen the project's traditional single-family image and work to offset the fact that units and lots are actually smaller.

To further instill buyer confidence in the quality of the homes, the builder offers each buyer a four-year warranty, as opposed to the one-year warranties typical in this market. The builder's success in pinpointing the market is evidenced by strong sales with only minimum marketing. The only media advertising for the project appears in the local *New Homes* magazine. Other advertising includes referrals and roadway signage. With these modest efforts, the model complex of four decorated units and a sales office receives 300 to 400 visitors per week.

Perhaps of some surprise to the builder is the project's popularity with Pacific Rim buyers. Asian immigrants have accounted for roughly 70 percent of the home sales. Referrals within this buyer segment are strong and often result in multiple home sales to extended family groups.

PROJECT DATA

LAND USE INFORMATION:
Site Area: 23.5 acres
Total Units: 205
Density: 8.7 units per acre
Typical Lot Size: 3,000 square feet
Parking Index: average of 2.6 per unit

LAND USE PLAN:

	Acres	Percent of Site
Open Space	11.3	48.1%
Buildings	5.5	23.4
Roads/Parking Area	6.7	28.5

UNIT INFORMATION:

Type	Square Feet	Number	Sales Price
2-bdrm./2-bath	850	18	$130,000
3-bdrm./2½-bath	1,245	57	$151,000
3-bdrm./2½-bath	1,405	82	$162,000
4-bdrm./2½-bath	1,685	48	$171,000

ECONOMIC INFORMATION:
Site Value: $6,673,775
Site Improvement Costs:

Excavation/Grading	$ 801,300
Sewer/Water/Storm Drainage	730,300
Paving/Striping/Signage	439,400
Curbs/Sidewalks	241,500
Public Area Landscaping	100,000
Utilities	198,200
Sound Walls	241,000
Total	$ 2,751,700

Construction Costs:

Structural Trades	$ 7,013,000
Finish Trades	2,195,000
Electrical	449,000
Plumbing	911,000
HVAC	610,000
Front Yard Landscaping	304,000
Total	$11,482,000
Total Hard Costs	$20,907,475

Soft Costs:

Fees/Permits	$ 1,273,600
Professional Services	245,400
Total	$ 1,519,000

DIRECTIONS:
From San Jose Airport, drive north on I-880 (Freeway 17) to Highway 84. Proceed west on Highway 84 one mile. Turn right on Ardenwood Boulevard, right on Paseo Padre Parkway, and right on Tupelo Street to California Meadows.

From Oakland Airport and Oakland Bay Bridge, drive south on I-880 and follow directions above.

DEVELOPER:
Kaufman and Broad South Bay, Inc.
39180 Liberty Street, Suite 101
Fremont, California 94538

PLANNER:
Frisbie and Associates
250-C Twin Dolphin Drive
Redwood City, California 94065

ARCHITECTS:
Richard C. Foust
P.O. Box 33203
Los Gatos, California 95031

Donald W. Simmons
6990 Village Parkway, Suite 206
Dublin, California 94566

PALOMINO HILL
LAKEWOOD, COLORADO

Michael Kephart

Traveling into unfamiliar territory can be disconcerting for anyone; for residential developers, the risks can be ruinous. Yet Carmel Homes of Denver decided to take this leap in 1986, betting it could use its extensive background in affordable, multifamily housing and apply it successfully to a single-family program in Lakewood, Colorado. This risk was increased by the state of the housing market in Denver, which had not only weakened considerably after several years of unprecedented volume, but had also become somewhat ill-defined and elusive.

DEVELOPMENT STRATEGY

The development strategy for Palomino Hill was simple: offer well-

Michael Kephart, AIA, is president of Kephart Architects, of Denver, Colorado, which specializes in designing homes, townhouses, condominiums, and apartments. Kephart is chairman of the Denver AIA Housing Committee.

designed and quality-built homes that would be larger in size and lower in price than competing products. The way to make this strategy succeed: create a product new and different enough to catch buyer attention, while ensuring that the house still satisfies the requirements of a cautious and traditional residential market.

The anticipated market segment for Palomino Hill was the entry-level buyer seeking affordable housing in the greater metropolitan area of Denver. Midway through conceptual design and planning, however, new market information demonstrated that the move-up buyer constituted a much larger part of the market than originally believed.

Thus, the Palomino Hill story also became a study in timely response, as both developer and architect studied and assessed early cues, and quickly adjusted design and planning to accommodate the needs of an additional and significantly different buyer profile.

■ **Affordability dictated a high degree of design repetition. To promote unit variety, the architect created a color palette of grays, browns, mauves, and blues accented by brightly colored trims. This wide-ranging color scheme broke with the regional norm but added a distinctive touch to the simple design of the houses.**

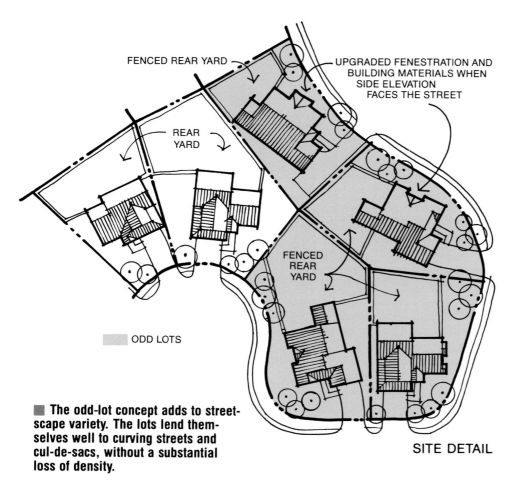

FENCED REAR YARD

UPGRADED FENESTRATION AND BUILDING MATERIALS WHEN SIDE ELEVATION FACES THE STREET

REAR YARD

FENCED REAR YARD

ODD LOTS

SITE DETAIL

■ **The odd-lot concept adds to street-scape variety. The lots lend themselves well to curving streets and cul-de-sacs, without a substantial loss of density.**

SITE AND APPROVALS

The Palomino Hill site is located in Lakewood, a suburban community west of Denver. The 8.78-acre infill parcel is served by a major arterial street, and is surrounded by an irrigation canal and a city park. Neighboring development includes a grade school, single-family housing, and a townhouse project. A basically level topography presented no engineering problems. Principal views focus either toward the Rocky Mountains or the city park.

The major planning constraint was that the density needed for the project to be affordable was six-plus units per acre, which required smaller lots than customary for single-family housing development in the area.

Thus, the project was subject to a PUD approval process. The Lakewood Planning Commission, other city officials, and neighboring residents viewed the proposed basic lot size of 50 feet by 90 feet as too small and frowned on the project as a whole. They feared the project would create a streetscape consisting of rows of garage doors. Because the planning solution was specifically tailored to alleviate this condition, community concerns were successfully addressed and the small lots were approved.

PLANNING

The principal planning goal for the site was to achieve a varied and pleasing streetscape within density requirements. Although the architect adhered to the average lot dimensions of 50 by 90 feet for most of the homes, these dimensions are varied on occasion for maximum planning flexibility. For example,

lots adjacent to public streets were made wider and shallower to allow for changes in orientation. Lot dimensions were also varied so that a maximum number of corner and cul-de-sac lots could be included in the plan. Curvilinear streets and slightly staggered setbacks were incorporated to further enliven the streetscape.

Of particular concern to the architect and developer were the lots bounded by South Garrison Street, the major artery serving Palomino Hill. Lakewood has no ordinance for government maintenance of public right-of-way areas, and because Palomino Hill would not include a homeowners' association, maintenance of this strip of land could not be assured.

To prevent the possibility that an unkempt "no man's land" would well up between the project's rear yards and Garrison Street, the houses in that area are adjusted so that frontages and rear yards are on interior streets, with side yards facing Garrison. Because side yards are rarely fenced, property lines are less apparent; homeowners will thus be inclined to extend their yard maintenance beyond actual property lines and include the right-of-way strip as part of their routine yard work.

ARCHITECTURE

In addition to maximum density yields, a project's affordability often relies on a high degree of design repetition, which can be aesthetically unappealing in a small-lot subdivision. To counteract this possibility, the architect incorporated a variety of designs with the proposed plans.

So that all plans offered at Palomino Hill could respond to the various lot sizes and orientation, each house is designed for two different front elevations: the first specifies a 50-foot frontage, and an alternate side elevation serves as

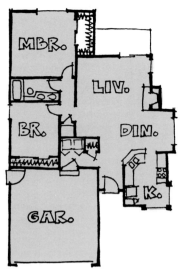

TYPICAL FLOOR PLAN

TYPICAL FRONT ELEVATION

■ The 1,109-square-foot floor plan provides two bedrooms and one bath at a price under $80,000. As shown below, it—as well as the other three floor plans—is designed so that either the front or side elevation may face the street, depending on the shape of the lot.

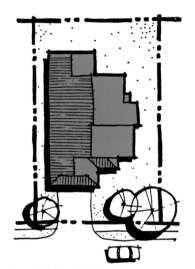

TYPICAL LOT

TYPICAL SIDE ELEVATION

■ On the typical 50-foot-by-90-foot lot, the view from the street is toward the narrow (front) part of the house. The side elevation is not visible from the street, and, architecturally, it is less detailed.

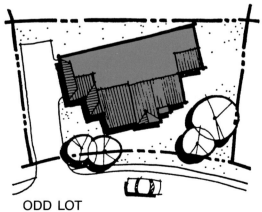

ODD LOT

ODD-LOT (STREET-FACING) SIDE ELEVATION

■ The wider but shallower odd lot requires that the house be rotated so that the side elevation faces the street and in effect becomes the "front" of the house. In this case, building materials and architectural details are upgraded to give a pleasant appearance from the street.

73

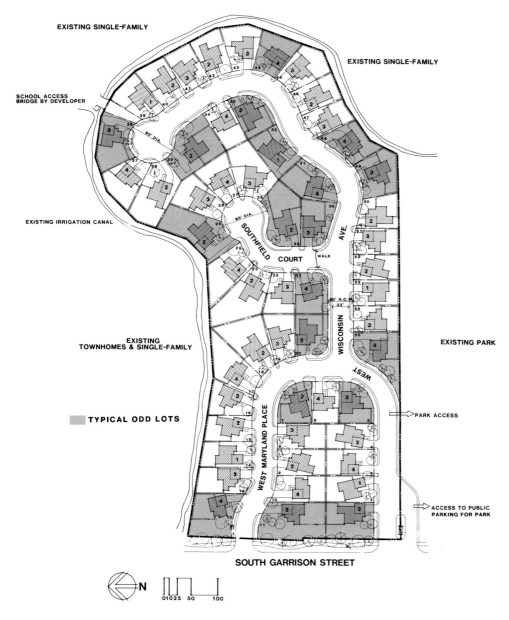

EXISTING SINGLE-FAMILY

EXISTING SINGLE-FAMILY

SCHOOL ACCESS
BRIDGE BY DEVELOPER

EXISTING IRRIGATION CANAL

SOUTHFIELD AVE.

COURT

WALK

WISCONSIN

EXISTING
TOWNHOMES & SINGLE-FAMILY

WEST

EXISTING PARK

■ TYPICAL ODD LOTS

WEST MARYLAND PLACE

PARK ACCESS

ACCESS TO PUBLIC
PARKING FOR PARK

SOUTH GARRISON STREET

N

0 10 25 50   100

■ **In the suburban community of Lakewood, Colorado, outside Denver, this 8.78-acre site is surrounded by park and detached residential uses. The developer achieved the required minimum density of six units per acre by using this alternate-width (odd) lot scheme. Also satisfied was the city's concern about too many narrow lots creating a streetscape dominated by garage doors.**

the front of homes placed on wider lots, or on lots where orientation is modified, such as those on Garrison Street. Side elevations that face the street are upgraded with additional brick treatment and dormer or recessed windows. Without substantially affecting engineering or construction costs, these minor variations help to animate the streetscape and increase the architectural appeal.

Materials and straightforward exterior forms are consistent with the prevalent style of the region, both

because affordability demands simplicity, and because the developer expressed justifiable reservations about departing significantly from the design norms of a highly traditional marketplace. A distinctive appearance was therefore achieved through the use of lively colors that are very different from those usually found in residential projects in the area.

Interiors respond primarily to the marketing information received on the move-up buyer. The 1,109- to 1,959-square-foot homes are larger than those originally planned, with particular emphasis given in larger floor plans to kitchens, baths, and master suites. Breakfast nooks are incorporated in kitchens. Principal living areas are designed with volume ceilings, and fireplaces are standard. Master suites are generously proportioned to accommodate seating and dressing areas; the attached baths are compartmentalized and fitted with dual vanities.

MARKETING

Although decorated models were planned for Palomino Hill, the program showed early signs of strong sales, and the developer abandoned this plan as an unnecessary expense. Marketing efforts relied primarily on signs and on minimal newspaper advertising to attract prospective buyers.

The location of Palomino Hill was central to buyer satisfaction; as an infill site, it is close to commerce, schools, recreation, and services. The site itself, next to a park, was also a draw.

Curvilinear streets effectively keep down traffic speed and constituted a major point favored by buyers. Buyers were also pleased with the floor plans, which they viewed as extremely functional and pleasant, and as adding to the value of their homes.

Price ranges were reasonable for both entry-level and move-up buyers, and financing was an added inducement. Because the developer owned his own finance company, all buyers were offered financing that was not only more conveniently obtainable, but also somewhat less costly than generally available from Denver financial institutions. Palomino Hill enjoyed immediate sales success, with all homes sold within a year of its opening.

PROJECT DATA

LAND USE INFORMATION:
Site Area: 8.78 acres
Total Units: 55
Density: 6.27 units per acre
Average Lot Size: 4,500 square feet

LAND USE PLAN:

	Acres	Percent of Space
Open Space	4.83	55%
Buildings	2.20	25
Roads/Parking Area	1.75	20

UNIT INFORMATION:

Type	Square Feet	Sales Price
2-bdrm./1-bath/optional master bath/ranch style	1,109	$ 79,250
2-bdrm./1-bath/optional master bath/optional 3rd bdrm./3 levels	1,404	$ 88,450
3-bdrm./2½-bath	1,638	$ 94,950
3-bdrm./2½-bath	1,644	$ 94,950
3-bdrm./loft or 4th bdrm./2½-bath	1,959	$105,450

ECONOMIC INFORMATION:
Site Value: $385,000[1]
Site Improvement Costs: $880,000[2]
Construction Costs: $32 per square foot

Notes:
[1]$7,000 per unit.
[2]$16,000 per unit.

DIRECTIONS:
From Stapleton International Airport/Denver, take I-70 west to Sheridan Boulevard and travel south on Sheridan to Mississippi Avenue. Head west on Mississippi to Garrison Street and turn south on Garrison for two blocks to Palomino Hill.

DEVELOPER:
Michael A. Kell
Carmel Homes
950 South Cherry, Suite 1100
Denver, Colorado 80222

ARCHITECT:
Michael A. Kephart
Kephart Architects
850 Lincoln
Denver, Colorado 80203

Robb Miller

LAKEMONT
SAN RAMON, CALIFORNIA

Phillip M. Hove

Although design and planning techniques for attached housing have steadily grown in sophistication since the days when "duplex" meant mirror-image floor plans and twin front doors, recent years have seen an unprecedented variety of density solutions. Once a method used primarily to solve the problems of land shortages, high interest rates, or incomes too low for detached homes, attached housing is coming into its own as a residential form that is preferred by a significant portion of the home-buying public.

Responding to buyer profiles that virtually did not exist in the 1950s, 1960s, and early 1970s, architects and planners are now being challenged not only to provide attached housing that meets higher-density requirements, but also to create residential forms that appeal to affluent and discriminating buyers in the retirement, empty-nester, divorced, and young-professional markets.

Many such buyers want attached housing for the familiar reasons of security, convenience, easy maintenance, and sociability. At the same time, they want homes that offer generous amenities and the type of

Phil M. Hove, AIA, is principal and chief of design at the Irvine, California, office of Berkus Group Architects—a nationally recognized firm of architects and land planners specializing in residential and commercial design for development clients throughout the western United States and Florida. A frequent speaker at industry seminars and conventions, Hove is a member of the AIA Housing Committee and serves on a ULI Residential Development Council.

Robb Miller

■ **The arch and glass block architectural treatment at the entrance to this duplex (plan five) unit reinforces the sense of individuality. Entrances to units are separated to promote privacy.**

76

privacy and individual identity traditionally associated with large-lot, single-family houses.

Working with the constantly evolving variables these social changes continue to generate, architects today are recommending solutions virtually no one considered 15 years ago—solutions that integrate innovation and tradition and thereby simultaneously serve contemporary uses while fulfilling the emotional need to own one's home. Lakemont represents one successful example of this synthesis.

DEVELOPMENT STRATEGY AND FINANCING

The developer of Lakemont initiated the project with two primary goals in mind: 1) to provide attached housing for move-up buyers which could compete successfully with the single-family detached product prevalent in the area, and 2) to create safeguards against potentially disastrous carrying costs in the event of an economic downturn. Using ownership and construction agreements unusual for attached housing programs, the Vermillion Group, Inc. (formerly Country Club Builders), achieved both of these goals.

Instead of treating Lakemont's site as one large lot, with buyers owning airspace of their individual units and a fraction of the common area proportionate to their units, the developer departed from tradition and subdivided their sites into individual lots for duplex and triplex buildings. Under this arrangement, buyers received fee titles not only to the airspace of their units, but also to their share of undivided interest in the lots themselves. On duplex lots, that share is 50 percent; on triplex lots, 33⅓ percent. Owners of ground-level units also receive an exclusive use easement for the rear yard area allotted to that building.

Robb Miller

The Vermillion Group found that its design strategy greatly increased the attractiveness of attached housing, successfully counteracting the stigma of not owning the land one's house sits on. Beyond that, the arrangement was tied to a provision that would enable the developer to modify construction as the project progressed.

Construction of the project was scheduled in phases, with approximately 50 units built in each of four phases. But, had the market turned sour, the developer had the flexibility to change this procedure. Using the individual lot arrangement, the developer could commit to construction of only the units on one lot. A buyer could select a duplex or triplex lot and, with the developer's assistance, acquire a construction loan for the new home. The title could then be transferred to the new owner, and construction could begin. If only one buyer was available for a duplex building, the developer could proceed, carrying the construction loan for the other half of the building.

■ The rear elevation of this duplex building illustrates the architect's intent to give it the appearance of a detached house. Large decks and patios allow room for outdoor living, and numerous windows open up views to surrounding open space.

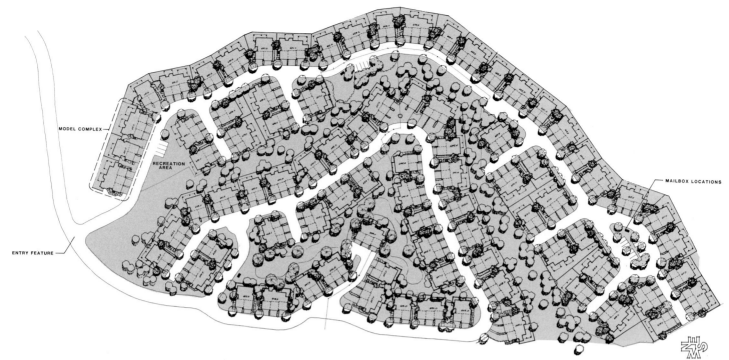

RECREATION
AREA

ENTRY FEATURE

MAILBOX LOCATIONS

■ The Lakemont site plan is based on a series of individual lots on which duplex and triplex buildings are located. While this lotting and ownership concept breaks with the traditional condominium approach, it achieves a density of nearly 16 units per acre. Located on a 13.65-acre site near San Ramon, California, the plan uses contour grading and terracing to soften the visual effect of the density and to maximize views to nearby lakes and the golf course.

This method could enable the developer to close escrow and transfer title earlier than in phased construction, thus helping him repay loans and realize profits more quickly. Under this arrangement, completion bond costs could apply only to individual buildings, rather than to an entire phase, resulting in another considerable savings. The arrangement could also be attractive to buyers, because it would give them more time to sell their existing homes, and to use tax write-offs on the interim interest paid on a swing loan. In addition to these advantages, this approach could permit limited revisions requested by new owners during construction.

However, the Vermillion Group has not needed to use this alternative. The first phase has 47 homes completed or under construction, and each unit has sold as soon as it was finished.

SITE

Located on 13.65 acres of rolling hillside in the San Ramon area of northern California, Lakemont is a pocket community of Canyon Lakes Country Club, a master-planned development of 1,060 acres that eventually will contain 3,100 for-sale and rental homes. Canyon Lakes is adjacent to Bishop Ranch, a growing industrial area that currently includes such anchor tenants as Chevron, Toyota, and Pacific Telephone, and that is expected to employ as many as 40,000 people.

Purchased in 1984 by the Vermillion Group, the Lakemont property is zoned for a density of 15 units per acre, with no restrictions on product type. The site is adjacent to an 18-hole championship golf course within Canyon Lakes Country Club: this location within the larger community was a major factor in determining the housing type.

PLANNING

The original master developer had received approval of a tentative plan of Lakemont specifying a series of three-story buildings with 12 units per building. Six units were to have one-car attached garages, and six were to have one-car detached carports. Six units would contain

900 square feet, with the rest ranging in size up to 1,800 square feet.

Rejecting this scheme, the Vermillion Group envisioned a program that would appeal to a variety of affluent buyers, while still providing the condominium density necessary for a profitable development. Turning to Berkus Group Architects of Orange County, California, the developer considered several plans that would provide maximum density and views in building forms that resembled single-family housing.

The final plan incorporates contour rather than vertical grading, which creates a terraced effect and softens the impression of density. The tiered system also provides for single-loaded streets on most of the lower pad, giving owners there unobstructed views across their street. Units on the upper pad face the golf course and a panoramic vista; some also enjoy views of the 15-acre lake. Rotating some of these buildings 10 to 15 degrees further enhances views toward the golf course and beyond. Of the 216 units, 171 have views of these amenities. The majority of the remaining units are carefully oriented to face an interior waterscape feature and landscaped greenbelt. While having the same density as in the original plan, dwelling units are contained in duplex and triplex buildings with attached two-car garages. Units range in size from 1,117 to 2,138 square feet.

The developer and architect intentionally are limiting amenities in Lakemont so that homeowners can enjoy those contained in the Canyon Lakes Country Club community (golf course, 15-acre lake, tennis courts, swimming pool, parks, and 24-hour guarded entrance gate). Within Lakemont, owners can take advantage of a private pool, spa, and cabana. Other exterior features include a lagoon with waterfalls and fountains, an entry monument with fountain, and a professionally landscaped greenbelt and pedestrian paths.

ARCHITECTURE

The architectural image at Lakemont reflects judicious combinations of contemporary forms with postmodern elements (such as glass block and ziggurat walls). Although the stucco and tile exteriors are more often associated with the traditional housing of southern California, they blend successfully with the architecture and the hillside site, making a subtle but distinctive design statement.

Five floor plans were developed for Lakemont, and are contained in either duplex or triplex buildings, both of which employ over/under, rather than side-by-side attachments. In the duplexes, a 1,117-square-foot unit and both two-car garages are located at street level; a 2,138-square-foot unit is on the second floor. In the triplexes, a 1,477-square-foot unit and a 1,802-square-foot unit are upstairs, while a 1,286-square-foot unit and three two-car garages are at street level.

Entrances are treated with particular care, to provide maximum privacy and separate identities, and to complement the single-family character of the buildings. Entrance to the ground-level unit in both duplexes and triplexes is treated as though it is the major entrance and is scaled in proportion to the large size of the building. Entrances to upper units are raised one-half level to separate vertically entrances located on the same side of the building (as in a triplex), and to animate the building mass of both the duplex and triplex. All entries are

■ **The plan for the first phase illustrates how individual lots were created for each duplex and triplex building. Buyers purchase the usual condominium air rights and a share of their individual lots (either 50 percent or 33 percent). Besides making it easy for buyers to understand what they "own," the lotting concept also makes it possible to phase the project on a lot-by-lot basis, if necessary.**

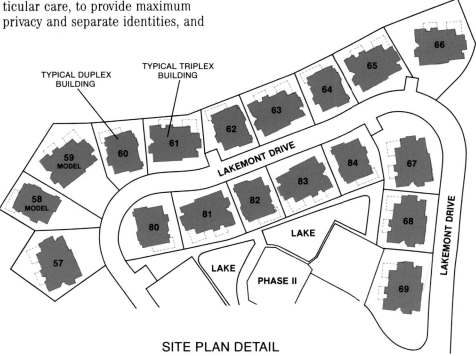

TYPICAL DUPLEX BUILDING

TYPICAL TRIPLEX BUILDING

SITE PLAN DETAIL

PLAN ONE
FIRST FLOOR OF DUPLEX BUILDING
2-BEDROOM/2-BATH
1,117 SQUARE FEET

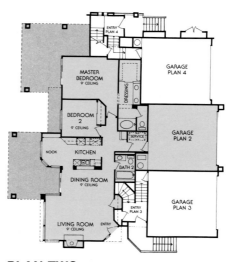

PLAN TWO
FIRST FLOOR OF TRIPLEX BUILDING
2-BEDROOM/2-BATH
1,286 SQUARE FEET

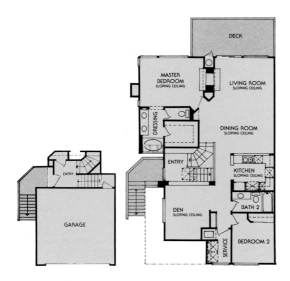

PLAN THREE
SECOND FLOOR OF TRIPLEX BUILDING
2-BEDROOM/2-BATH/DEN
1,477 SQUARE FEET

PLAN FOUR
SECOND FLOOR OF TRIPLEX BUILDING
3-BEDROOM/2-BATH/LOFT
1,802 SQUARE FEET

■ The luxury units, ranging in price from $156,900 to $208,900, were designed for young professional singles, young couples, and empty nesters. Popular features of the floor plans include attached garages, access to outdoor space, and the sense (from the interior) of living in a detached house. About 50 percent of the units were purchased by divorced buyers.

PLAN FIVE
SECOND FLOOR OF DUPLEX BUILDING
3-BEDROOM/2-BATH/FAMILY ROOM
2,138 SQUARE FEET

Robb Miller

sheltered for privacy. Each unit has a second entrance from its attached garage, providing security and convenience that is unusual in many attached garage designs.

All garages face the street. To avoid an unrelieved bank of garage doors, the architect staggered building setbacks; streets are curved in conformance with the contours of the terraces. To further reduce the visual impact of garages, architectural elements are used to place garage doors in shadow. One-story rooflines soften the building silhouette; balconies and fenestration over garages draw the eye up and away from the garage.

Wherever possible, each of the five plans is designed to promote the feeling of living in a detached house. The unit on the lower level stretches the width of the building, providing views to the back yard

■ To minimize an unrelieved vista of garage doors, building setbacks are staggered and streets are curved. Also, architectural elements surround garage doors to set them in shadow; balconies and fenestration help to draw the eye up and away from garages.

Robb Miller

■ The raised entry of this plan three model leads to the open living/dining/kitchen area. The pass-through above the kitchen sink area allows unobstructed views to the primary living area and interaction during social gatherings.

■ **Skylights and glass blocks bring abundant natural light into plan five's master bedroom. Not pictured is the small outdoor deck located off this master bath.**

sate for the absence of a private yard.

Interior spaces also are designed to lessen the effect of households living over or under each other. Roof plates for lower units are nine feet high rather than the standard eight feet; instead of having the usual six-and-one-half-foot height, windows are eight feet high, and begin as low as six inches from the floor, rather than 22 to 30 inches. Upstairs, ceilings are two stories high and are punctuated with skylights to admit natural light, to enliven the area, and to make units seem more spacious. In all units, major living areas are given the best views.

MARKET

The image of detached single-family houses projected by the development, the two-car garages, and the open and dramatic style of the floor plans was a major asset used in the marketing program. The original market profiles presented to the architect included young, dual-income buyers, mature homeowners who wanted smaller quarters without loss of luxury, and high-income single professionals. Upon further investigation, another profile emerged—the divorced buyer, primarily female, who has accounted for about 50 percent of sales. Readjusting design criteria, the architect developed the 1,477-square-foot unit to accommodate two unrelated people sharing the same home. With widely separate sleeping areas, this plan allows for agreeable roommate arrangements. The attached garages also appealed to women buyers. Prices of $156,000 to $209,000 are approximately $40,000 below those of comparable units in the area.

from virtually every room, an advantage not enjoyed by ground-floor residents of more traditional attached programs. Upstairs, decks are oversized—to create more than token outdoor living space—and function as large private patios; they provide expansive views to the back yard and beyond, and partially compen-

PROJECT DATA

LAND USE INFORMATION:
Site Area: 13.65 acres
Total Units: 216
Density: 15.8 units per acre
Parking Spaces: 516[1]
Parking Index: 2.39

LAND USE PLAN:

	Acres	Percent of Site
Open Space	4.17	30.5%
Buildings	5.32	39.0
Roads/Parking Area	2.02	14.8
Lagoon	0.49	3.6
Private Space (Rear Yard)	1.65	12.1

UNIT INFORMATION:

Type	Square Feet	Number	Sales Price
2-bdrm./2-bath	1,117	36	$156,900
2-bdrm./2-bath	1,286	48	$169,900
2-bdrm.+/2-bath	1,477	48	$183,900
3-bdrm./2-bath	1,802	48	$208,900
3-bdrm./2-bath	2,138	36	$208,900

ECONOMIC INFORMATION:
Site Value: $9,720,000[2]
Site Improvement Costs:

Units	$1,676,808[3]
Lagoon	$ 182,000
Landscaping	$ 405,580

Amenities Cost: $37,500 (estimate)[4]
Development Fees: $1,207,008[5]
Construction Costs: $16,822,512[6]
Homeowner Fee: $61.74 to $83.13 per month

Notes:
[1]Does not include parking on driveways.
[2]$45,000 per unit.
[3]$7,763 per unit.
[4]Includes pool and cabana.
[5]$5,588 per unit.
[6]$77,882 per unit.

DIRECTIONS:
From San Francisco International Airport, take U.S. 101 north to the Bay Bridge exit. Cross the Bay Bridge and stay in the right lanes; watch for Walnut Creek/Highway 24 exit and travel through Oakland and Pleasant Hill. Take I-680 south to the Crow Canyon exit and travel east through San Ramon to Lake Shore Drive. Turn right onto Lake Shore Drive and right again at the gatehouse for Canyon Lakes Country Club. Follow the road to the Lakemont project at the top of the hill.

DEVELOPER:
Vermillion Group, Inc.
10 Crow Canyon Court, Suite 100
San Ramon, California 94583

ARCHITECT:
Berkus Group Architects
26 Corporate Park
Irvine, California 92714

From Townhouses to...

For centuries the townhouse has provided affordable housing for urban dwellers. Within the efficient site layout allowed by a grid street pattern, densities of 30 to 40 units per acre were commonplace. To reestablish the townhouse concept in a nongrid subdivision, however, the building form and site plan concept must be analyzed anew.

...ATTACHED SINGLES

The basically linear configuration of urban townhouses can be broken into "attached singles" for suburban sites. The attached singles concept individualizes units through a variety of techniques to establish an image of detached housing. These principles work best on two-, three-, and four-unit buildings, but may also be applied to six- and eight-unit buildings.

Attached singles are generally sited at a density of seven to 10 units per acre, with units ranging in size from 900 to 1,800 square feet.

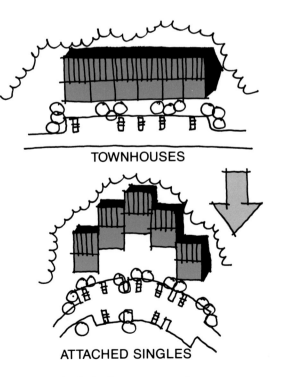

TOWNHOUSES

ATTACHED SINGLES

■ Attached singles assume a less linear configuration than traditional townhouses while achieving a suburban density of 10 units per acre.

From the street elevation, attached singles strive for a single-family detached appearance.

There is an obvious trade-off between unit differentiation and density, whereby closely spaced linear buildings and parking can achieve densities of around 20 units per acre. Attached singles are especially suited to difficult sites where clustering and grade changes are often required.

In terms of site planning objectives, common wall length can be minimized by sliding units back or pushing them forward on the site. This works particularly well in three-plex and four-plex buildings, where a landscaped courtyard can result, becoming a central focus. An additional goal is to increase the overall linear footage of exterior walls for windows, affording more views and natural light for interior rooms.

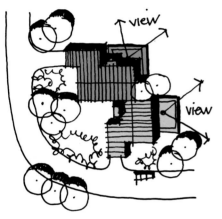

Separating the entrance of one house from the entrance to the adjacent house creates the image of a detached house.

Other site plan techniques may allow units to turn a corner if the street layout permits, with entries and orientations shifted 90 degrees. This technique successfully presents a separate unit facade from each front elevation.

Juxtaposing one-story with two-story units will vary rooflines dramatically and further emphasize individual units. Varying floor elevations at the party wall between units will also help to define the units while accommodating natural differences in the topography.

Grade changes and roofline variety are techniques used to promote unit identity.

Garages, if provided, can be grouped so that the party wall is moved forward, giving more privacy to the front entrance area. This also helps minimize pavement area off the street and concentrates parking areas.

In the internal design of attached singles, it is particularly important to orient features that face the outdoors, such as windows and decks, so that privacy is safeguarded. The construction cost of units will probably fall somewhere below that of detached singles but above that of townhomes, due to the individual articulation of each unit.

...COACH HOMES

A second popular descendant of the rowhouse is the coach home, which combines interior townhouse units with stacked flats at the ends of the building. This building hybrid allows density to increase while maximizing the open space exposure to four units at the ends of the building instead of the standard two units.

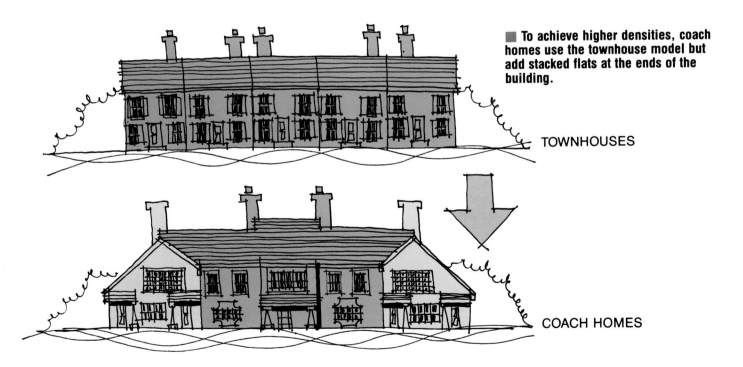

■ To achieve higher densities, coach homes use the townhouse model but add stacked flats at the ends of the building.

TOWNHOUSES

COACH HOMES

Typically, coach homes range from 900 square feet to 1,800 square feet and can be sited at 10 to 14 units per acre. All units can accommodate one- or two-car attached garages and grade-level entrances. The upper-level, end flat can be reached by internal stairs from a ground entrance that also has direct access to the garage. Coach homes work well on sites with grade changes. Exterior orientations of stacked end units can vary with the grade to increase privacy and make it possible to have two ground-level patios.

Garage exposure on the street is again an issue. As with high-density detached products, the ratio of the garage expanse to that of the total unit should be reviewed. If the expanse of the garage exceeds 40 percent of the total unit width, the entrance and the streetscape could suffer.

To further increase density, townhomes may also be combined with back-to-back end unit flats. On hilly sites, this may include the two-thirds split concept, with two-story units on the uphill side and three-story units on the downhill side. These combined factors may allow the coach home concept to approach a density of 20 units per acre.

■ **When topography permits, each stacked unit can have access to ground-level patio space.**

...STACKED TOWNHOUSES

The popularity of living on one level also has advanced a hybrid
style of townhome that combines the familiar two-level townhouse
stacked over a single-level flat. With appropriate topography, this plan
may be extended to include two levels down and two levels up; all
units would share a common entry level.

A prime concern of the stacked townhouse is vertical circulation.
The use of several techniques can achieve a graceful entrance to the
upper level. A private interior staircase from a grade-level entry porch
to the second-level unit is favored. Other plans for the second-level
unit include a partially elevated front door with 50 percent of the rise
from an exterior landscaped design and the balance internalized. In
both cases, the lower-level unit needs a graceful, individualized
entrance as well.

■ **Density can be increased by stacking a conventional townhouse over a single-level flat.**

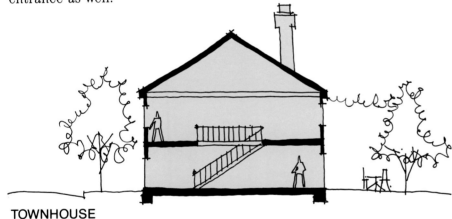

TOWNHOUSE

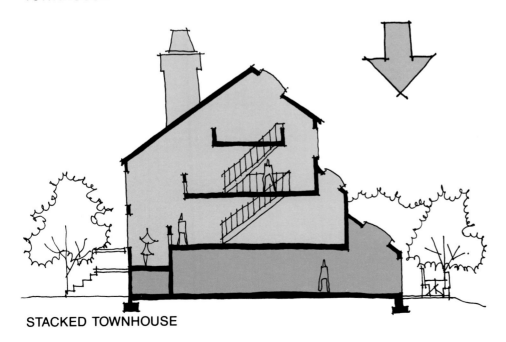

STACKED TOWNHOUSE

...TOWNHOUSE MEWS

In both urban and suburban settings, linear townhouses can be organized in pairs to constitute new building types for increased density. Townhouses may be sited front-to-front or back-to-back to concentrate entrances along an open space.

The back-to-back grouping of open space is a variation of the urban prototype. The essence of urban townhomes is found in tight rear yards separated by screens for privacy. The concentration of front-to-front entryways may be more suitable to tight infill sites, where rear building areas are needed for automobile access and garage placements.

The townhouse mews concept has been successfully applied in both urban and suburban settings. Because relatively high densities can be achieved, the product works well on small urban infill parcels. It also works well on larger suburban parcels, where higher densities and attached garages are concurrent objectives.

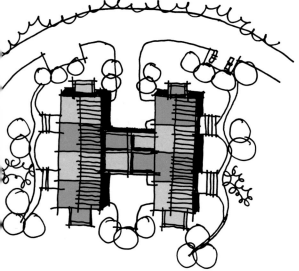

TYPICAL SITE PLAN

■ **The townhouse mews is created by placing two rows of townhouses front-to-front, or, in this example, back-to-back, with a common driveway located in between. Deck areas are located behind the units with some extending over the driveway.**

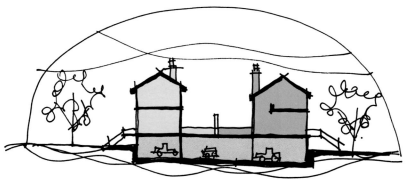

TYPICAL SECTION

WHITMAN POND
WEYMOUTH, MASSACHUSETTS

Paul J. Carroll

In a market with a surplus of larger and older attached housing, Whitman Pond Village effectively demonstrates how appropriate design and planning can mitigate the disadvantages traditionally associated with higher-density pro-

Paul J. Carroll, AIA, is head of Paul J. Carroll Associates based in Boston, Massachusetts. His design practice includes commercial and office buildings, shopping centers, health care facilities, and large-scale residential projects. Carroll is a member of the National AIA Housing and Codes Committees.

grams. A townhouse community of 11 seven-unit clusters on six acres, Whitman Pond Village employs open interior planning to create an illusion of space, making each unit seem larger than its 680 to 800 square feet. To further diminish the impression of density and to promote socializing among neighbors, each cluster shares an entrance courtyard. And although the units are small in comparison to other attached housing in the area, high-quality construction and materials give them the substantial character that encouraged many renters to become first-time homeowners.

■ Instead of plotting these townhouses in a linear pattern, the architect grouped them into compact clusters that measure only 90 feet in length; thus, road and utility costs are reduced. The clusters also permit at least five of the seven units to have more than two exposures to the outdoors.

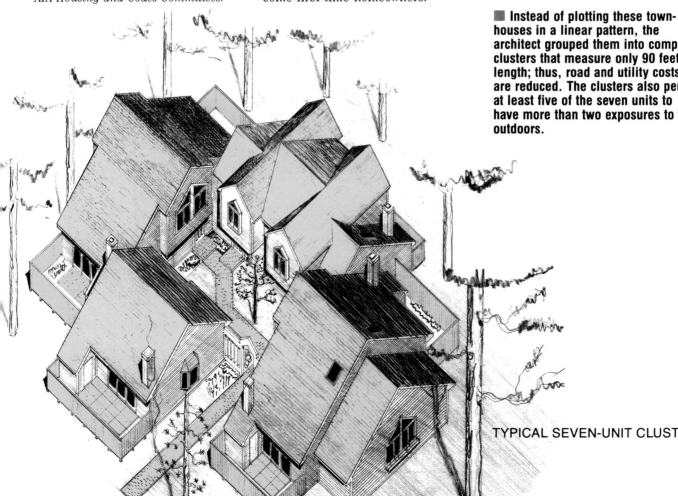

TYPICAL SEVEN-UNIT CLUSTER

■ The central courtyard provides a point of entrance to each of the seven units grouped within the cluster. High-pitched roofs and clapboard siding follow the traditional New England style.

DEVELOPMENT STRATEGY

The developer's intent at Whitman Pond was to provide traditional, yet individualized, townhouses; to create homes that offer style and privacy; and to offer buyers the attributes that foster pride of ownership. The prime objective was to build housing at affordable prices for a market whose annual incomes range from $20,000 to $30,000. Although not directly subsidized, the project was the first to come on line under a Massachusetts program offering below-market mortgage interest rates to first-time buyers.

Modular construction and a fast-track construction program created significant cost reductions. However, an efficient site plan helped most to minimize construction costs. The site concept led to a reduction in road surface and utilities, thereby lowering dramatically the per-unit cost of site improvements.

SITE

Whitman Pond Village's site was a passed-over, nonconforming parcel in a primarily single-family residential area. The land was relatively inexpensive because of large rock outcroppings that limited its development potential. A bonus for the developer was an adjacent lake with bath houses, a public recreational facility that eliminated the need to budget for on-site amenities.

PLANNING

Essential to the reduction of construction and maintenance ex-

penses was siting unit clusters around entry courtyards. With typical townhouse planning, a seven-unit building measures at least 140 feet to 160 feet in length. Structures at Whitman Pond total only 90 feet in length, allowing significant infrastructure cost savings.

Each of the 11 seven-unit clusters is arranged in a pinwheel configuration, with a landscaped entry courtyard at the center and grade-level patios for each unit at the perimeter. This concept afforded a yield of 12.8 units per acre, with 66 percent of the site remaining in open space. Shared open space compensated for the higher density by providing outdoor living areas and increased opportunities for communal activity.

Each building contains a mix of one- and two-bedroom units. Five units in each structure have more than two exterior exposures for maximum light and ventilation. The 20-foot-by-20-foot foundation of each

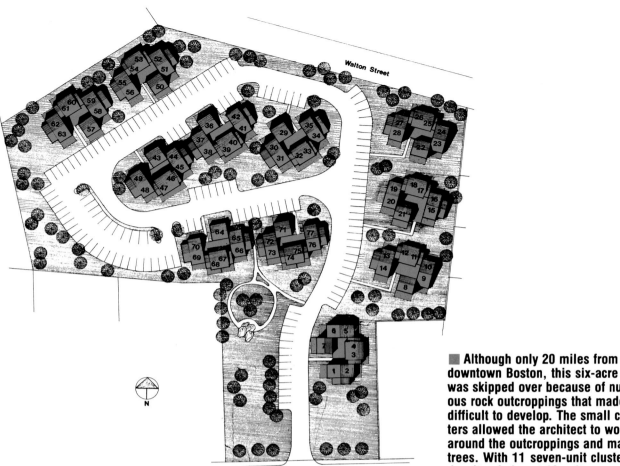

Walton Street

Lake Street

SITE PLAN

N

unit allowed the one- and two-bed-room plans to be interchanged as sales dictated.

Existing rock formations were used to good advantage as a land-scape element, complemented by the retention of many mature oaks and elms. Distinctive gates identify entries to unit clusters.

■ Although only 20 miles from downtown Boston, this six-acre site was skipped over because of numer-ous rock outcroppings that made it difficult to develop. The small clus-ters allowed the architect to work around the outcroppings and mature trees. With 11 seven-unit clusters, a density of almost 13 units per acre was achieved.

■ Modular and prefabrication con-struction techniques were used to maintain affordability without com-promising quality. Each unit has an at-grade, fenced patio located around the perimeter of the cluster.

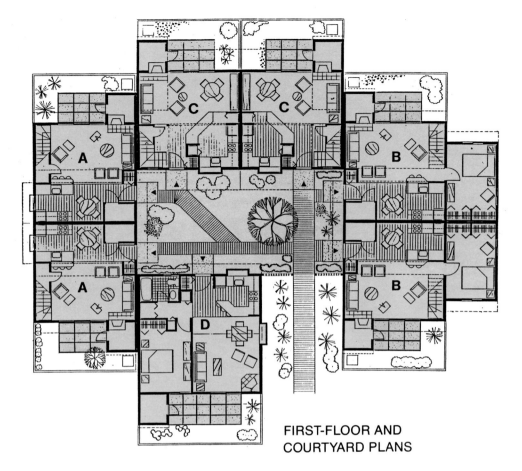

FIRST-FLOOR AND
COURTYARD PLANS

ARCHITECTURE

Many of Whitman Pond's buildings are modular components. With off-site prefabrication, labor costs were reduced and the construction schedule was compressed—an added benefit in New England's long winter season. Four-foot building increments, an interchangeable unit plan, energy-conserving common walls, and back-to-back plumbing afforded additional economies.

Whitman Pond Village's design incorporates many amenities not commonly found in affordable housing. Among these features are volume ceilings, private patios, spiral stairs, fireplaces, and air conditioning. Within the constraints of prefabricated components, the architecture is an updated rendition of forms and materials traditional in the New England design vocabulary—white clapboard, high-pitched roofs, and a rambling footprint.

APPROVAL AND FINANCING

A streamlined development application process allowed the town's planning board to approve plans and drawings in only one day. At a time when the market rate was 14 percent, the Massachusetts Housing Finance Agency offered mortgage financing at 10 percent interest, with only a 5 percent downpayment.

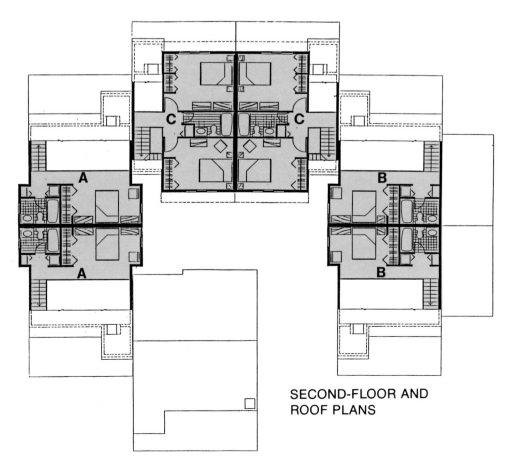

SECOND-FLOOR AND
ROOF PLANS

■ **The 20-foot-by-20-foot unit pads can accommodate any of the four floor plans. This flexibility allowed units to be built in accordance with market demand. Most of the 77 units—which ranged in price from $53,900 to $65,000—were purchased by first-time homebuyers.**

MARKETING

With a smaller, denser product, the marketing challenge was to convince buyers that, with a small initial investment, they could own homes for the same monthly cost as renting. Minimal advertising coupled with the attractive financing package resulted in sales of all 77 units within six months, at prices ranging from $53,900 to $65,000. As anticipated, most buyers are young, first-time homeowners. This award-winning concept was repeated successfully in Washington, D.C., and New Hampshire.

PROJECT DATA

LAND USE INFORMATION:
Site Area: 6 acres
Total Units: 77
Density: 12.8 units per acre
Parking Spaces: 149
Parking Index: 1.9 spaces per unit

LAND USE PLAN:

	Acres	Percent of Site
Open Space	4.00	66.6%
Buildings	1.33	22.1
Roads/Parking Area	0.68	11.3

UNIT INFORMATION:
Number of Townhouse Units: 77
Size: 680 to 800 square feet
Program: 2-bdrm./1-bath; 1-bdrm./1-bath
Sales Prices: $53,900 to $65,000

ECONOMIC INFORMATION:
Site Value: $350,000[1]
Land Improvement Costs: $385,000[2]
Construction Costs: $40 to $42 per square foot
Homeowner Fee: $50 per month (originally)

Notes:
[1]$4,545 per unit.
[2]$5,000 per unit.

DIRECTIONS:
From Logan Airport, take Southeast Expressway to Route 3 south; exit Route 3 south at Exit 16A. Turn right on Route 53 (second traffic light), turn left on Pleasant Street (first traffic light), turn right on Lake Street (first traffic light), and proceed to Whitman Pond Village, on left.

DEVELOPER:
Fox Properties
47 Winter Street
Post Office Box 29
Weymouth, Massachusetts 02189

ARCHITECT:
Paul J. Carroll and Associates
30 The Fenway
Boston, Massachusetts 02115

AWARD:
• Grand Award: *Builder* magazine, Best Small Attached Housing Project, 1984

THE COACH HOUSES OF TOWN PLACE
BOCA RATON, FLORIDA

Quincy R. Johnson III

The inspiration for Lexington Homes's development of The Coach Houses of Town Place came from the firm's success with its Lexington Green coach home project at the PGA National Resort in Palm Beach Gardens, Florida.

In the early 1980s, Boca Raton's strong economic base and its midpoint Gold Coast location between Fort Lauderdale and West Palm Beach made it a hot spot for buyers of new and used homes. With a strong high-technology employment base, as well as a plentiful number of financial and medical institutions, the area was drawing a large population of young executives who wanted a Boca Raton address but could not afford a single-family home. A second market segment wanted to move down from detached housing.

DEVELOPMENT STRATEGY

Lexington Homes realized it could tap the target markets if it offered smaller, more affordable residences with upscale features and amenities. The key was to design a community with a higher density,

---

Quincy R. Johnson III, AIA, MIRM, is president of Quincy Johnson Associates Architects/Planners, based in Boca Raton, Florida. The firm has designed housing projects in 22 states. Johnson is a member of the National AIA Housing Committee, a frequent speaker at housing industry forums, and a monthly columnist for Florida Home Builder *magazine. He is also an active member in the Institute of Residential Marketing.*

---

but without sacrificing the style and amenities important to these buyers.

To ensure the success of the new product, the developer sought a location close to Boca Raton's major thoroughfares and shopping attractions and, in 1983, purchased a 34.87-acre site from Arvida Corporation for $150,000 per acre. The site borders two high-traffic roads, St. Andrews Boulevard and Palmetto Park Road, and provides easy access to both the interstate highway and Florida's Turnpike. It is within walking distance of Town Center, a major regional mall. The property fit the corporate philosophy of selecting sites at prestigious locations with high visibility.

The community is part of Arvida's Town Place planned unit development, which features an extensive tennis and aquatic center. Residents of The Coach Houses at Town Place can apply for membership in Arvida's club system, which includes several country clubs both locally and across the state—another important consideration in Lexington's decision to purchase the property.

A long list of other developers building in Town Place helped establish an upscale image in the local marketplace. Project architects Quincy Johnson Associates proposed a "coach home" concept for 312 residences at a density of 8.9 units per acre.

SITE

Before construction, Lexington spent $23,000 per unit in a concerted effort to develop its new property within the natural ambience of Boca Raton. More than 800 trees were carefully transplanted, including many mature live oaks and palms. A slough filled with native maple trees on the northern perimeter was preserved, and a three-acre lake was created in the middle of the planned community, satisfying both stormwater management and aesthetic concerns. The lake also provided the developer with an inexpensive source for additional fill on the low-lying site.

PLANNING

The coach home plan specified 35 two-story eight-plex buildings and eight two-story four-plex buildings. Lexington was particularly interested in a product offering attached garages since the majority of the competition at the time was not providing them. The development team decided to use a curvilinear land plan to avoid a "barracks"-like massing that would not be readily accepted in the Boca Raton market. The double entry plan and curvilinear loop prevented horizontal massing of buildings and made it easy to find individual addresses.

The four-plex buildings were planned to fit in corner areas of the site where the eight-plex buildings could not be accommodated sufficiently. The curvilinear layout allowed for a maximum number of these units to border premium locations on the lake or slough.

Much of the native vegetation on the south perimeter of Palmetto Park Road was left intact. Landscaping was added to buffer the units from traffic while still allowing a view of the property from Palmetto Park, a major road. Two highly visible entrance treatments were planned off St. Andrews, which created attractive "windows" focusing on and highlighting the models.

■ **To provide both affordability and low maintenance, the architect used a coach home design that combines townhouses and stacked flats within eight-plex and four-plex buildings. The 312-unit project is located on a heavily landscaped 35-acre site, and achieves a density of 8.9 units per acre. Amenities include two pools, a three-acre lake that provides for stormwater retention, and a large wooded nature preserve.**

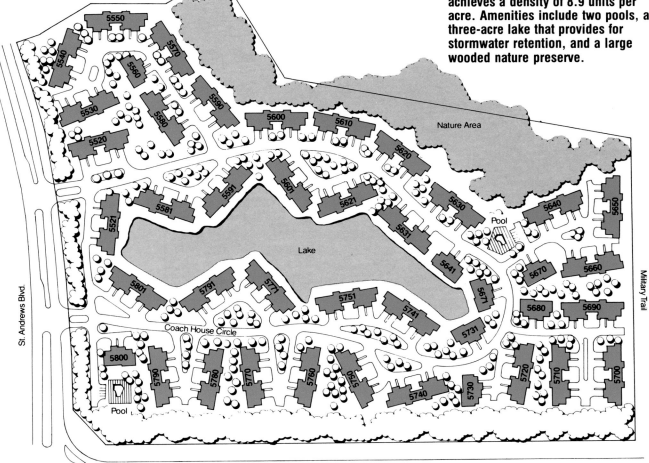

This site plan indicates the developer's intent. It is subject to change without notice.

■ Each unit enjoys a private entrance featuring a covered archway beneath a tiled barrel roof that carries out the "Spanish village" architectural theme. Lush landscaping is a major selling point in this tropical Florida setting.

ARCHITECTURE

All of the buildings at The Coach Houses of Town Place were designed in southern Florida's dominant "Spanish village" architectural style. Each structure features a Spanish barrel tile roof with cedar trellises.

Lexington's coach home experience at PGA National suggested some minor modifications to these successful designs. The developer switched from wood to concrete caps on the exterior perimeter walls and specified metal rather than wood garage doors to ensure a longer, more maintenance-free material.

While some consumers in the Boca Raton area might prefer a two-car garage to the one-car garages provided, the developer believed

such an addition to the design would create a more expensive product without a matching increase in demand. The garage adds approximately $4,500 to $6,000 to the construction cost of each residence.

Individual entries are removed from each other. For second-story residences, a mid-level entry is positioned from a half-flight of exterior stairs. This entry opens into a foyer that offers a strategic resting point, and simulates a sense of the split-level residence popular in the northern United States. Second-floor units also have private, inside stairways to the garage, with the space beneath these stairways providing ample storage.

The Coach Houses of Town Place offer four different floor plans catering to specific market profiles.

Plan A is a two-bedroom, one-bath residence with 1,025 square feet of living space. It features a great room design, long angled views to the outside, and a compact master bedroom with an off-set wall that provides a sitting area. The guest bedroom has a double-door entry and can be used as a den. Plan A is targeted to the large singles market or as a starter home for a married couple without children. The one-bath design keeps the price down without sacrificing other amenities.

Plan B is a two-bedroom, two-bath, 1,400-square-foot design offering twin master suites. The unit has a large master suite and ample living and dining room areas. The kitchen's eat-in area extends onto the balcony, providing a glassed area for casual meals. It also divides the large screened patio into two distinct areas—one off the master bedroom and the other off the living and dining rooms. Plan B is suited for the typical empty nesters or seasonal "snow bird" couples. Both plans A and B are first-floor residences, with plan B always situated at the end of a building.

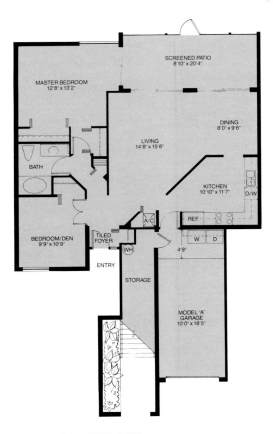

PLAN A—2-BEDROOM/1-BATH
SIZE: 1,025 SQUARE FEET
PRIMARY MARKET: SINGLE PROFESSIONALS, YOUNG COUPLES
LOCATION: FIRST FLOOR

PLAN B—2-BEDROOM/2-BATH
SIZE: 1,400 SQUARE FEET
PRIMARY MARKET: EMPTY NESTERS, "SNOW BIRD" COUPLES
LOCATION: FIRST FLOOR AT END OF BUILDING

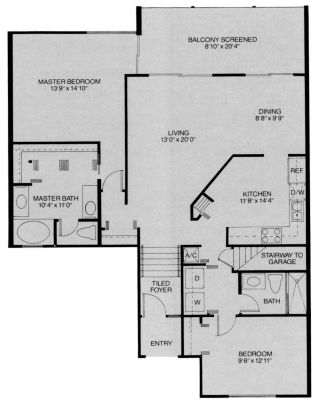

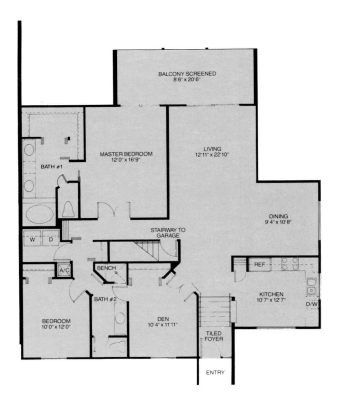

PLAN C—2-BEDROOM/2-BATH
SIZE: 1,275 SQUARE FEET
PRIMARY MARKET: MOVE-UP BUYERS, YOUNG COUPLES, EMPTY NESTERS
LOCATION: SECOND FLOOR

PLAN D—3-BEDROOM/2-BATH
SIZE: 1,600 SQUARE FEET
PRIMARY MARKET: MOVE-UP BUYERS (AFFLUENT FAMILIES), EMPTY NESTERS
LOCATION: SECOND FLOOR AT END OF BUILDING

■ Vaulted ceilings and paddle fans—even in first-floor units—add volume and comfort to the living and dining areas.

Robert Stein

Plan C is a two-bedroom, two-bath, split-level plan with 1,275 square feet of living space. It is an expanded version of the A model, with larger bedrooms and a laundry room. This unit appeals to the move-up home buyer, the young married couple who might have one child, or the empty nester who is ready to move down from a single-family residence.

Plan D has three bedrooms and two baths with 1,600 square feet of living space. Its features include a formal living and dining room, den with double-door entry, and guest bath designed with one, two, or three access points to accommodate a second or third master bedroom

suite. The large master suite has a double-door entry, and double vanities in the bath. Plan D was designed to accommodate the more affluent move-up family needing a residence with more space, or empty nesters who need a den or study. Both plan C and plan D are second-floor residences, with plan D always at the end of the building.

Vaulted ceilings further enhance the perception of single-family living, especially in plans A and B, where consumers are pleasantly surprised to find volume spaces in first-floor residences of two-story buildings. Each residence includes a large, fully covered and screened patio or balcony, with access from both living room and master bedroom, as well as a roomy L-shaped kitchen with comfortable breakfast area. Bathrooms feature ceramic tiling, custom cultured marble vanity tops and tubs, and oversized mirrors; plans B, C, and D offer compartmentalized bathrooms. All units have indoor laundry areas, except plan A, where washer and dryer facilities are in the garage. Recreational amenities within the community include two heated swimming pools with sundecks.

MARKETING

A Fort Lauderdale advertising and public relations firm publicized the community in local newspapers, and trade and relocation publications. Lexington also hired a marketing/broker relations director to work closely with local brokers and real estate agents, providing them with a flow of current information. Units purchased through the Boca Raton and Delray Beach Board of Realtors account for approximately 70 percent of sales.

To date, more than 200 residences have sold at The Coach Houses of Town Place. Some of the more recent sales were the result of the community's positive referral service. Contributing to the sales success is the fact that six area builders and eight realtors are residents in the community. At least a dozen residents brought friends and relatives into the neighborhood, including one buyer who encouraged six friends and four relatives to purchase homes. The developer estimates that 60 percent of sales are to single professionals and young married couples with no children. Approximately 10 percent of residents

■ Glass-enclosed breakfast nooks offer a relaxing lakefront view of one of the community's outdoor amenities.

Robert Stein

have children, and an additional 30 are "snow birds" or empty nesters from the Northeast.

Buyer consensus is that these coach homes offer—at moderate prices—many of the advantages of single-family housing. Some buyers have taken advantage of the affordability and purchased two residences, maintaining one as an investment property. Especially praised are the first-floor volumes, space-maximizing interior planning, garages with direct unit access, and the substantial recreational amenity package.

PROJECT DATA

LAND USE INFORMATION:
Site Area: 34.87 acres
Total Units: 312
Density: 8.9 units per acre
Parking Spaces: 624
Parking Index: 2 spaces per unit

LAND USE PLAN:

	Acres	Percent of Site
Open Space	16.14	46.3%
Buildings	7.66	21.9
Roads/Parking	7.74	22.2
Lake	3.33	9.5

UNIT INFORMATION[1]:

Location	Type	Number	Square Feet	Sales Price
A) 1st floor	2-bdrm./1-bath	78	1,025	$ 97,500
B) 1st floor	2-bdrm./2-bath	78	1,400	$125,000
C) 2nd floor	2-bdrm./2-bath	78	1,275	$114,000
D) 2nd floor	3-bdrm./2-bath	78	1,600	$143,000

ECONOMIC INFORMATION:
Site Value: $5,230,000[2]
Site Improvement Costs: $3,432,000[3]
Construction Costs: $8.6 million for first 200 units[4]
Total Hard and Soft Costs: $17,622,000 for first 200 units[5]
Amenities Costs: $200,000[6]
Homeowner Fee: $143 per month

Notes:
[1]Each unit has one-car attached garage. Plans B and D are always located at the end of the building.
[2]$16,762 per unit; $150,000 per acre.
[3]$11,000 per unit; includes fees, lake, landscaping, irrigation, and two heated swimming pools with sundecks.
[4]Originally $30 per square foot; now up to $35 per square foot.
[5]$88,110 per unit.
[6]Two swimming pools plus ancillary facilities.

DIRECTIONS:
From Palm Beach International Airport, take Interstate 95 south to Palmetto Park Road; go west on Palmetto Park to St. Andrews Boulevard (second traffic light); project is on corner of Palmetto Park Road and St. Andrews.

From Lauderdale International Airport, take Interstate 95 north to Palmetto Park Road; go west on Palmetto Park to St. Andrews Boulevard (second traffic light); project is on corner of Palmetto Park and St. Andrews.

From Florida's Turnpike, exit at Glades Road; go east on Glades approximately 1.5 miles to St. Andrews Boulevard and south on St. Andrews to project entrance.

DEVELOPER:
Lexington Homes
5521-A Coach House Circle
Boca Raton, Florida 33432

ARCHITECT:
Quincy Johnson Associates, Architects/Planners
949 Clint Moore Road
Boca Raton, Florida 33431

RIVERPLACE
NEW HAVEN, CONNECTICUT

K. Zane Yost

In 1981, affordable ownership housing in the city of New Haven, Connecticut, was severely restricted. More than half of the demand in the New Haven labor market area was for housing in the $30,000 to $72,000 range. However, less than 10 percent of the residential units being produced were priced below $72,000. Within the city, only 44 units of condominium housing had been built that year, and these were selling at prices ranging from $90,000 to $95,000.

In an effort to spark a revitalization of the area, New Haven's Redevelopment Agency announced a design competition for a 4.5-acre stretch of Front Street in Fair Haven, a section of the city settled in the 17th century. The project was awarded to architect Zane Yost and market researcher John Scott based on a Victorian-style townhouse/flat mix. The city liked the "friendliness" of the design in relationship to the older buildings in the neighborhood.

Winning the competition gave Yost and Scott, who formed the Riverfront Development Corporation, the right to buy the land for $76,000. This reduced land cost, combined with the higher density allowance, made possible a riverfront development of upscale housing at affordable prices.

DEVELOPMENT STRATEGY AND FINANCING

As there were few desirable housing opportunities within the buying power of young families and one- or two-person households, Riverplace was designed to offer affordable city living, recreation, and proximity to employment and cultural activities within a true neighborhood setting.

Zane Yost, AIA, is president of Zane Yost and Associates, Inc., of Bridgeport, Connecticut, which has done the land planning and designs for over 7,000 housing units throughout the Northeast. Yost is a member and past chairman of the National AIA Housing Committee and is a recognized speaker on housing issues.

■ The Victorian architectural style blends well with the surrounding neighborhood, which dates back to the 17th century. Most units are offered with an optional one-car garage, with the remainder of the parking area provided in small, off-street lots.

To convince the city of their commitment to bring the project to reality, the developers contributed $150,000 toward a riverside park promised by the city as a key amenity for the project.

The 1981–1982 financial environment was not conducive to development. Interest on construction financing was 18.5 percent. But the complex approval process for a city-sponsored infill project moved slowly, and when approvals were finally in place in 1984, the New Haven Savings Bank financed a $2 million construction loan at 12.5 percent interest.

THE SITE

The 4.5-acre site is located in a historic district just 10 minutes from downtown New Haven, in a declining quasi-industrial neighborhood. The sloping stretch of city land along the Quinnipiac River was a scrap metal yard, after years of being home to oyster fishermen. Above the site stood historic Victorian homes.

Because the site was zoned for a mix of industrial, residential, and business uses, the developer applied to the New Haven Planning Commission for designation as a planned development district. This zoning ordinance allowed 20 units per acre, or a total of 88 units in a townhouse/flat mix with three-story flats reminiscent of the historic New Haven "triple decker" and townhouse over a flat.

Because it was an urban infill site awarded by the Redevelopment Agency, plans had to be in keeping with the goals for the revitalization of the Fair Haven Renewal Area and, in particular, the Quinnipiac Riverfront.

APPROVALS

The site was also in a floodplain and the Coastal Area Management Zone, which required finished floors

of living areas to be at or above the established flood level, in this case, 11 feet above mean sea level. As the site was located in the Quinnipiac River Historic District, separate approvals were needed for the Historic District Commission and the State Historic Preservation Office.

In addition, the city promised the people living in the historic houses on East Pearl Street above the site that their views of the river would not be obstructed. This called for public hearings with neighborhood owners reviewing plans and requesting design changes.

Although working drawings were available as required within 90 days, it took almost three years to gain all the approvals. This time lapse worked in the developer's favor, as the shifting economy provided a more conducive environment for the construction of affordable housing.

These delays also allowed the city time to clear the site of scrap iron and storage tanks, restructure Front Street, and rebuild the Grand Avenue bridge leading to the site (at a

■ **Multiple markets made up of first-time buyers, singles, and young professional couples could be targeted because of the mixture of product types being offered. All of these markets appreciated the convenience offered by the in-town location.**

cost of $4 million). The city also rehabilitated commercial buildings along Grand Avenue leading to the site, and appropriated $1.3 million toward developing the park.

PLANNING

Sensitive architectural and planning solutions were implemented at Riverplace. With a total of 88 units, and 20 units per acre, the feeling of density was softened by a skillful mix of product types including: Victorian townhouses; two-story "Cape Cods," and "triple deckers," which dominated New Haven at the turn of the century.

The concept of townhouse over one-bedroom flat presented the

Chambers Street

Second Street

East Pearl Street

Pierpont Street

Front Street

D/D/D*   E/E/E   B   A/C   D/D/D*   F

■ **As seen from Front Street between Second and Pierpont, this portion of the Riverplace plan illustrates how product types are mixed within building clusters. Unit plans include stacked flats (plans D and E), townhouses (plan B), townhouses over flats (plans A and C), and freestanding one-family houses (plan F).**

problem of providing a desirable private outdoor space for overhead units. With the use of retaining walls, the one-bedroom flat is level with the grade in front and has a side yard, while the townhouse opens to the rear with its private yard. The city required that river views from existing homes on the adjacent hillside be preserved. Buildings were configured with varying heights so that adjacent houses could overlook them and have clear view corridors. The sloping hillside lent itself to a three-story configuration that allows parking under one- and two-story townhouses.

ARCHITECTURE

To integrate Riverplace with its historic neighborhood, the designers chose a distinctive Victorian architecture in a stick style with balconies, bay windows, and dormers. Tall narrow windows with ornamentation, scalloped shingles, eave brackets, hand-built stair rails, and white picket fences were also offered. Most units have three-sided exposure; all have views of the river and park and either a private backyard, balcony, or porch. Inside, material quality is reinforced through recessed lighting, traditional hardware, and fireplaces.

Riverplace offers a mixture of housing products. One model is designed as a detached, two-story Cape Cod with a garage under it. It takes its design from the early fishermen's homes in the area. The traditional lobster "crib" under the original version of this home has been adapted as a two-car garage concealed with lattices. Another model is based on the New Haven triple decker, with two units on each of the three levels in a townhouse-style building. The triple decker units range in size from a 960-square-foot one-bedroom unit, one bath to a 1,092-square-foot two-bedroom unit with eat-in kitchen, walk-in laundry room, and two walk-in closets in the master bedroom.

The stacked townhouse plans combine the familiar two-level townhouse over a single-level flat. An affordable one-bedroom, one-bath, downsized unit of 612 square feet has a galley kitchen with serving bar, a large dining area centered on a bay window, two walk-in closets in the master bedroom, and access to generous attic storage.

MARKETING

Riverplace responded to the city's affordable housing shortage. It offered one-, two-, and three-bedroom units of 612 to 1,478 square feet, priced at $65,000 to $85,000. Construction costs averaged about $42 per square foot, for a total of approximately $4.5 million.

The project opened for presales in June 1984, almost three years after the successful bid for the land. Interest rates and demand had improved significantly. Financing eased to between 13 to 14 percent. The new economic climate, combined

■ The 4.5-acre project site offered the advantages of a riverfront location near downtown New Haven, Connecticut, and the disadvantages of being in a declining, partially industrial neighborhood. The linear site configuration presented another challenge. The architects created a 20-unit-per-acre, mixed-product plan that capitalized on views of the river and the emerging market for housing convenient to downtown services.

with the location, attractiveness, and affordability of the units, promoted a very lively sales pace of 10 units per month.

An on-site sales trailer was equipped with graphically rendered one-quarter-inch floor plans, finishes, and upgrades. The grand opening was scheduled to coincide with Fair Haven Day, which attracted thousands of people to the site in a

**PLAN C—FLAT UNDER
  TOWNHOUSE
1-BEDROOM/1-BATH
612 SQUARE FEET**

**PLAN A—TWO-STORY TOWNHOUSE OVER FLAT
2-BEDROOM/1½-BATH
1,224 SQUARE FEET**

■ **Plan C is a traditional Victorian townhouse located above an affordable, single-level flat. The entrance to the plan A flat unit is at grade while the entrance to the townhouse unit is on the second level of the building.**

■ **Riverplace incorporates several units of two-story townhouses over single-level flats. The lower-level flat is popular for its affordability and single-level design. In some locations where topography permits, the townhouse has access to a ground-level patio to its rear.**

festival celebration. Riverplace T-shirts were distributed and a great deal of interest was generated. Deposits were taken and all of the first phase was sold out before construction began. One furnished model, a townhouse, was done as part of the second phase.

The market has included first-time buyers, singles, and young professional couples who enjoy Riverplace's convenience to shopping, churches, restaurants, employment, and public transportation.

Riverplace has acted as a catalyst for development along the riverfront. Between January 1985 and June 1986, proposals for developments comprising 600 residential units were presented to city planning and zoning boards; currently, 530 units along the east and west banks of the Quinnipiac River are completed and occupied, and another 200 are under construction.

Nearly 500 housing units have been completed or are under construction in the area immediately surrounding Fair Haven's redevelopment land and historic district. As would be expected, land costs have soared. In 1982, developers paid approximately $7,500 per unit for unsubsidized land; today, the price is about $50,000 per unit.

■ **Interiors featured traditional design elements such as tall, narrow windows, corner fireplaces, recessed lighting, crown molding, and chair rails.**

PROJECT DATA

LAND USE INFORMATION:
Site Area: 4.5 acres
Total Units: 88
Density: 20 units per acre
Parking Index: 1.5 spaces per unit[1]

UNIT INFORMATION:

Program	Type	Square Feet	Garage	Sales Prices[2]
A) Townhouse	2-bdrm./1½-bath	1,224	Optional	$154,900
B) Townhouse	2–3-bdrm./2½-bath	1,478	1	$179,900
C) Flat	1-bdrm./1-bath	612	Optional	$ 79,900
D) Flat	1-bdrm./1-bath	960	Optional	$119,900–$124,900
E) Flat	2-bdrm./1-bath	1,092	Optional	$125,900–$130,000
F) Cape Cod	3-bdrm./1-bath	1,413	1	$165,900

ECONOMIC INFORMATION:
Site Value: $76,000[3]
Construction Costs: Approximately $4,500,000[4]
Site Improvement Costs: $700,000[5]

Notes:
[1]Includes 40 garage spaces.
[2]At presales (1984), units were priced from $65,000 to $85,000.
[3]$864 per unit.
[4]$42 per square foot average.
[5]$7,954 per unit.

DIRECTIONS:
From Bradley International Airport in Hartford, Connecticut, take Bradley International connector (Route 20) east to I-91. Take I-91 south to Exit 6. Turn right onto Blatchley Avenue, travel one block, then turn left onto Lombard Street. Continue on Lombard to North Front Street and the Quinnipiac River. Turn right onto North Front Street and continue past Grand Avenue to South Front Street. Riverplace is on the right.

DEVELOPER:
Riverfront Development Corp.
100 Crown Street
New Haven, Connecticut 06510

BUILDER:
Revesco Inc.
10 Oxford Road
Milford, Connecticut 06460

ARCHITECT:
Zane Yost & Associates, Inc.
144 Island Brook Avenue
Bridgeport, Connecticut 06606

MARKETING:
Scott-Fitton & Company, Inc.
100 Crown Street
New Haven, Connecticut 06510

AWARD:
• *Builder* magazine, Best Project of the Month, June 1986

SEA COLONY
SAN DIEGO, CALIFORNIA

Dale Naegle

I n southern California the urban homestead is perceived as a living situation in which one's car resides a door's thickness away from oneself. In short, the garage is attached.

In the late 1970s, the young first-time buyer looking for affordable, in-town housing had to settle for apartment-type stacked flats. Houses with attached garages were not available in densities greater than 10 units per acre, and lower-density programs were usually beyond the financial reach of young buyers.

Yet demand was very strong for affordable housing located close to the city center. This was particularly true in San Diego, which was experiencing tremendous population growth related to its academic institutions, high-tech industry, and desirable climate. But infill sites zoned for apartments in density ranges of 14 to 28 units per acre were extremely expensive. To have density yields increased, developers of land zoned for lower densities were required to go through the planned unit development (PUD) approvals process; discretionary approvals made this a very risky option for them. The townhouse mews offered one solution to these problems at Sea Colony.

Dale W. Naegle, FAIA, is president of Naegle Associates, a San Diego, California–based architectural and planning firm specializing in residential and commercial projects. Naegle has lectured abroad on residential development issues.

DEVELOPMENT STRATEGY

The townhouse mews eventually built at Sea Colony was conceived before a site was found that would yield the needed 18 to 22 units per acre. This density range was selected because it would not require variances or negotiations related to the city's PUD ordinance.

The mews concept was promoted to several developers in the area; Lion Properties recognized its potential and committed resources to purchase and develop an appropriate property. The architect/developer team refined the initial concept and applied it to 270 units to be constructed near Nimitz Boulevard, the infill parcel later marketed as Sea Colony.

As a result of the original pricing of these units, downpayments on them were only slightly higher than a total of the first and last months' rents plus the security deposit required for local, upgraded apartments. Prospective buyers immediately recognized this equity ladder and started climbing.

SITE PLANNING AND ENGINEERING

The unique mews concept at Sea Colony was developed for a 13-acre infill parcel with a natural cross slope of 3 percent to 8 percent. Four townhouse plans with attached garages are included in the program, and are grouped into six-unit lineal buildings.

Garages are submerged four and one-half feet, allowing each building to be classified as a two-story, Type

V nonrated building. This reduced construction costs, as a three-story, Type V structure would have required a one-hour fire wall rating, with more expensive drywall installation, and second exits from the top floor. Construction savings are also realized from the cross slope, which allows driveways to drain naturally.

Each plan has one or two bedrooms on the upper level, with a living and dining area at mid-level and a garage at the lower level; all levels are connected by interior stairways. The living/dining level is four feet above grade; access is from a half-flight of stairs leading from a pedestrian pathway. Window sills along this entry path are six feet above grade to visually separate occupants from visitors.

In the units with party walls on both sides, the outdoor space occurs at the middle level. Over the garage

entries of these units, a patio "bridge" extends across the 30-foot-wide driveway to the building sharing the drive. At the center of the bridge, a six-foot fence runs parallel to these buildings, and perpendicular to the buildings at the party wall, thus creating 15-foot by 15-foot private balconies. This design was used in lieu of the usual six-foot cantilevered balcony, which would not have offered privacy from balconies across the drive, or screened activities in the motor court.

Balconies for end units are eight feet wide and 14 feet long, and do not stretch across the driveway. To safeguard privacy, they have solid walls that extend three feet above the living room level; the tops of the balcony walls rise eight feet above the pedestrian pathways.

Each six-unit building is attached by bridge patios to another six-unit building. These 12-plex con-

■ The Spanish Mediterranean architecture reflects San Diego's heritage. Building materials of stucco and tile are affordable and require little maintenance.

figurations are sited perpendicular to the private collector roads, which accommodate guest parking. Each drive serves 12 garages, and ends in open space. This building arrangement displays two end units to the collector road, rather than the longer side elevation, thus concealing the actual density of the project.

Entry paths are densely landscaped—to promote privacy for each unit and an established character for the site. Recreational amenities include a clubhouse, swimming pool, and spa, all located at

In this mews plan, six townhouse units are grouped in a linear building. Two six-plex buildings are then placed back-to-back to form the basic 12-unit cluster. A shared driveway is located between the two buildings and one-half level below grade to provide access to garages. Decks extend from the rear of the units and over the driveways to provide outdoor living space.

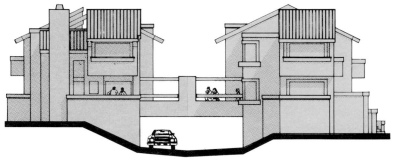

END ELEVATION

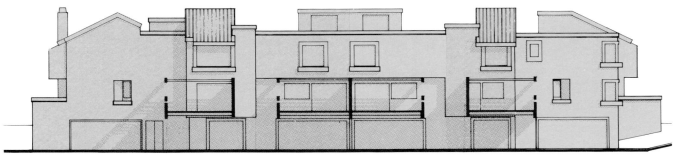

SECTION OVER DRIVEWAY/ELEVATION OF REAR OF UNITS

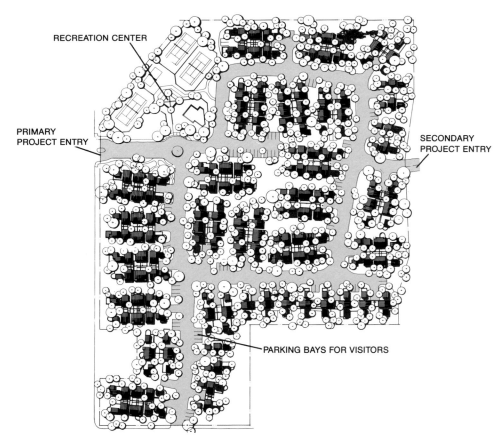

RECREATION CENTER

PRIMARY PROJECT ENTRY

SECONDARY PROJECT ENTRY

PARKING BAYS FOR VISITORS

SITE PLAN

the project entrance. Tennis courts placed along Nimitz Boulevard buffer traffic noise and provide additional privacy for the community.

ARCHITECTURE

The exterior design of Sea Colony reflects the climate and building materials of southern California. The style is Spanish Mediterranean, and colors are in a range of earth tones for both roof tiles and stucco.

Located on a 13-acre infill site close to downtown San Diego, California, Sea Colony used a townhouse mews plan to meet the strong local demand for condominiums from young, first-time buyers. Affordability depended largely on reaching an apartment density of over 20 units per acre; the mews design met this density requirement without looking like a typical apartment project. Each unit also has an attached garage to further distinguish it from an apartment.

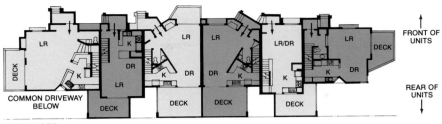

COMMON DRIVEWAY BELOW

FIRST FLOOR

FRONT OF UNITS

REAR OF UNITS

COMMON DRIVEWAY BELOW

SECOND FLOOR

FRONT OF UNITS

REAR OF UNITS

■ **The typical building contains six one- and two-bedroom units ranging from 843 to 1,322 square feet. Interior units (those with two party walls) have decks facing the rear of the building that extend over the driveway, while end units have decks along the side of the building at grade level. Located below each two-story townhouse is an attached one- or two-car garage.**

TYPICAL FLOOR PLANS

Entrance stairways and balconies are of stucco, proportioned to enhance the buildings without the need for additional materials, such as wood, that require more maintenance.

The half-flight entrance stairway for each home twists and turns to provide maximum privacy and a sense of identity. Inside, floor plans range in size from 843 to 1,322 square feet, and incorporate angled walls to animate interior spaces and delineate room functions without obstructing views. By providing as much openness as possible within limited square footage, this design works to overcome the "apartment" feeling associated with high-density housing.

MARKETING

Because of pent-up demand for affordable housing in this area, marketing for Sea Colony was minimal. One year before completion, the project was sold out, with prospective buyers standing in line for the opportunity to purchase units. Lion Properties successfully repeated this product on six other sites throughout San Diego, and to date, the concept has been applied to more than 2,000 housing units.

PROJECT DATA

LAND USE INFORMATION:
Site Area: 13 acres
Total Units: 270
Density: 20.76 units per acre
Parking Spaces[1]: 675
Parking Index: 2.5 spaces per unit

ECONOMIC INFORMATION:
Site Value: $1.1 million
Site Improvement Costs: $612,000
Construction Costs: $5,870,000[2]
Amenities Costs: $45,000[3]
Homeowner Fee: $45 per month[4]

UNIT TYPES:

Type	Square Feet	Number	Opening Sales Price[5]	Garage Spaces[6]
1-bdrm./1-bath	843	21	$34,500	21
2-bdrm./1-bath	867	53	36,500	53
2-bdrm./2-bath	995	68	39,500	136
2-bdrm./2-bath	1,101	80	42,500	160
2-bdrm./2-bath	1,322	48	49,000	96

Notes:
[1]One- and two-car garages.
[2]About $20 per square foot.
[3]For three lighted tennis courts.
[4]At opening.
[5]Year of sale, 1975.
[6]The 843- and 867-square-foot units each have one garage space and one assigned surface lot space; guest parking is provided at a ratio of .5 spaces per unit.

DIRECTIONS:
From Lindbergh Field, take Harbor Drive west to Nimitz Boulevard and turn right. Turn right onto Chatsworth and left onto Voltaire. Follow Voltaire to Sea Colony Drive.

DEVELOPER:
Bill Scott
Lion Property Development
1669 North Hotel Circle, Suite 200
San Diego, California 92108

LANDSCAPE ARCHITECT:
Kawaski Thailaker & Associates
3776 Fourth Avenue
San Diego, California 92103

ARCHITECT:
Naegle Associates, Inc.
2210 Avenida de la Playa
La Jolla, California 92037

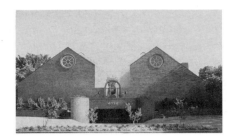

WYCLIFF CONDOMINIUMS
DALLAS, TEXAS

Jack Craycroft

I n 1982, Dallas was approaching the peak of an unprecedented growth period, accompanied by a boom in real estate. Speculators were driving up land costs in the face of strong demand for housing of all kinds, as well as for commercial developments. Interest rates, although beginning to moderate from all-time highs, were hovering around 14 percent. These high interest rates combined with apartment rents of $0.65 to $0.70 per square foot to make homeownership difficult.

Dallas, the archetypal Sunbelt city, was growing beyond its employ-

Jack Craycroft, AIA, is head of Craycroft Architects, Inc., based in Dallas, Texas. The firm has designed over 150,000 housing units and numerous commercial buildings, hotels, and country clubs. Craycroft is a past Dallas Chapter AIA president and a member of the National AIA Housing and Design Committees.

ment centers without an effective mass transit system. Its central business district was and remains strongly vibrant, resulting in near-gridlock on an overcrowded freeway system. Thus, a need existed for close-in housing for affluent adults without children. Because condominiums had been accepted as a housing alternative, both as converted apartments and as newly built communities, they represented the preferred solution.

DEVELOPMENT STRATEGY AND FINANCING

The developer, an architect who was expanding into project development, had two objectives: 1) to create a living environment for private use, and 2) to demonstrate planning concepts that would encourage inner-city redevelopment on the expensive sites available in Dallas.

Because of high land costs, a rental project was not feasible. A

■ In the typical mews design, units face each other and onto the linear central courtyard. Private patios are at the rear of each unit in the side yard setback area. This urban version of the mews concept locates all parking in a common underground garage with individual entrances to each of the units from the garage. The courtyard level sits about four feet above grade, while the garage is submerged about four feet below grade.

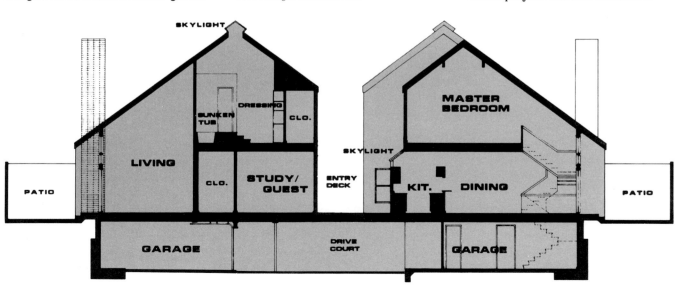

■ The 14,350-square-foot site for this mews design condominium project was created by combining two former single-family detached lots. About two miles northwest of downtown Dallas, Texas, the site is located on a very busy street in a transitional neighborhood. Curb cuts allow for easy right turns into and out of the site. Security features include a gate at the courtyard entrance and controlled access to the parking garage.

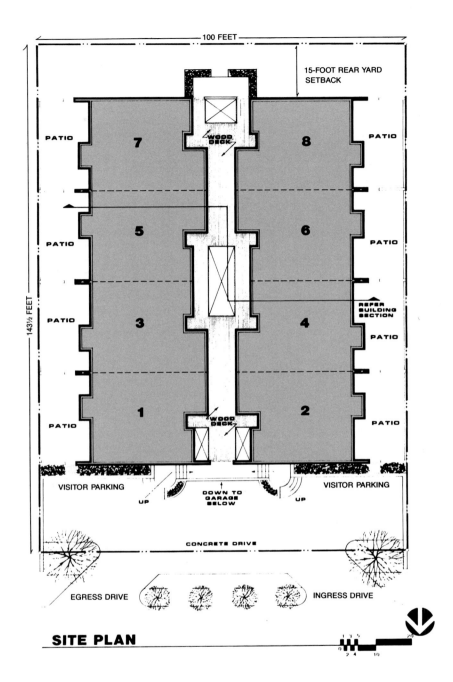

SITE PLAN

neighborhood bank arranged a simple interim construction loan for the condominium development, and as a backup, it required a takeout loan guaranteeing available funds for end loans at an unspecified interest rate.

SITE

The developer acquired two adjacent residential lots, both zoned for apartments, in the Oak Lawn area about two miles northwest of downtown Dallas. Oak Lawn is a community in transition, located between the central business district and one of Dallas's premier residential areas, Highland Park. As a result of a large regional planning study, Oak Lawn's zoning allows low-rise multifamily, mixed-use developments, and office and commercial uses. Existing Oak Lawn development, however, is somewhat uneven in quality, largely due to the fact that many old single-family houses were converted to other uses before the new planning policies were adopted.

A greenbelt with a landscaped creek winding through the heart of Oak Lawn, as well as several well-nurtured parks, make the community one of the most attractive in Dallas. Turtle Creek Boulevard, one of the city's prettiest streets spanning the greenbelt, is the main artery between downtown and Highland Park.

The development site, which is 100 feet by 143.5 feet, is located on the westbound portion of a major east/west street. For sales purposes the developer determined that visibility and convenient access outweighed the possible disadvantage of Wycliff Avenue's high volume of traffic. Fortunately, a stop sign 150 feet west of the site slows traffic and diminishes noise.

PLANNING AND ARCHITECTURE

Because land was costly, the developer used the maximum density allowed by the zoning, achieving 25 units per acre with the eight-unit condominium. Market research and financial considerations dictated the need for a minimum 1,400-square-foot unit.

■ Dramatic volume ceilings, indirect lighting, hardwood floors, skylights, and architectural staircases appeal to the discriminating target market of single professionals and childless couples.

The angled driveway approach to the project facilitates autos entering it from busy Wycliff Avenue. To reduce traffic noise, the units were designed to face into an interior courtyard located behind a landscaped wall. Because of concerns over security in this transitional neighborhood, a telephone-controlled locked gate was installed at the courtyard entrance to the development. Access to parking garages is restricted by an automatic door opener system.

The mews design takes advantage of the site's four-foot elevation above the street. From the entry drive, a ramp descends half a level to the

basement level, where garages for each unit are located, as well as utility and storage areas. To reinforce the feeling of a single-family detached home, each unit also has private access via an inside stairway leading from the garage onto the unit's main floor. Guest parking is at street level with two sets of exterior stairs leading down half a level to the main entry gate.

All units have the same floor plan with guest entrances from the main-level decks. Each home's main level includes the living room, dining room, kitchen, and a small guest bedroom/study with an adjoining full bath and walk-in closet. Of primarily floor-to-ceiling glass, the far wall of the living room overlooks the 14-by-26-foot private fenced patio that runs the length of the room, and visually extends the living room to the patio fence. Also along that wall are the fireplace and two sets of French doors.

The upper level offers a large loft master bedroom that overlooks the 22-foot-high living room and the patio. The master bedroom includes a split-level bath with his-and-her walk-in closets and a dressing area. The master bath has a skylight, a sunken Jacuzzi tub, a glass-enclosed shower, twin vanities, and a separate commode compartment.

To satisfy the target market, the developer incorporated dramatic volume spaces, open floor plans, skylights, fenced and landscaped patios for each unit, kitchens and baths with full amenities, ample storage space, and individual double garages. Helping to ensure privacy for each unit are the downward-pitched roof, the wing walls, and the patio fence.

The contemporary exterior, punctuated with round windows six feet in diameter and the security gate arch, provides a touch of postmodernism. In each of the four end units, the round window is above eye level. Exterior brick is a slightly

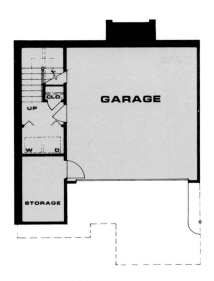

LOWER LEVEL

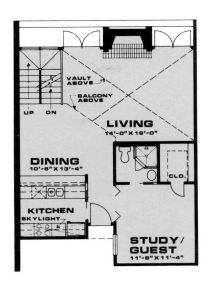

MAIN LEVEL

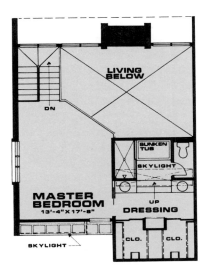

UPPER LEVEL

■ Units are designed to appeal to young urban professionals who desire a sophisticated, secure in-town location. All units feature luxurious master bedrooms and baths with large walk-in closets on the upper level. The builder allowed buyers to select most of the interior finishes. Buyers also spent an average of $15,000 per unit in upgrades.

glazed hard-iron, spot-blend of mauve, copper, and dark brown. The stucco is a medium-value gray, and painted trim around windows, roof, and patio is off-white with gray contrasts.

MARKETING

The target market—two-income, childless couples—determined the design of double garages, twin vanities, and two master walk-in closets. Two months after the developer's personal unit was merchandised as a model, the seven remaining units were sold. The single buyers (five men, two women) ranged in age from early 20s to early 50s, and were employed in management positions either downtown or nearby.

Before formal marketing began, all units were completed except for interior finishes. With these, choices for paint, flooring, other decorator

■ Extensive use of glazing and French doors opening onto the private patios provide abundant light and a "frame" for the fireplace. The contemporary interior design proved popular with the buyers.

items, and patio landscaping, were left to the individual buyers. Buyers spent an average of $15,000 more than the stated allowance upgrading flooring and adding amenities like bookshelves, patio decks, and hot tubs.

Two sales were transacted in cash. The other buyers arranged their own financing with only one using the prearranged end loan financing. All units were sold within six weeks.

Sales resulted from on-site signage, networking with realtors, and small ads run in the major daily newspaper. The developer paid a 3 percent real estate commission on four units. The end units sold for $185,000 and the interior units for $170,000.

Buyers responded not only to the favorable location of the Wycliff Condominiums, but also to the manageable size of the program. With only eight units, the Wycliff project promotes easygoing and "instant" neighborliness. The homeowners' association is free of the friction that sometimes develops in large attached programs, and all community decisions are made cooperatively and informally.

PROJECT DATA

LAND USE INFORMATION:
Site Area: 14,350 square feet
Total Units: 8
Density: 24.4 units per acre
Building Site Coverage: 5,740 square feet[1]

UNIT INFORMATION:
8 1,400-square-foot 2-bdrm./2-bath units[2]
8 400-square-foot garages[3]
Sales Price Range: $170,000 to $185,000

ECONOMIC INFORMATION:
Site Value: $229,600[4]
Construction Costs: $900,000[5]
Total Cost: $1,129,600
Per-Unit Cost: $141,200

Notes:
[1]40 percent of site.
[2]Total of 11,200 square feet.
[3]Total of 3,200 square feet.
[4]$16 per square foot for 14,350 square feet.
[5]Hard and soft costs at $62.50 per square foot.

DIRECTIONS:
From Dallas/Fort Worth Airport (DFW), take exit south out of airport. Turn left on Highway 183, which merges with Highway 114 south to Dallas. Stay on 114 going toward Dallas; 114 merges with Highway 35 east, heading south to Dallas. Stay on 35 east to Oak Lawn exit. Turn left (north) on Oak Lawn and follow to Wycliff Street. Turn left on Wycliff; the Wycliff Condominiums are in the second block.

DEVELOPER:
The Craycroft Interests
4131 N. Central, #1200
Dallas, Texas 75204

ARCHITECT:
The Craycroft Architects, Inc.
4131 N. Central, #1200
Dallas, Texas 75204

From Breezeway Buildings to...

A common prototype used for garden-density attached housing has been two- or three-story flats with breezeway exterior circulation and stairs. Breezeway buildings are generally linear in nature, with units bound together on three common walls. Originally, breezeways with stair towers separated the units and acted as fire buffers required by codes. This building type generally allowed only one out of four walls of a unit to have access to light and air.

...EIGHT-PLEX BUILDINGS

At a similar density, the eight-plex (or eight-unit) building offers some major advantages for both interior areas and site plan considerations. It provides two contiguous exterior walls at 90-degree angles to allow light and ventilation into units. In two-story buildings, alternate open space orientations can overcome the "stacked" deck problem and increase privacy. Interior private stairs, with grade-level entrances, and second-level lofts may be incorporated to upgrade units on the upper floor.

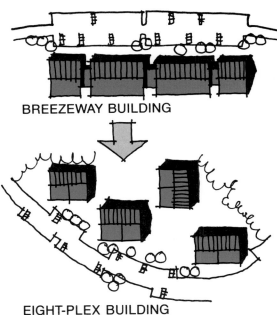

BREEZEWAY BUILDING

EIGHT-PLEX BUILDING

■ **The eight-plex configuration increases each unit's exposure to light and air and maintains a density comparable to breezeway buildings.**

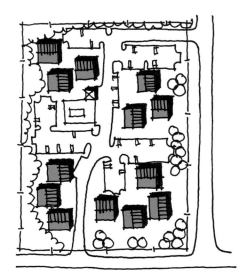

TYPICAL SITE PLAN

■ The smaller eight-plex buildings provide an opportunity for more creative site planning and usable pockets of open space.

In terms of site planning, the eight-plex concept can provide a more interesting land plan. Buildings may be rotated on an axis to create variations throughout the site and maximize the exposure of units to open space. Floor plans generally range from 600 to 1,400 square feet with densities between 10 and 16 units per acre.

...COURTYARD BUILDINGS

Breezeway or townhouse buildings increasingly are being designed with a "courtyard" orientation to concentrate entrances at one well-defined central area, while all private exterior orientations focus out on the building perimeter. The courtyard is a time-honored planning concept that evokes feelings of security and community. Combined with an appropriate elevational concept, such as the manor home, the courtyard works particularly well for the vertically stacked flats often found in breezeway buildings.

In the entrance courtyard, individual doors or porches may be grouped into portico areas. Access to second-level units may include a common grand stairway leading to a common balcony. After entering the door of the unit, one climbs a stairway to the living area.

With courtyard homes or other higher-density attached prototypes, the garage often is omitted or removed from the building. The idea of freestanding garages located throughout the site as landscape elements can be skillfully incorporated into the site concept. Offering the option of a garage will provide a market advantage, while the garages themselves can act as perimeter buffers or privacy screens for certain areas within the site.

■ The stacked flats found in breezeway buildings can be grouped around a central courtyard amenity.

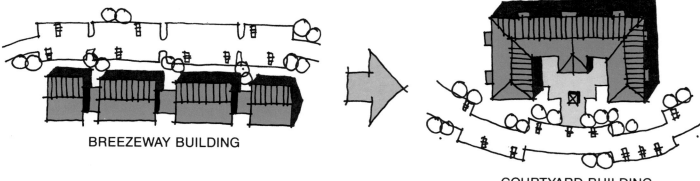

BREEZEWAY BUILDING

COURTYARD BUILDING

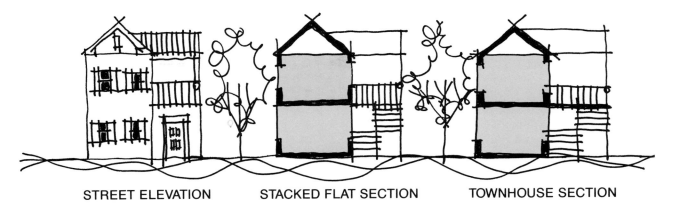

| STREET ELEVATION | STACKED FLAT SECTION | TOWNHOUSE SECTION |

...STACKED UNIT INFILL BUILDINGS

Redeveloping urban areas makes it possible to build infill housing, often raising the density above that of the housing type originally occupying the site. The new housing may replicate the earlier style to maintain the urban fabric, but internal floor plans may be reconfigured to increase unit yield. This recalls the subdividing of townhouses into flats during the industrial era.

Contemporary stacked infill programs may take a myriad of different forms, varying according to regional—and neighborhood—architectural styles. Indeed, responding to context is the hallmark of successful infill housing. Interior unit plans must resolve the same lifestyle concerns of other prototypes.

Although not a direct descendant of the breezeway design, contemporary stacked unit infill projects display several of the qualities and design constraints inherent in breezeway buildings. The narrow and deep lots typical of many older residential neighborhoods dictate a linear design and create design difficulties when, after serving only a single unit, they are redeveloped for two or more units.

One approach has been to stack the units and orient them to the side, rather than the front, of the lot. This solution draws on the historical "side house" design popular in the southern states during the 17th and 18th centuries. A porch or balcony positioned on the extreme side provides an area for outdoor enjoyment. The narrow house enjoys maximum cross ventilation. The side house certainly is not the only solution for tight infill parcels, but its use in Europe and the South has proven efficient for generations.

■ Stacked flats on urban infill sites often draw on historical housing designs such as the "side house" concept. With unit modifications, the side house design can also accommodate townhouses or a combination of flats and townhouses.

119

WOODBRIDGE APARTMENTS
ORLANDO, FLORIDA

Victor A. Mirontschuk

Even in fast-growing markets like Orlando, Florida, competition among multifamily rental properties can be keen. As a development boom reaches maturity, subtle architectural distinctions can become vital to marketing success. The developer, Whitemark, Inc., understood that principle when planning the 168-unit Woodbridge Apartments. Knowing that approximately 1,000 competing apartment units would flood the market when Woodbridge became available, Whitemark set ambitious parameters for design innovation.

DEVELOPMENT STRATEGY

Capitalizing on real estate investment trends, Whitemark formulated a development and leasing strategy to maximize the project's potential for institutional sale. Rapid lease-up at high pro forma rents facilitates institutional investment. To that end, Whitemark sought a strong architectural identity that would expand immediately Woodbridge's market share and support higher rents.

In a competitive market dominated by conventional apartment architecture, the developer recognized

Victor A. Mirontschuk, AIA, is president and founder of EDI Architecture/ Planning and directs operations of the firm's offices in San Francisco, Houston, and Philadelphia. Mirontschuk was appointed in 1987 to the National AIA Housing Committee. He is a frequent contributor to industry periodicals and a guest lecturer at national trade conventions, conferences, and seminars.

that the property's appeal would be boosted significantly by endowing the project with two of the benefits associated with single-family housing: spaciousness and privacy.

SITE PLANNING

Often the most challenging aspect of a land plan is not architectural, but governmental. Woodbridge's 9.32-acre site was subject to Florida's environmental regulations mandating that postdevelopment water runoff not exceed predevelopment runoff. Because of this consideration, as well as required building setbacks of 50 to 100 feet, more than three acres of the site could not be used for buildings.

Ponds frequently are used for water retention. However, this alternative would have required a lake of nearly 9,600 square feet, effectively eliminating the land for one of the 21 eight-plex buildings. Instead, water retention is accomplished through the use of a meandering stream, which winds through the site and is spanned by several decorative wooden bridges.

The site concept also incorporates driveways at the required width of 32 feet, and 1.75 parking spaces (10 feet by 20 feet) per unit. Resulting density is approximately 18 units per acre, but the 21 eight-plex structures are scattered throughout the site to promote the perception of open space.

As standard bearer of the project's image, an elaborate community center with pool, tennis courts, and clubhouse visually dominates the project's main entry.

■ With the first-floor living rooms projecting beyond the second floor, volume ceilings could be created on both levels. Each unit on the first floor is entered at a different corner of the building; on the second floor, two units share one set of stairs but their front doors are set 20 feet apart to strengthen each unit's identity.

ARCHITECTURE

In addition to affording each unit a desirable corner location, the two-story, eight-plex format provides other design solutions. Under the Southern Building Code, buildings with more than four dwelling units per floor must have two means of egress. Ordinarily, apartment buildings address this requirement with stair halls. The eight-plex plan avoids this encumbrance by providing open stairways at opposite ends of the structure, which allows each unit a private entrance. Entries are carefully designed to enhance individual unit identity; downstairs units are entered at four different

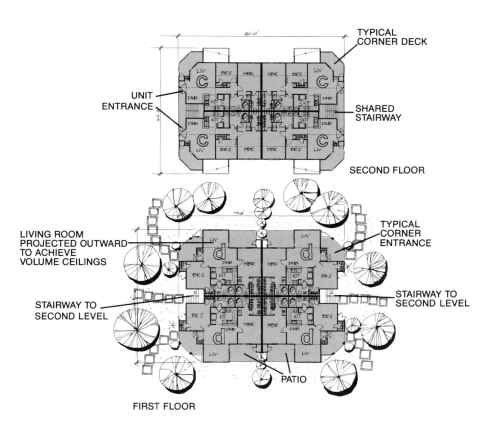

TYPICAL EIGHT-PLEX BUILDING

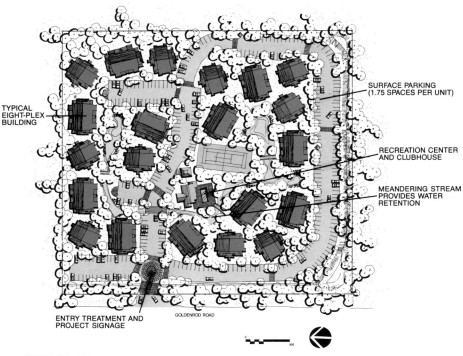

SITE PLAN

■ Despite a flooded apartment market in Orlando, Florida, all 168 of these apartments were leased within six months as a result of careful site planning, architectural design, and the provision of amenities. The meandering stream running through the project allows for water retention without loss of buildable area. While open space seems abundant, the 21 eight-plex buildings provide a density of about 18 units per acre.

A-634 S/F 2ND FLOOR

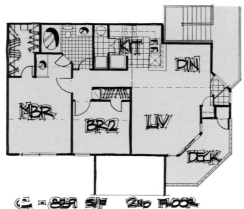

C-829 S/F 2ND FLOOR

B-724 S/F 1ST FLOOR

D-939 S/F 1ST FLOOR

■ Four floor plans, ranging from 634 to 939 square feet, are offered. Units A and B make up one of the eight-plex buildings, while units C and D form another building combination. One advantage of the eight-plex design is that it allows every unit to be located on a corner of the building.

points in each building. Upstairs units share stairways in pairs; front doors, however, are placed some 20 feet apart.

Volume, the effective method for increasing the sense of spaciousness in high-density housing, is often limited to second-floor apartment units. At Woodbridge, the second floor could be termed "an apartment builder's dream": a perfect rectangle with most ceilings sloping upward to a dramatic height of 12 feet. However, the Woodbridge design incorporates volume ceilings in first-floor units as well. Downstairs living rooms project out from beneath the upper floor, allowing 12- to 14-foot-high ceilings with high glass windows that minimize the presence of the upstairs unit.

With the projected first-floor living areas, the high-pitched roofs have been further extended, bringing the rooflines closer to eye level. These design elements reduce the apparent scale of the buildings.

Each first-floor unit has a patio; second-floor units have decks that wrap around the building corners. Exteriors are finished with stucco and cedar siding. All units have 42-inch-wide bathtubs; washers and dryers; individual heating, hot water,

■ Volume ceilings in every unit helped to distinguish units, setting them apart from the strong local competition. Because each unit has a corner location in the building, outdoor views could be maximized.

■ With the projected first-floor living rooms, the high-pitched roofs have been further extended, bringing the rooflines closer to eye level. The buildings are finished in stucco and cedar siding.

and air conditioning units; open serving counters from the kitchens; and private master-bedroom dressing areas with vanities and sinks. Units range in size from a 634-square-foot flat with one bedroom and one bath to a two-bedroom, two-bath unit with 939 square feet.

MARKETING

Interest from passersby triggered preleasing of the project during construction. Within six months of completion, the property was 100 percent leased, representing a pace 30 percent faster than had been initially projected. A limited-run billboard and apartment guide advertisement constituted the only formal marketing efforts before full occupancy was reached.

Residents are primarily professionals employed at a nearby university and medical center. The target market—singles, couples, and roommates in their 30s—responds favorably to the privacy, aesthetics, and amenities of the apartment community. According to residents, careful interior space planning, coupled with volume ceilings and corner placement of all units, gives the impression of spaciousness within the relatively small square footages.

The developer provided an extensive amenity package that includes community pool, hot tub, tennis courts, clubhouse with wet bar, excercise room, saunas, and valet laundry service. These sophisticated, above-market features raise Woodbridge above its competition, making possible higher per-unit rents.

PROJECT DATA

LAND USE INFORMATION:
Site Area: 9.32 acres
Total Units: 168
Density: 18.0 units per acre
Parking Spaces: 294
Parking Index: 1.75 spaces per unit

LAND USE PLAN:

	Acres	Percent of Site
Open Space	3.4	37%
Buildings	3.1	33
Roads/Parking Area	2.8	30

UNIT INFORMATION:

Type	Square Feet	Number	Monthly Rent
1-bdrm./1-bath	634	40	$435
1-bdrm./1¼-bath	729	40	$455
2-bdrm./1¼-bath	839	44	$520
2-bdrm./2-bath	939	44	$550

ECONOMIC INFORMATION:
Site Value: $1,090,000
Construction Costs: $3,293,000[1]
Site Improvement Costs: $987,000
Engineering Fees: $28,000
Sewer/Water Tap Fees: $280,000
General Site Preparation Costs: $679,000
Amenities: $95,000[2]

Notes:
[1]$25 per square foot.
[2]Includes pool, tennis courts, club/spa interiors.

DIRECTIONS:
From Orlando International Airport, take Cimarron Boulevard north to University Boulevard. Go right on University Boulevard to Goldenrod Road, and right on Goldenrod Road approximately one-half mile to Woodbridge Apartments.

DEVELOPER:
Whitemark, Inc.
611 Chapman Road
Oviedo, Florida 32765

ARCHITECT/LAND PLANNER:
EDI Architecture/Planning
3731 Briarpark, Suite 300
Houston, Texas 77042

CIVIL ENGINEER:
Donald W. McIntosh & Associates
2200 Park Avenue North
Winter Park, Florida 32789

CONSULTING ARCHITECT FOR CODES RESEARCH/CITY APPROVALS:
Fugleberg/Koch Associates
1600 E. Amelia Street
Westland, Florida 32803

Phokion Karas

THE BOATYARD
FALMOUTH, MASSACHUSETTS

John D. Bloodgood

The Boatyard was developed in response to a growing market of affluent buyers seeking secure waterfront homes for weekends and vacations. Originally a storage

John D. (Jack) Bloodgood, FAIA, MIRM, is president of Bloodgood Architects, of Des Moines, Iowa, and Boston, Massachusetts. Bloodgood serves as design consultant to Professional Builder *magazine and is an active participant of ULI serving on a Residential Development Council and as vice chairman and juror on the ULI Awards Committee.*

area for boats and nautical paraphernalia, the site had been passed over as an unattractive and unpromising one until the Green Company recognized its potential and purchased it in 1982. Although other kinds of housing were readily available to buyers of secondary homes, luxury attached housing was scarce. The Boatyard was conceived in response to this demand.

DEVELOPMENT STRATEGY

Development strategy was based on two primary goals: to achieve the eight-unit-per-acre density required

■ **Once a neglected boat storage yard, this four-acre site was transformed into a setting for 32 luxury townhouses selling for up to $350,000. The units are contained in four large buildings clustered around paved motor courts to reach the developer's density requirement of eight units per acre. The unit A plan was specifically designed to allow the townhouses to turn corners, thus breaking up the linear pattern.**

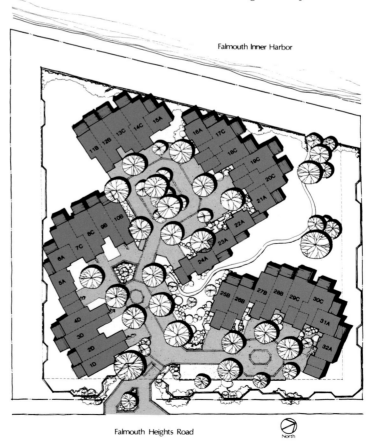

Falmouth Inner Harbor

Falmouth Heights Road

North

for profitable development on a very expensive parcel; and to do so without compromising the design criteria for luxury housing. For zoning acceptance, styling was to blend with the traditional character of the Cape Cod waterfront homes that surround the Boatyard site.

As is frequently the case for residential attached products, profit was to be achieved by a swift sales pace, so the emotional appeal of a familiar-looking home environment was more important than intellectual considerations of a challenging product design. The developer knew that the target market wanted a community that was fully landscaped, complete, and ready to move into. Matarazzo Design of Concord, New Hampshire, integrated planning and landscape treatment to achieve this end, and the site projected an established character before opening day.

SITE AND PLANNING

The Boatyard site is a level, four-acre parcel overlooking the inner harbor of Falmouth, with a boat storage facility on one boundary and a resort motel on the other. The principal constraint was between the site and the waterfront, where parking access to a private marina was to remain.

The primary planning goal was to capitalize on the harborfront view and develop as many homes as possible without allowing the density to smother the appeal of the site. To meet this goal, building types originally designed for linear siting were planned instead in staggered courtyard configurations. Major living spaces are elevated one level above grade to optimize harbor views while screening the marina road.

Exterior grade-level areas are used to accommodate automobiles, with units clustered around landscaped motor courts paved in geometrically patterned concrete. The plants and paving make the courts

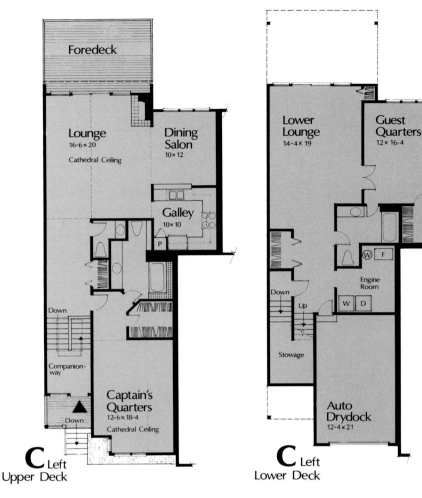

C Left
Upper Deck

C Left
Lower Deck

look like plazas rather than parking lots, deflecting the visual impact of the automobiles.

An undulating fence around the perimeter of the site gives privacy and accommodates additional pockets of landscaping. Careful planning at the entrance includes a divided drive and gatehouse island, and emphasizes a sense of arrival, security, and importance.

ARCHITECTURE

Floor plan design at the Boatyard emphasizes primarily harbor views from second-floor spaces. Master suites, kitchens, and principal living/dining areas are on the homes' second levels, with ground-level areas designed to accommodate secondary sleeping and living spaces, and garages. To make the climb to main living areas more palatable to

■ The largest of the three floor plans is unit C, which contains 1,850 square feet, with two bedrooms and two and one-half baths. To reinforce the nautical theme of the project, sales brochures employed sailing terms to explain unit and project features.

125

■ Exterior architecture is inspired by the Cape Cod style. Cedar shingles give a weathered look while heavy white trim and lattice screening provide contrasting accents.

■ The paved courtyards take on the appearance of Old World plazas with their use of materials and geometric forms. To give the project an instantly finished look, mature plantings and lush landscaping are used extensively around the courtyards and at unit entrances.

■ Large glass areas are at the rear of the houses and usually face the waterfront. To further capitalize on views, primary living areas are located on the second floors of the houses.

the target market, the transition from ground level to the upper main level is eased by the front entry's being raised one-half level. Entry is from individually designed timber steps and platforms that retain the grade against the building to provide areas for heavy landscaping with mature trees and shrubs.

Substantial volumes are employed in the 1,350- to 1,850-square-foot homes to make moderate room sizes seem larger and more impressive; skylights add natural light and visually expand the space. Particular emphasis is placed on kitchens and baths, where appointments and finishes include such luxury touches as recessed lighting, plant shelves, high-gloss laminates, and platform tubs. Used generously, these elements mesh to bring a feeling of true luxury to the modestly proportioned homes.

Exterior design employs traditional forms and materials of Cape Cod, and assembles them in a fresh, updated style. Cedar shingles have a weathered color. Simple white trim, vinyl-clad sash, and sharply pitched roof forms combine to tie the buildings to the familiar character of the surrounding area, and to make the clustered housing units less obtrusive at a density that is higher than that of other parcels in the immediate area.

MARKETING

With a waterfront site and a clear objective of marketing to affluent empty nesters and retired buyers, the developer quickly established a nautical theme as appropriate for attracting real "boaters," as well as those who have dreamed of living directly on a scenic Cape Cod waterfront.

Of the Boatyard's 32 homes, 28 have harborfront views, a fact that was emphasized in all marketing elements—community name, sales brochure, signage, and advertising. The nautical theme was also carried through in the model and sales office to focus on the many pleasing images associated with waterfront living.

126

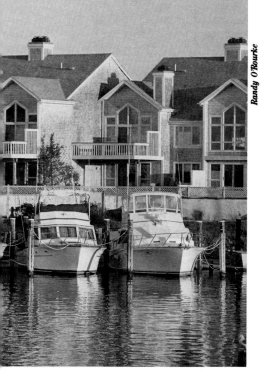

■ **Private exterior space extends around the perimeter of the buildings and is oriented toward views. By carefully positioning the clusters, the architect provided waterfront views for 28 of the 32 units.**

The settled, established appearance achieved by the abundant landscaping and uncluttered design was vital in marketing to the targeted buyers; in fact, the successful integration of the built structures with the landscaping generated favorable comment from virtually all prospective buyers.

The project was constructed and marketed in three phases; each marketing phase included presales for one-third of the units in that phase, followed by a combination of radio and print advertising and buyer referrals, which generated subsequent sales as construction progressed. For all phases, sales were well ahead of production.

PROJECT DATA

LAND USE INFORMATION:
Site Area: 3.95 acres
Total Units: 32
Density: 8 units per acre
Parking Spaces: 76
Parking Index: 2.4 spaces per unit

LAND USE PLAN:

	Acres	Percent of Site
Open Space	2.220	56.1%
Buildings	0.910	23.1
Roads/Parking Area	0.740	18.7
Amenities[1]	0.075	0.9

UNIT INFORMATION:[2]

Type	Number	Square Feet	Opening Price Ranges
2-bdrm./2½-bath	10	1,350	$145,000–250,000
2-bdrm./2-bath	12	1,650	$155,000–270,000
2-bdrm./2½-bath	10	1,850	$200,000–350,000

ECONOMIC INFORMATION:
Site Value: $635,000[3]
Site Improvement Costs:

Excavation/Backfill/Sewer	$	48,930
Grading		18,200
Paving		250,393
Landscaping		119,170
Other[4]		112,775
Total	$	549,468[5]

Total Construction Costs: $3,500,000[6]

Average Construction Costs per Unit:

Structural	57,496
Carpentry	4,300
Electrical	3,630
Plumbing	4,050
HVAC	4,808
Other[7]	18,716
Total	$ 93,000

Amenities Costs: $37,000[8]
Development Fees: $230,000
Homeowner Fee: $250 per month

Notes:
[1] Includes pool and walks.
[2] Garages total 28 with six detached.
[3] $19,843 per unit.
[4] Includes pool construction, walkway to pool, fencing, gatehouse, and retaining wall.
[5] $17,171 per unit.
[6] $74.40 per square foot.
[7] Includes cabinetry, paint, appliances, and miscellaneous finishing costs.
[8] Pool and cabana.

DIRECTIONS:
From Logan Airport in Boston, take Route 3 south to Route 6 west. Follow Route 6 west to Route 28 south and continue through Falmouth Center. Turn right on Falmouth Heights Road and follow approximately one-quarter mile to the Boatyard.

DEVELOPER:
The Green Company
46 Glen Avenue
Newton, Massachusetts 02159

LANDSCAPE ARCHITECT*:
Matarazzo Design
9 Hills Avenue
Concord, New Hampshire 03301

ARCHITECT*:
Bloodgood Architects, P.C.
3001 Grand Avenue
Des Moines, Iowa 50312

*Joint office located at Four Thirteenth Street, Charleston Navy Yard, Boston, Massachusetts 02129.

AWARD:
• 1984 Grand Award Winner: *Builder* magazine's Builder's Choice competition.

Randy O'Rourke

CHARLESTON PUBLIC HOUSING
CHARLESTON, SOUTH CAROLINA

Richard H. Bradfield

Charleston, South Carolina, is well known for its fierce pride of place and vigilance in protecting its distinctive architectural heritage. This active port city on the South Carolina coast was settled more than 300 years ago, and has adopted as its motto, "Charleston protects her buildings, customs, and laws."

Charleston boasts many "firsts": it was one of the first planned cities in colonial America; it established America's first chamber of commerce, first museum, first Georgian theater, and first municipal college. In 1931, Charleston became the first city to pass legislation establishing a historic district, and this district is the largest in the country, encompassing approximately 1,000 acres and more than 3,000 buildings.

In 1985, Charleston scored another first, receiving a Presidential Award for Design Excellence from President Ronald Reagan in a White House ceremony, the only such award ever presented for a public housing development. In 1986, the same development earned an Honor Award from the American Institute of Architects at the annual convention in San Antonio, Texas.

BACKGROUND

In the summer of 1978 the Housing Authority of the City of Charleston received the first allocation of funds for construction of new public housing in more than 10 years. The housing was to be for low- and moderate-income families, some of whom were being displaced by revitalization activities within the city's historic district. The architectural firm of Bradfield Associates, Inc., of Atlanta, Georgia, was chosen to design the project because of its proven record in the development of public housing.

The easy approach would have been to select a single approvable site and build the entire project in one location. But the Housing Authority Board of Commissioners and its executive director, Donald J. Cameron, as well as Charleston Mayor Joseph Riley, were committed to placing the new housing in the historic district even though many Charlestonians clearly opposed it. Cameron and Richard H. Bradfield, head of the architectural firm Bradfield Associates, Inc., thus began the long and tedious search for an appropriate site.

In all, more than 100 sites were reviewed before the final eight sites for the 67 units of housing were designated in 1981. The final sites had to meet the criteria established by the Housing Authority; they had to be vacant sites zoned for multi-family residential use; they had to

Richard H. Bradfield, AIA, is president of Bradfield Associates, Inc., in Atlanta, Georgia. He has had over 30 years of experience in multifamily housing and in housing for the elderly and the handicapped, for both the public and private sectors. Bradfield currently is involved in several projects providing shelter and transitional housing for the homeless. He is a member of the National AIA Housing Committee and numerous professional and charitable organizations. Bradfield was the 1987 recipient of an Atlanta Chapter AIA Award for Community Service.

TYPICAL SITE PLANS

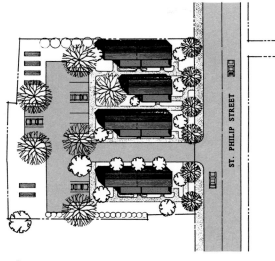

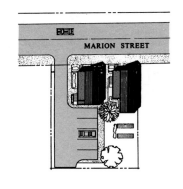

ST. PHILIP STREET SITE

AMHERST STREET SITE

MARION STREET SITE

be unlikely candidates for private redevelopment; they had to have all utilities readily available; they had to be for sale (the Authority did not want to use condemnation as a means of acquisition, even though it had the power to do so); and they had to be small enough so that dwelling units would not be concentrated in any one location. Five of the sites were within the boundaries of the historic district; the other three were in nearby areas being considered as additions to the district. The number of units per site ranged from two to 15, with an average density of about 12 units to an acre.

DESIGN REQUIREMENTS

The development was funded by a loan through the Department of Housing and Urban Development; therefore, HUD guidelines regarding site selection and local building standards were to prevail. In addition, the Housing Authority and the city architect suggested that the designs reflect careful consideration of

the existing fabric, the adjacent structures, and the general streetscape of the area for each new development.

The sites themselves imposed certain restrictions on the design: typical Charleston lots are only 25 to 30 feet wide and about 120 feet deep. However, depth can vary from 100 to 200 feet. These narrow lots are a product of the early 18th century practices of taxing based on the amount of street frontage.

Because most of the sites were in the historic area, the standards established by the city's Board of Adjustment and Board of Architectural Review, as well as standards set by the State Archives Commission and the President's Advisory Council on Historic Preservation, had to be met, and each agency had the right to review the design.

Aside from the specific technical or historic standards to be satisfied, the attitudes and prejudices of the neighborhoods, all of which were based upon existing public housing examples, had to be overcome. This was the most difficult task to be

■ The 67 units of the project are located on eight sites in and around the historic district of Charleston, South Carolina. Typical lots in the historic area are 25 to 30 feet wide and about 120 feet deep (but can range from 100 to 200 feet deep). The eight sites varied widely in size, depending on the number of lots that could be combined, but the side house prototype proved flexible enough to work well under all conditions.

faced by the Housing Authority and the architect. That it was accomplished is testimony to the tenacity of the Board of Architectural Review members and the elected city officials who addressed a constant barrage of criticism from their constituents.

THE SOLUTION

Because of the myriad of standards, the numerous agencies empowered to review and pass upon

129

■ Only one room wide, the side house prototype fits the historical lotting pattern of the area and allows good cross ventilation—an important feature in this subtropical climate.

proposed designs, and the modest budget, the design team had to find some common ground that would convey Charleston's architectural character, regardless of location. It also had to incorporate sufficient design repetition to economize on construction.

South Carolina HUD standards dictated a brick veneer, and because of HUD's maintenance experience, nothing else would be accepted. The HUD standards also required concrete curbs and gutters for all drives and parking areas—a practice inconsistent with Charleston's built environment. The architect made a firm decision, however, to design for

Charleston and not for HUD. Once this decision was made, the real character of Charleston housing began to emerge in the design.

A prototype was chosen, based on another Charleston first: the 18th century "single house" or "side house," which is long and narrow and fits nicely on the narrow Charleston lots. Only a single room wide, these buildings provided adequate cross ventilation and worked well in the subtropical climate of this coastal city. A covered porch on the west or south side offered shade and an opportunity to enjoy the prevailing off-shore breezes. Privacy was achieved by placing a false entry on the street side of the porch; the remaining side yard was fenced along the street to make "good neighbors."

Wherever one turns in Charleston, one sees the side house. Whether the house has a single floor or several, whether the side yard is an elaborate garden or only a few square feet, whether the home is an extravagant mansion along the Battery or the meanest cottage on Coming Street, the good things learned from the side house have prevailed.

To economize in the construction of this prototype, the architect consulted local builders who had restored some of the modest houses in the area. They were able to capture the character of the old details with new, inexpensive materials. Railings

were to be milled from standard two-by-fours, balusters were to be stock two-by-twos, and columns were simply four-by-fours with chamfered edges. They even found a local manufacturer to furnish the characteristic S-curved shutter holdbacks. Because the native cypress that clad the majority of the old side houses proved too expensive, California cedar was used instead, with the finished side placed against the sheathing so that the natural grain was exposed.

Initial HUD reviews were devastating. Pages of comments cited nonconformities. Off the record, certain HUD personnel confided that they felt the project was doomed as long as the Housing Authority persisted in proposing such radical departures from "typical public housing." Through a series of conferences, the architect and the executive director of the Housing Authority explained the concept, and ultimately prevailed. Among their most persuasive points was that the materials proposed were not extravagant, nor was their application unusual. When the designs were thoughtfully considered, the HUD staff conceded that, though the end result was certainly different, the various systems employed were practical, efficient, and affordable.

Due to Charleston's somewhat depressed construction industry, the low bid received to construct the project was 4 percent below the budget. The total construction contract resulted in a square-foot cost of only $27.06. HUD and the Housing Authority were elated and the construction began immediately.

■ Building materials remain in character with the architecture of Charleston's historic area, while also proving to be inexpensive. In addition, the uncomplicated design helped keep down construction costs.

TYPICAL FRONT ELEVATION

TYPICAL SIDE ELEVATION

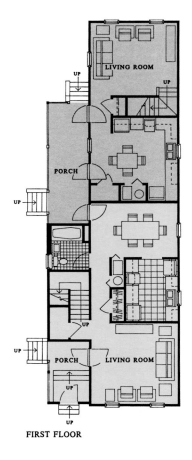

FIRST FLOOR

TWO- AND THREE-BEDROOM DUPLEX

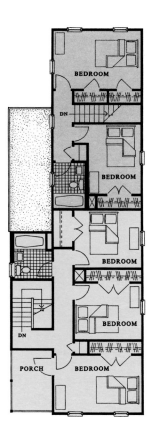

SECOND FLOOR

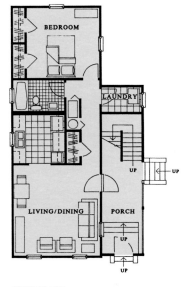

FIRST FLOOR

ONE-BEDROOM DUPLEX

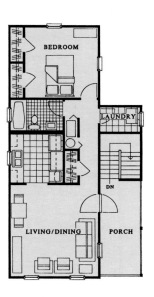

SECOND FLOOR

■ Designed for low- and moderate-income families, floor plans range from 659 square feet for one-bedroom/one-bath units to 1,279 square feet for three-bedroom/two-bath units. Units are arranged either in the traditional stacked-flat pattern (shown here in the one-bedroom duplex plan) or in a two-story design (as shown in the two- and three-bedroom duplex). Outside the historic area several four-bedroom units were built.

THE RESULT

On scattered infill sites ranging from 0.18 to 1.4 acres, 67 Charleston families now have homes of which they can be proud. This public housing did not reduce property values on adjacent sites, nor did it deter private investors. Most important, it did not inhibit the efforts of the communities to continue the rehabilitation and restoration of the historic sections of Radcliffeborough, Elliot Island, Cannon Borough, or Eugely Lands.

In fact, on Amherst Street on the city's east side, nearly 50 percent of the lots had been vacant. The new housing serves as an example of good investment to neighboring communities, while development in this neighborhood has returned for the first time in more than 20 years.

The tenants of the new housing take pride in their homes and, consequently, in themselves. The Housing Authority happily has found this pride manifested in the tenants' marked interest in caring for the property. Most residents enjoy taking part in the maintenance and repair of their own apartments; many have planted flowers and additional shrubbery to supplement the landscaping in their small, but pleasant, yards. One tenant registered her only complaint. "It should be mine," she chortled, "I take care of it."

The initial resistance by homeowners to public housing in their neighborhoods has virtually disappeared. Many have reacted with renewed vigor in the rehabilitation and revitalization of their own homes. In many areas, new private construction has begun on lots immediately adjacent to the public housing.

PROJECT DATA

LAND USE INFORMATION:
Site Area: 5.83 acres[1]
Total Units: 67
Density: 11.5
Parking Spaces: 102
Parking Index: 1.5 spaces per unit

UNIT INFORMATION:

Type	Number	Square Feet
Historic Sites		
1-bdrm./1-bath	12	693
2-bdrm./1-bath	7	907
3-bdrm./2-bath	12	1,279
Other Sites		
1-bdrm./1-bath	6	659
2-bdrm./1-bath	4	915
3-bdrm./2-bath	17	1,138
4-bdrm./2-bath	9	1,350

ECONOMIC INFORMATION:
Site Value: $343,342
Site Improvement Costs: $564,144
Building Costs: $1,681,543
Development Fees: $135,000
Total Development Cost: $3,359,916[2]

Notes:
[1]Spread over eight sites.
[2]$50,148 per unit.

DIRECTIONS:
From Charleston airport, take Interstate 26 to Charleston. Follow I-26 to the directional signs for Charleston's historic district. Enter the historic district; the most publicized site is at 149 Coming Street.

OWNER/ARCHITECT:
Housing Authority of the City of Charleston
20 Franklin Street
Charleston, South Carolina 29401

Bradfield Associates, Inc.
Post Office Box 52426
Atlanta, Georgia 30355

AWARDS:
- Presidential Award for Design Excellence, Ronald Reagan, 1985
- Federal Design Achievement Award, National Endowment for the Arts, 1984
- Honor Award, American Institute of Architects, 1986
- Award of Merit, Georgia Chapter AIA, 1984
- Honor Award for Excellence in Housing Project Design, National Association of Housing and Redevelopment Officials, 1986
- Innovative Design Award, U.S. Department of Housing and Urban Development

From Mid-Rise Block Buildings to...

Historically, mid-rise buildings in the four to eight-floor range might be categorized as rectangular blocks with straightforward building forms. Double-loaded corridors with stair towers at the ends defined the building form as a linear slab of variable height. Parking was provided on site—at grade level and adjacent to the building. Densities ranged from 30 to 40 units per acre.

...COURTYARD BUILDINGS OVER PLATFORM PARKING

With rising land costs, contemporary mid-rise buildings are calling for subsurface parking below the building footprint. This concept often provides additional freedom in the site layout for green space and landscaping.

The increased cost of structured parking must factor into the development pro forma. In some cases, land is priced for lower density and the decked parking allows higher density at a lower per-unit land cost. In other instances, a higher-end product will absorb the increased cost of parking.

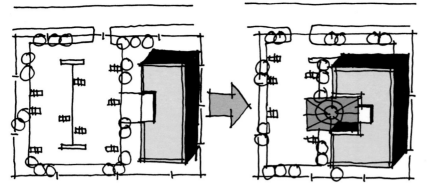

SURFACE PARKING

UNDERGROUND PARKING WITH
COURTYARD BUILDING ENTRANCE

■ Density and land efficiency increase when resident parking is
placed underground, below the building. Often, visitor parking is still provided in a surface lot with at-grade
access to the building's main
entrance.

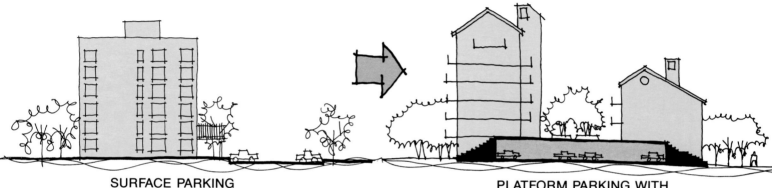

SURFACE PARKING

PLATFORM PARKING WITH
CENTRAL COURTYARD

■ Higher densities can be achieved
by placing parking beneath a courtyard platform. The courtyard also offers a valuable open space amenity.

In many cases, the substructure parking is single-level in nature
with direct access to the surrounding grade. Topographic differences
may allow two parking levels, both accessible from natural grade level
at different points on the site. The shape of the parking bays will play
a major role in the building configuration above them. Many decked
mid-rise buildings are rectangular shapes, approximately 65 feet wide,
which corresponds to the double-loaded parking below. In other cases,
the parking roof deck may form a platform atop which is the first floor
of the building and the open courtyard.

Both vehicular, pedestrian, and visitor circulation becomes complex
in mid- and high-rise buildings. The convenience of covered parking
with direct internal access to elevators is a marketing benefit that
generally justifies cost premiums. Some outside visitor parking at
ground level must also be provided, along with a comprehensible visitors' entrance to the building.

With the platform parking concept, an elevator lobby can be included at the parking level with a minimum loss of parking spaces. For courtyard mid-rise buildings, a gracious, landscaped stairway from the natural ground level may provide access to the common, central area.

...TERRACED BUILDINGS

The unit plan forms the basic building block or shape of the mid- and high-rise building. There may be hundreds of units with the same unit plan within the building. Therefore, a meticulously developed layout is essential.

Often the building layout can be changed vertically. By dropping off units from the ends of a building a terraced effect can be achieved. This will allow bulky structures to decrease in size as they increase in height. Further, the roof of a unit may then become the outdoor terrace for one above.

...ARTICULATED BUILDINGS

In mid-rise buildings, the structure's image is probably less significant to the resident than in lower-density housing. However, many directions are being pursued in terms of design. One general trend is toward articulated building forms.

It may be argued that lower-scale mid-rise buildings were developed to bridge the gap between traditional low-density suburban housing and high-rise towers, which often are perceived as institutional and somewhat sterile buildings. By keeping the building height to five or six stories and by introducing low-rise symbols like gables, sloped roofs, chimneys, balconies, and other elements, a design team can create a more friendly image that appeals to the middle-income market—the market most likely to be targeted for infill and medium-density housing.

■ With the right topographic conditions, two levels of parking can be provided with each level having its own at-grade entrance.

■ The contemporary mid-rise building is breaking away from its former rectangular box image with the use of more articulated building forms such as terracing and varied rooflines.

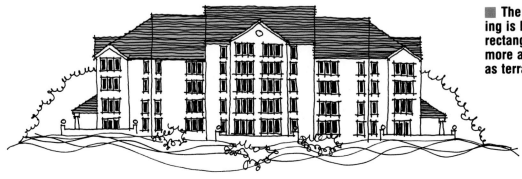

BISHOPS PARK
RALEIGH, NORTH CAROLINA

David Furman

B ishops Park, a 138-unit condominium project on a central
Raleigh infill site, adapts the
early 1900s architecture of surrounding neighborhoods to contemporary attached housing forms. In
an established area of single-family
homes built primarily in the 1910s
and 1920s, historically sensitive design and high construction standards paid off in terms of neighborhood and market acceptance.
Bishops Park gained immediate attention in a market not accustomed
to the project's density and relatively
high cost per square foot, and the
design quality made it easier to ob-
tain needed variances. As a bonus,
community support of the first
phase expedited the approvals and
permitting process for subsequent
phases.

**■ Parking is provided under the
buildings, partially below grade, and
is screened from view by landscaped
brick retaining walls. Architectural
features—such as articulated brick
work, gables, and round attic windows—recall regional design elements and help to reduce the scale of
the buildings.**

*David F. Furman, AIA, is president
and owner of David Furman/Architec-
ture, in Charlotte, North Carolina. He
specializes in the development of innovative housing concepts that emphasize
quality of designs in the multifamily
industry. Furman's writing has been
featured in major architecture
periodicals.*

DEVELOPMENT STRATEGY

The developer wanted to create a
community rather than a project, offering three distinctly different
phases aimed at different markets.
With an infill site surrounded by established residential areas, the developer realized that, historically, appropriate design and density-mitiga-
ting features would be critical to
both agency approvals and eventual
sales.

The architect's solution was a
program of 138 stacked flats sited
around courtyards and integrating
many of the traditional design elements found in neighboring single-
family homes. The three phases are
different but related in their design,
creating cohesive variations on a
theme and forming an interesting
progression through the site.

SITE

In 1982, the developer purchased
a 7.2-acre site from the Methodist
Home for Children. Located one and

one-half miles from downtown Raleigh, the parcel was part of a 77-acre orphanage that was one of the last inner-city developable areas in northwest Raleigh. To the north of the 77-acre tract is the Hayes-Barton neighborhood, generally considered one of the oldest, finest residential areas in the Raleigh area. East and south of the site are other established neighborhoods, primarily of single-family homes built in the 1910s and 1920s. To the west is an older neighborhood of townhouses centered around Cameron Village, a fine established shopping center.

The site lies less than one mile north of the intersection of Glenwood Avenue with Wade Avenue, which leads west to Interstate Highway 40, the main route to Research Triangle Park and Durham, and east to Downtown Boulevard, the principal northern entrance to downtown Raleigh. Thus, Bishops Park is highly accessible to employment centers.

The project site had been partially occupied by three residences; two of these were moved to other locations and one was demolished. The terrain of the entire site is gently rolling, offering opportunities for creative use with varied levels for building entrances and views. Groves of large oak trees throughout the tract add to the attractive, park-like setting.

PLANNING AND ARCHITECTURE

The design challenge at Bishops Park was to design a four-story building that would incorporate new architectural ideas while reinforcing a residential image. The program meets the challenge with buildings adapting architectural elements from the 1910s and 1920s, when most housing in surrounding neighborhoods was constructed. Careful attention was given to landscape details—such as walls, paving, and plantings—that would enhance the appearance of the project and reduce the effects of higher density. As a result, although the gross density is 19 units per acre, all units have pleasant views and good access.

The 48-unit first phase contains 24 residences in each of two buildings that are similar in appearance but varied in floor plans. The buildings are integrated with the site and neighborhood through exterior architectural features. They are covered with cedar shingles on the first two floors and stucco on the third floor. Architectural counterpoints—such as decorative chimneys, bay and round "attic" windows, gables, brackets, and stylized keystone shapes—help delineate smaller masses to maintain a human building scale, and also echo design elements of nearby neighborhoods and regional residential styles.

To achieve a hierarchy of space upon entry, buildings are paired around a paved and landscaped courtyard from which all units are entered. The courtyard is ringed with entry decks and a "plaza level" terrace, creating an interesting variety of space. Stairs and an elevator are located on the perimeter of the courtyard.

The physical amenities of the site were carefully preserved. Building pads and parking areas were situated to preserve as many large trees and as much open space as possible. The dissimilarities in floor plans of the two first-phase buildings were partly due to this concern: locations of individual unit stacks were adjusted to existing landscape conditions. Parking lots were set close to buildings to disturb the site as little as possible. The first phase includes a swimming pool and private driveway that serves 90 units in the other two phases.

Within the unit cluster, covered outside stairways and corridors link the units, leaving the internal courtyards open to the sky. Although the courtyards are small (35 to 40 feet at their widest), the variety of horizontal and vertical space provided by the stairways and building setbacks gives an illusion of greater space. The feeling of spaciousness is carried over into the units: all units have covered porches off living rooms and most enjoy unobstructed views in two directions as well as into the courtyards.

■ The landscaped courtyard serves as the central focus for the 18 units within the typical phase II building. The brick courtyard is located at grade (the first level) while the plaza terrace is located on the second level (both shown here). The door shown at the upper right leads to compartmentalized attic storage spaces.

■ Units in the typical phase II building are stacked in three levels with a parking garage below one side of the building and attic storage space above the other side of the building. Taking advantage of the gently sloping site conditions, the design team located the parking area—accommodating one car per unit—partially underground. The two- and three-bedroom/two-bath units, grouped around a ground-level courtyard, range in size from 1,120 to 1,640 square feet and were marketed to both empty nesters and young professionals.

PHASE II BUILDING—LEVEL 1

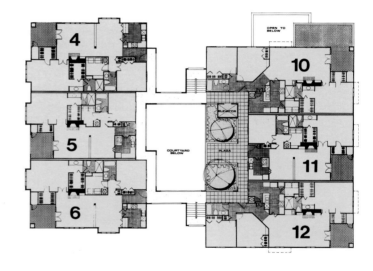

PHASE II BUILDING—LEVEL 2

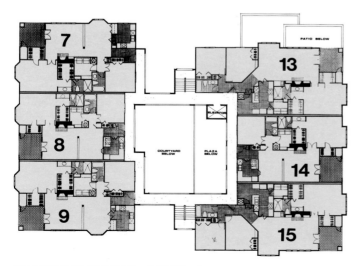

PHASE II BUILDING—LEVEL 3

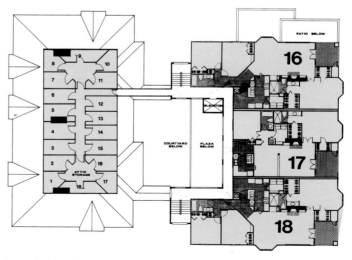

PHASE II BUILDING—LEVEL 4

City Park

WASHINGTON STREET

WASHINGTON STREET

PHASE II—BUILDING 4
DEVELOPMENT SITE

PHASE III
DEVELOPMENT SITE

PHASE II

PHASE I

pool

GLENWOOD AVENUE

Buildings in the second phase are designed to appeal to a somewhat higher-income and older market. The 66 units are larger (1,120 to 1,640 square feet), with covered platform parking, elevator access, and higher-grade finishes.

The rolling top of the site was incorporated to seclude second-phase parking—one car per unit—under the higher side of the building. (Additional parking was provided on the site for a second car per unit.) With access to the garage at the end of the building, the parking was hidden behind retaining walls, with the first level above but close to grade level. Placing parking facilities under unit clusters allowed higher density while preserving open space.

Because half of the building is at grade and the other half is over the parking area, the third level of the high side aligns with the attic of the low side. Each unit has access to a large attic storage room.

Exteriors of the second-phase buildings are brick with a band of shingles around the top floor. Rooflines are more regular than those of the earlier buildings, but design details such as round and bay windows, decorative chimneys, and keystones recall the first-phase building design. Porches that can be enclosed or left open are provided for each unit.

The construction of the second phase was slab on grade with a steel frame, incorporating metal composite floor decks and masonry walls for the parking garage. Regular wood frames, with floor and roof trusses, were used on top of the elevated slab and on the half of the building at grade level. The 24-unit third and last phase consists of a single cluster designed much like the first-phase buildings, centered around a courtyard with an elevator.

Landscaping was planned with the same sensitivity to detail, aided considerably by the architecture of the buildings. Because exterior wall materials were brought down to

■ Set on a 7.2-acre site in central Raleigh, North Carolina, Bishops Park achieves a density of over 19 units per acre without conflicting with its surrounding, low-density neighborhood. The site plan is based on three phases of three- and four-story buildings, each containing up to 18 stacked flats clustered around a central courtyard. Buildings in the second phase also feature parking located beneath the building (partially underground). The building clusters allowed many of the mature trees located on the site to be preserved.

ground level, foundations did not have to be hidden with shrubbery. Other architectural treatments covered transformers, condensers, and trash stations. This allowed the landscaping design to concentrate more fully on major elements such as the project entrance, site borders, interior access, and the pool area.

The main entrance is flanked by brick columns, on one of which a pink granite slab is engraved with the project's name. The internal drive is laid with Z-pavers, creating a herringbone pattern much like cobblestones. The inverted crown road has a storm drain and flush brick curbing that allowed a narrower road and eliminated grading for swales that would have required the removal of more trees. Turf stone is used in parking areas to protect tree roots. Brick walls encircle the buildings and pool, adding an established character to the project and, along Glenwood Avenue, effectively hiding parking spaces from the street. The pool offers lounging areas, both shaded and sunny, and is also surfaced with Z-pavers. The internal courtyards are treated with similar care, providing easily maintained plantings and seating areas.

APPROVALS

Development on this infill site required the cooperation of city officials to adjust and interpret provisions in zoning and building code requirements that would have eliminated some of the most distinctive features of the design, including the preservation of trees and open space and the provision of internal courtyards.

A number of special approvals were required from the planning commission, including a text change in the zoning ordinance to permit unit entrances to be located on the courtyard instead of on a public

street and to allow parking within 30 feet of the buildings. Special approval was required from the health department for the use of concrete pavers at the pool, from the Board of Adjustment for the height of the wall, and from the city's engineering department for the road construction and paving. Rezoning was not required, as the existing designation for office and institutional uses allowed residential use subject to city review and approval of precise plans. The design won the approval and cooperation of officials, minimizing delays.

MARKETING

The first phase of the project was expected to attract young professionals and perhaps a few empty-nester couples, although the third-floor walkup was seen as a potential discouragement for older residents. This market identification was proved accurate by actual sales, which were mostly to young single people and childless couples aged 30 to 40. The project also has a few older couples and more single occupants than expected. The minimum household income of residents is $35,000 to $40,000 per year, with

some occupants earning substantially more.

Interestingly, most residents are not first-time buyers but rather have moved from previously owned homes. Some were moving up from lower-cost homes but most were attracted by Bishops Park's uncommon style and favorable location. Buyers commended the privacy and efficient planning of individual units, as well as the established character of the overall community. The developers found relatively little market resistance to prices that represented high per-square-foot values for the area.

The marketing strategy concentrated on substantial advertising to establish project identity, stressing the distinctive architecture and the developer's track record in Charlotte's Fourth Ward, a well-known inner-city housing area. As most buyers were not looking for new homes in this established residential area, a description of the location and driving instructions proved useful. Most sales were made before construction. Later phases have benefited from the image established by publicity for the first phase and from the presence of an on-site sales office and model.

■ **Each phase II building is divided in half with parking located below the taller of what appears to be two separate structures.**

Interior units—those with no corner exposure—proved most difficult to market. In subsequent phases, building clusters were designed to minimize interior units or maximize light by stepping these units out.

In this market, two baths are almost a necessity and ample kitchen cabinets are an asset. Buyers moving from single-family homes expect the convenience of two baths and extra storage space.

Top-floor units, which feature vaulted ceilings, were popular even with the three-floor walkup. The added luxury and privacy were important enough to buyers to warrant the extra cost.

The obvious quality of construction—exemplified in paving materials, walls, and other exterior design features—assured buyers that long-term maintenance costs would not be excessive.

PROJECT DATA

LAND USE INFORMATION[1]:
Site Area: 7.2 acres
Total Units: 138
Gross Density: 19.2 units per acre
Parking Index: 1.92 spaces per unit

ECONOMIC INFORMATION:
Site Costs[1]: $1,144,000[3]
Construction Costs per Unit[2]:
Hard Costs .... $75,680[4]
Soft Cost plus Amenities[1] $13,750
Total Hard and Soft Costs $89,430
Average Total Cost per Unit[2]: $97,720

LAND USE PLAN[1]:

	Acres	Percent of Site
Open Space	3.5	48.6%
Buildings	1.3	18.1
Roads/Parking Area	1.7	23.6
Walks, Courts, Amenities	0.7	9.7

UNIT INFORMATION[2]:
Four buildings constitute the "parking-under" phase (phase II) of Bishops Park. The units were enlarged progressively in reaction to the market response in favor of larger, more expensive units. One buyer actually bought two units and customized them into one double-sized, double-priced dwelling.

Building	Unit Type	Number	Square Feet	Sales Price
I	A	6	1,120	$105,000
	B	6	1,290	$115,000
	C	6	1,460	$135,000
II	A	3	1,120	$110,000
	B	3	1,290	$120,000
	C	12	1,460	$140,000
III	D	6	1,380	$130,000
	E	6	1,640	$165,000
IV	A	3	1,120	$115,000
	B	3	1,290	$ 25,000
	C	12	1,460	$145,000

Notes:
[1]For entire site including other different phases.
[2]Information specific to 66 units in building types under which parking is located (phase II). The other 72 units in Bishops Park are of a different, less expensive building type and are not included in this report.
[3]$8,290 per unit.
[4]$55 per square foot average.

DIRECTIONS:
From Raleigh/Durham Airport, follow Interstate Highway 40 east and continue on Wade Avenue to Glenwood Avenue. Turn south on Glenwood Avenue to Washington Street on right (300 yards). Or follow U.S. Highway 70 east from airport to Interstate 64 beltway and continue two miles on Glenwood Avenue to Washington Street on right. Bishops Park is on the west side of Glenwood Avenue north of Washington Street.

DEVELOPER:
Martin Development Group, Inc.
2305 Randolph Road
Charlotte, North Carolina 28207

ARCHITECT:
David Furman/Architecture
508 East Boulevard
Charlotte, North Carolina 28203

LANDSCAPE ARCHITECT:
Hunter, Reynolds, Jewell, P.A.
Elmwood
16 North Boylan Avenue
Raleigh, North Carolina 27603

AWARDS:
• *Builder* magazine, Builder's Choice Awards, 1985
• AIA Award, 1986
• Sir Walter Raleigh Award, 1984

CRANE PLACE
SENIOR CITIZEN HOUSING
MENLO PARK, CALIFORNIA

Robert T. Steinberg

Crane Place, a mid-rise apartment complex for senior citizens in Menlo Park, California, is located on an irregularly shaped site in an affluent neighborhood adjacent to the downtown area. Although the project looks neither dense nor subsidized, it is both: 93 studio and one-bedroom units and communal facilities are situated on slightly less than a single acre, with construction and operating costs federally subsidized through HUD's now-expired Section

Robert T. Steinberg, AIA, is president and chief executive officer of The Steinberg Group, architects, in San Jose, California. He is a member of the National AIA Housing Committee.

8 program. Residents pay 30 percent of their gross income and government subsidies make up the difference, up to designated market rates.

The entire project is planned around a central courtyard to maximize light and air, provide views, and offer opportunities for outdoor activity in a controlled, secure environment particularly appealing to senior citizen residents.

DEVELOPMENT STRATEGY

With an extreme shortage in the area of housing for the elderly, demand for such apartments was not an issue in formulating a development strategy; instead, the major challenge was to locate and acquire

■ The limited street frontage presented a design challenge; the building had to be large enough to accommodate a variety of functions while not so large that it would overpower other buildings in the neighborhood. It is weighted to the rear of the site, terraced to reduce its scale, and sheathed in cedar shingles to blend with the wooded setting.

available, affordable land and use it to its fullest potential to help fill this housing void.

The contract was awarded as the result of a competition among eight developer/architect teams with a single stated purpose: to construct 93 units of senior citizen housing in the Bay Area for a maximum cost of $3.5 million. The winning entry was a collaboration of The Steinberg Group, architects, and sponsor Peninsula Volunteers, Inc., a nonprofit group dedicated to providing services and activities for the elderly.

SITE AND PLANNING

From the outset, the site selected by the sponsor posed the major design problem, and ultimately determined the viable, innovative solution of a courtyard concept. Street frontage of the flag-shaped site was minimal, yet it had to accommodate a variety of critical functions, including a driveway and off-street passenger loading area, a landscaped front entrance, a pedestrian ramp and stairway, auto access to the underground garage, and a food service facility delivery entrance that doubles as a fire emergency access. In addition, the program placed the building's reception area, security offices, and several administrative offices at or near the front entrance.

These requirements, coupled with the need to retain several mature oak and redwood trees, compounded the siting difficulties and ultimately prescribed the design solution: to place communal and service functions at street frontage in a low-rise configuration, and to step back toward the wider, rear portion of the site in an L configuration for greater mass and density for residential units. The entire complex was oriented toward a courtyard, which would allow maximum use of skylights, and clerestory and conventional glazing.

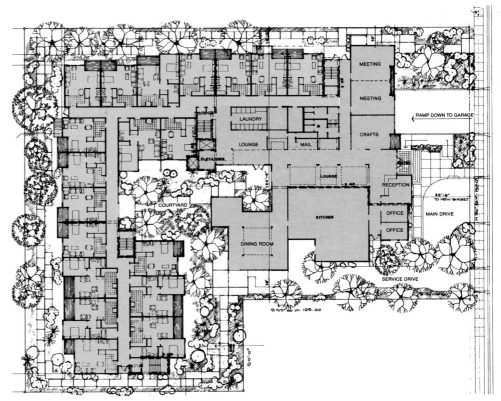

SITE/BUILDING PLAN

ARCHITECTURE

Placing the bulk of residential units toward the rear of the site posed another design challenge: locating elevators so that they would be convenient to the main entrance, yet far enough into the building to avoid long, institutional corridors leading from elevators to apartments. The latter was done, and the entrance problem was solved by developing a significant building amenity for residents and guests at street level: a unique, 100-foot-long pedestrian spine that begins outside the building's glass entry doors and moves inside to link the entrance with the elevators.

Along this "pedestrian street" are all of the communal/social/activity areas of the facility, including lounges, gift shop, craft areas, library, and dining room—all of which are generously glazed to maximize natural light and their relationship to the central courtyard.

■ Designed as housing for the elderly in Menlo Park, California, Crane Place comprises 93 apartments located on a one-acre infill site. The project also features ancillary facilities including lounges, a dining room, a central courtyard, and underground parking for 35 cars. To lessen the visual impact of the density, units are concentrated primarily at the rear of the site, and the building mass is terraced down toward the street frontage.

Thus, what might have been merely a passageway became instead an active and vital center of building activity—a gathering place or "town square" in which residents can socialize informally and participate in community life.

Despite high density, the L-shaped plan also allowed for what became another of the building's

■ A "pedestrian street" (top) links the front doors to the courtyard located at the interior of the site. Opened to the outdoors by means of skylights and conventional glazing, this corridor serves as an activity hub with lounges (above), dining room, shops, and activity rooms located along its path.

most important amenities—the courtyard. In addition to providing light, air, and views for the units facing it, the courtyard is designed to encourage residents to participate and become involved in the outdoors and with each other. It is a "living area" that offers informal seating/conversation areas amid the mature oak and redwood trees and other plantings; a fountain with fish; varied surface areas; and the well-articulated surrounding building, which provides background texture. An exercise walk around the perimeter of the building—also landscaped with trees, plantings, and bench/rest areas—supplements the central courtyard space and also provides landscaped views for rear units.

Complementing the secluded, communal, and primarily shady interior courtyard is a roof garden on the top floor at the front of the building, which offers an alternative outdoor setting—a sunny, private aerie overlooking the neighborhood. Thus, tenants can choose between two types of outdoor environment.

The building's exterior was designed to blend with the natural setting through use of wood-frame plywood and wood shingles that weather naturally. Large glassed expanses provide maximum light and views for building residents.

To avoid unappealing views from the courtyard or apartments of an equipment-laden roof on the single-story kitchen/dining facility, mechanical equipment is concealed with an enclosed penthouse. Stacked and terraced with louvers and varied material textures, the penthouse actually creates another design element, giving the courtyard as viewed from above the appearance of a multilevel plaza.

In the building's residential zones, apartments are located on both sides of corridors whose length is diminished visually by several right angle "jogs" with varying de-

sign treatments that both orient residents and visitors and serve as small rest stops, if needed. (They have, in fact, been dubbed "bus stops" by the residents and are yet another area for informal socializing.) Glazing at the end of each hallway and along some corridor sections overlooking the courtyard permits natural light to penetrate deep into the building.

Of the 93 apartments in Crane Place, two-thirds are 410-square-foot studios and one-third are 540-square-foot one-bedroom units, each with a small kitchen and bathroom. Ten percent of the units are designed specifically for handicapped residents.

Unit layouts place sleeping areas in small niches out of direct view. Special consideration was given to many design features geared specifically to the mature residents, including custom kitchens with cabinets and appliances requiring minimal reaching or stooping; compartmentalized bathrooms entered via cased openings; handrails; and security systems.

Every unit has either a balcony or a patio to provide private, personal outdoor space, extending the living area—which can be used often because of the mild climate—and allowing residents to enjoy nature. Extensive use of windows further expands the perception of space in the compact units.

APPROVALS

Although HUD officials were pleased with the design and proposal from the development team, city officials were less than enthusiastic, citing the high density, the low parking-per-unit ratio, and the large building mass in this primarily residential neighborhood. Following a redesign process and a lengthy city approval procedure, the project was approved and constructed.

■ The compact apartment units are designed to make maximum use of space. Each unit features a separate sleeping alcove, small kitchen, and individual balconies or patios to expand the visual and functional space.

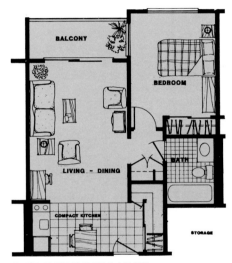

ONE-BEDROOM UNIT
514 SQUARE FEET

STUDIO UNIT
410 SQUARE FEET

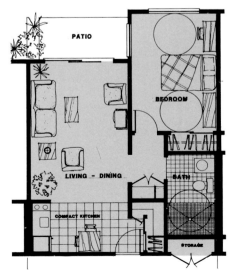

ONE-BEDROOM WHEELCHAIR
  UNIT
540 SQUARE FEET

STUDIO WHEELCHAIR UNIT
410 SQUARE FEET

■ Residents can select either the one-bedroom or studio unit, each of which features a kitchen and bath. Both floor plans are offered in a slightly modified design to accommodate residents confined to wheelchairs.

MARKETING/PROJECT SUCCESS

The success of the project has been called phenomenal, both because the units were rented immediately with only minimal marketing, and because the project's design has fostered so much enthusiasm and communal spirit.

The functional plan; the high-density site; the pedestrian walkway with its lounges, shops, dining room, and activity areas; the garden courtyard; and the sensitive design of individual units combine to create a much sought-after residence for seniors. Crane Place has a waiting list of two to five years for future occupants.

■ **Mature pine trees were preserved around the perimeter of the site and within the central courtyard. Units facing the perimeter of the building enjoy a view of the exercise walk and the dense landscaping.**

Russell Abraham

PROJECT DATA

LAND USE INFORMATION:
Site Area: 0.99 acres
Total Units: 93
Density: 93.94 units per acre
Parking Spaces: 35 spaces in underground garage
Parking Index: 0.41 spaces per unit

LAND USE PLAN[1]:

	Acres	Percent of Site
Open Space	0.47	47.5%
Buildings	0.47	47.5
Other	0.05	5.0

UNIT TYPES[2]:

Type	Square Feet	Number	Monthly Rental Range	Garage
studio/1-bath	410	66	$711	No
1-bdrm./1-bath	514–540	27	$767	No

ECONOMIC INFORMATION:
Site Value: $460,000[3]
Construction Costs: $3,308,766[4]
Site Improvement Costs: $108,847
Off-Site Work[5]: $56,200

Notes:
[1]Amenities cannot be separated.
[2]Ten units are equipped for handicapped.
[3]$4,946 per unit.
[4]$42.52 per square foot.
[5]Storm drainage improvements mandated by the city.

DIRECTIONS:
From San Francisco Airport, take Highway 101 south to Willow Road exit. Go west on Middlefield Road; turn right onto Ravenswood and left onto El Camino. Follow El Camino to Oak Grove Avenue and turn right. From Oak Grove Avenue turn left onto Crane Street: 1331 Crane Street is on the left side of street.

DEVELOPER:
Peninsula Volunteers, Inc.
800 Middle Avenue
Menlo Park, California 94025

ARCHITECT:
The Steinberg Group
60 Pierce Avenue
San Jose, California 95110

AWARDS:
• 1982 Grand Award, Pacific Coast Builder's Conference/*Builder* magazine
• 1981 Merit Award, Red Cedar Shingle Handsplit Shake Bureau

THE BARONY ON PEACHTREE
ATLANTA, GEORGIA

Lloyd W. Bookout with
William W. Howell

It is almost impossible to think of Atlanta without the word "Peachtree" coming to mind. One might also recall the prestigious Buckhead neighborhood of north Atlanta, or visions of stately southern mansions set on large, tree-lined lots. All of these impressions offered both opportunities and constraints for the developers of the Barony on Peachtree condominium building.

For generations, the Buckhead area has been home to Atlanta's

William W. Howell, AIA, is chairman and chief executive officer of the Monarch Group, Inc., real estate developers, and president of William Howell and Associates, Inc., architects, both based in Atlanta, Georgia. He is a member of the National AIA Housing Committee.

wealthiest and most powerful families. But as land costs increase and demands for higher-intensity land uses mount, Buckhead is showing signs of change. New residents are settling for both smaller homes and smaller lots just to live in this neighborhood only a few miles from downtown. The trend toward higher density is especially prevalent along Peachtree Road—often called the Park Avenue of Atlanta—where townhomes and garden-density condominiums have gradually become commonplace.

The Barony on Peachtree was a pioneer of mid-rise luxury condominiums in Atlanta. Located on a 1.32-acre site, the nine-story building contains 56 two-bedroom, two-bath units. Each floor contains eight units along a double-loaded corridor. Two levels of parking for 104

■ **The main entrance off Lindbergh Drive (right) provides vertical separation of automobile and pedestrian traffic. The elevated pedestrian plaza connects to an at-grade entry courtyard and transit stop off Peachtree Road (left).**

■ The gabled roof and other exterior design features emphasize the residential character of the building. After sales began, blue window awnings were installed to add color, promote entry identity, and provide shade to solariums.

cars are located beneath a platform that also serves as a pedestrian plaza. The building features modern security technology and offers maintenance-free living to Atlanta's growing urban market.

DEVELOPMENT STRATEGY

The concept for the 1.32-acre site, as proposed by its original developer based in Jacksonville, Florida, provided for only 10 units of approximately 10,000 square feet each—a viable concept for a Florida project. With an estimated sales price of $1 million each, these units were targeted for a very select market. Having built similar units successfully in other urban markets, the developer proceeded with building design and the required rezoning.

Subsequent to project approvals, a marketing study cautioned that the select group of buyers that was needed for mid-rise condominiums in this price range might not exist—even in Buckhead. Instead, the study suggested a potentially untapped market for smaller two-bedroom, two-bath units selling in the range of $125,000 to $150,000. The targeted buyers would be young professionals seeking a location close to employment centers, transit lines, shopping, entertainment, and restaurants. Using this revised strategy, the developer formed a joint venture with a local Atlanta developer, and initiated a redesign effort.

SITE

Peachtree Road, the primary north-south corridor through Buckhead, acts as a major transit line connecting downtown Atlanta with the rapidly developing Lenox area to the north. The development of office buildings, hotels, and retail uses in and around Lenox has spurred demand for nearby residential uses. Although Atlanta's rapid transit system (MARTA) does not extend down Peachtree, it is easily reached by bus connections.

The Barony is located on the site of two former single-family houses, which the developer acquired in 1982 to undertake higher-intensity residential uses consistent with development trends on surrounding parcels. Expensive townhomes front on Peachtree Road immediately north and west of the Barony. Just to the south and across Peachtree, a new 19-story apartment building has recently been constructed. These projects have met with considerable success in the marketplace despite steep rents and sales prices often in excess of $400,000.

Although higher densities are now accepted along Peachtree Road,

development intensity drops off quickly within one block either east or west of it. Immediately east of the Barony is the Peachtree Heights residential neighborhood, characterized by large single-family homes and spacious grounds. Residents of this neighborhood have resisted the encroachment of higher-density uses, and sensitive planning and design solutions are often necessary to avoid zoning battles.

APPROVALS

When the architect and the local joint venture partner became involved in the Barony project, the site had already been rezoned to provide a floor/area ratio (FAR) of 1.5. This zoning change had required three months of public hearings and had been opposed by some of the local residents in the Peachtree Heights neighborhood. The new development team was anxious to avoid another lengthy public hearing process, especially one that might result in a lower FAR than already existed.

Atlanta's zoning regulations permit redesign of previously approved buildings by an "administrative variance" process, whereby no new public hearing is required. Although this process can be gone through in less than one month, it requires that the redesigned building conform to the previously approved FAR and to the same setback and height limitations. To avoid potential controversy and to expedite approvals, the development team set out to design a new building that conformed both to the approved development standards and to the latest market study.

PLANNING AND ARCHITECTURE

The primary design challenge was to maximize the number of units on the site in order to offer them in the targeted price range. Marketing studies advised that the city's minimum parking ratio of 0.67 spaces per unit would be insufficient for this market segment. Although many residents of the project would use public transportation to commute to work, they would also own automobiles and would expect convenient parking. The minimum ratio of 1.5 spaces per unit suggested by the market study added to the challenge to maximize the site's development potential.

■ Ranging in size from 1,323 to 1,479 square feet, the two-bedroom/two-bath units were designed to appeal to young professionals wanting to be close to transit and city services. The Hanover plan, featuring two master bedroom/bath suites, is popular with unrelated buyers sharing a unit. Plan B (not shown) is similar to the plan D unit but is about 150 square feet smaller.

PLAN A—THE HANOVER
1,339 SQUARE FEET

PLAN C—THE EDINBOROUGH
1,399 SQUARE FEET

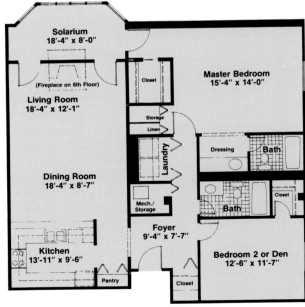

PLAN D—THE BUCKINGHAM
1,479 SQUARE FEET

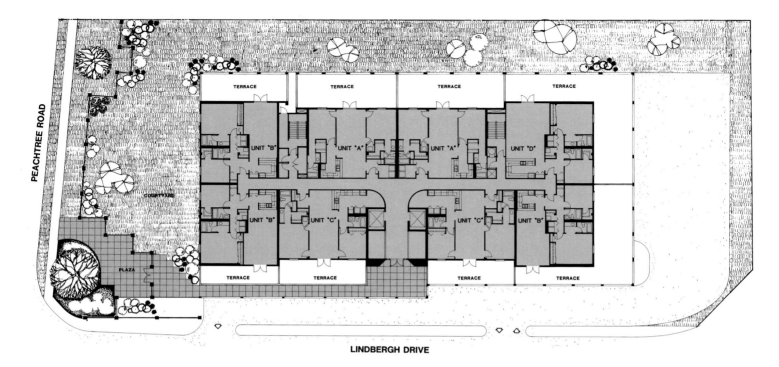

PEACHTREE ROAD

TERRACE TERRACE TERRACE TERRACE

UNIT "B" UNIT "A" UNIT "A" UNIT "D"

COURTYARD

UNIT "B" UNIT "C" UNIT "C" UNIT "B"

PLAZA

TERRACE TERRACE TERRACE TERRACE

LINDBERGH DRIVE

■ **Located five miles from downtown in Atlanta's prestigious Buckhead neighborhood, the Barony on Peachtree contains 56 luxury condominium units at a density of 42.4 units per acre. The seven floors of residential units (eight units per floor) rest on a platform that provides a courtyard and circulation area for pedestrians. Two levels of resident parking are located below the platform.**

To meet these challenges, the architect designed a building that provided seven, eight-unit stories on top of a two-level platform parking garage. Because the site sloped down to the east, ground-level vehicular drives could be built off Lindbergh Drive. The parking garage platform maintains the same grade as Peachtree Road and serves only pedestrian traffic moving between the main entrance to the building and Peachtree Road.

The orientation of the rectangular-shaped site presented another design problem. The long side of the parcel fronts on Lindbergh, which was the logical entry to the building. But the developer wanted to satisfy the marketing program's objective that the building have a Peachtree Road address and identity. Thus a pedestrian entrance facing Lindbergh Drive was created at the platform level and was connected to Peachtree Road via a pedestrian plaza. The plaza was designed to relate closely with the intersection of Peachtree and Lindbergh, which serves as a transit stop. As a result of these design so-

lutions, the Barony is readily identified with Peachtree and vehicular and pedestrian traffic are separated.

Perhaps the design team's greatest challenge was to create a midrise residential building that would be architecturally compatible with the adjacent single-family neighborhood—an eclectic collection of traditional regional styles. Many of the homes, however, reflect the influence of Atlanta architect Neil Reed, who was responsible for the design of dozens of the area's buildings constructed in the 1920s. The Barony's architects used several elements of Reed's design to blend the project with the surrounding neighborhood and to enhance the building's residential scale and appearance.

Reed's influence on the Barony can be seen in the columns of bay windows that serve as the solarium for each of the units, in the arched windows, in the pediment at the entrance to the building, and in the light colors of the trim and the cementitious, stuccolike coating. The residential scale of the building is reinforced by the gabled roof. The total effect is that of a building with a clearly defined bottom, middle, and top, similar to most single-family homes.

To promote a sense of space within the building, each floor has nine-foot-high ceilings. The elevator lobbies extend up two stories on every third floor while large windows located in each of the lobbies provide light and views outside. Curved walls have been used to soften the effect of the corridors. Units receive maximum light through bay windows and the enclosed solarium that comes with each unit. In its treatment of both exterior and interior design elements, the Barony has attempted to achieve a residential scale and quality comparable to those of the single-family residences for which Buckhead is famous.

MARKETING

Marketing efforts are oriented heavily to professionals and to individuals relocating to Atlanta from the Northeast and areas where midrise condominium living is commonplace. Several of the units have also sold to empty nesters and retirees who desire a maintenance-free lifestyle but want to stay in the Buckhead area. Each unit is offered with standard features such as marble entries, crown molding, a microwave oven, and one parking space. Some of the parking spaces are laid out in tandem, accommodating two cars parked front to back; these spaces are offered on a first-come, first-served basis.

At the time of its opening, the Barony was a relatively new product to the Atlanta market. Thus, an aggressive and specifically targeted marketing program was undertaken at the onset of development. Sales would likely have benefited by the provision of on-site amenities. The developer considered including an exercise room and a spa, but dropped them from the plan because of concerns about space. As

anticipated, many of the prospective buyers have been young professionals who would have appreciated having such amenities.

Many buyers immediately wanted to customize their units to fit their personal tastes and lifestyles. Customizing requests included not only decorating, but also items such as the location of walls, the design and size of closets, and the type of cabinetry provided. To the extent feasible, the developer attempted to accommodate the buyers' requests. In working with these buyers, the developer recognized a possible market for condominium "shells" (rather than turnkey units) that could be designed to fit a buyer's needs. This marketing approach would involve buyer participation in the layout of the rooms and in the selection of finishing details such as flooring and kitchen and bathroom appointments.

Initial sales were slower than anticipated, primarily because the de-

◼ **The popular indoor solariums, shown here behind a glass block wall, add light and expanse to living rooms. Solariums were considered similar to porches and were not counted against the building's floor/area ratio limitation.**

veloper did not at first offer a convenient loan package and because the mid-rise condominium product was unfamiliar in the Atlanta area. Sales improved significantly, however, when the developer secured a source to "warehouse" the loans. For buyers already in residence, favored features are the security of the building and parking, extensive glazing, the prestigious mid-town location, and the conveniences of living in a condominium building.

PROJECT DATA

LAND USE INFORMATION:
Site Area: 1.32 acres
Total Units: 56
Density: 42.4 units per acre
Building Area[1]: 85,933 square feet

Floor/Area Ratio: 1.5
Site Coverage: 23,296 square feet[2]
Parking Spaces: 104 spaces
Parking Index: 1.86 spaces per unit

UNIT INFORMATION:

Type	Program	Square Feet[3]	Number	Sales Price
A) Hanover	2-bdrm./2-bath	1,339	15	$142,000–$159,000
B) Windsor	2-bdrm./2-bath	1,323	14	$139,000–$163,900
C) Edinborough	2-bdrm./2-bath	1,399	14	$140,000–$165,900
D) Buckingham	2-bdrm./2-bath	1,479	13	$155,000–$186,900

ECONOMIC INFORMATION:
Site Value: $640,000
Site Improvement Costs:

Demolition/Excavation/Backfill	$ 112,440
Grading	60,760
Paving/Curbs/Sidewalks	26,500
Landscaping	35,000
Storm Drainage	7,979
Total	$ 242,679

Construction Costs:

Structural	$1,282,696
Carpentry	219,324
Electrical	339,169
Plumbing/HVAC/Sewer/Water	552,445
Sprinklers	82,144
Elevators	152,931
Other	1,928,562
Total	$4,557,271

Total Hard Costs[4]: $5,439,950
Total Soft Costs: $200,000

Notes:
[1]Building square footage excludes indoor solariums.
[2]40 percent of site.
[3]Unit square footage includes indoor solariums.
[4]Hard costs include site acquisition, improvement, and construction costs. Average cost per unit is $97,150.

DIRECTIONS:
From airport: Take Interstate 85 north to Peachtree Road exit (immediately after I-75/I-85 split). Turn left (north) on Peachtree Road (State Highway 9) and proceed approximately two miles to Lindbergh Drive.

From downtown: Follow directions above or proceed north on Spring Street (State Highway 9), which becomes Peachtree Road. The project is about five miles from the downtown business district.

DEVELOPER:
Peachtree Barony Venture
(a joint venture of Milajest Inc. & AB Ventures)
P.O. Box 888506
Atlanta, Georgia 30356

ARCHITECT:
William Howell & Associates
1355 Terrell Mill Road
Building 1484, Suite 200
Marietta, Georgia 30067

GENERAL CONTRACTOR:
Marvin M. Black Company
P.O. Box 888506
Atlanta, Georgia 30356

MARKETING/SALES:
Coldwell Banker
5252 Roswell Road, #202
Atlanta, Georgia 30342

From High-Rise Slab Buildings to...

High-rise buildings differ from lower-density, mid-rise buildings in several ways. While the mid rise may have open corridors, decks, or stairs similar to garden-density buildings, the high rise is almost always an internalized, highly secure, self-contained structure. The high rise is also more likely to be set on a valuable, urban site where construction costs are at their highest and circulation and service become even more difficult.

While the mid-rise building may cling to the ground plane for identity, the high rise is associated with a skyline image. In the past, is-

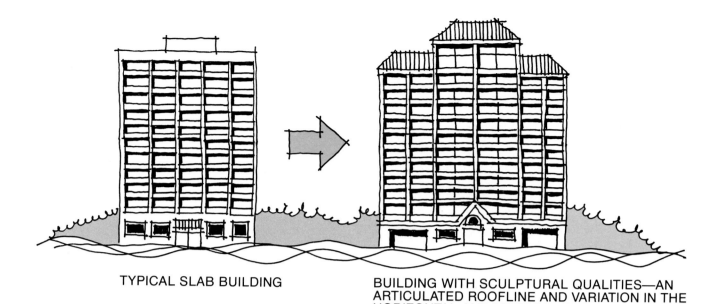

TYPICAL SLAB BUILDING

BUILDING WITH SCULPTURAL QUALITIES—AN ARTICULATED ROOFLINE AND VARIATION IN THE HORIZONTAL AND VERTICAL DESIGN ELEMENTS

■ Varied heights, roofline articulation, and changes in texture and materials are design techniques used to achieve more personable, sculptured housing towers.

sues like location, address, views, amenities, and convenience generally have superseded building image. But with the growing acceptance of high-rise living spreading across the country, these buildings are taking on new and more exciting forms.

SCULPTURED TOWERS

Gradually, high-rise structures are becoming more articulated. They are following the trend set by commercial office towers that seek to establish identities for their corporate owners by making a unique impression on the city skyline. From the Transamerica Tower in San Francisco to the AT&T Tower in New York City, corporations are learning that secondary benefits can accrue from distinguished architecture.

Housing towers increasingly are being integrated with other uses such as office, retail, and institutional activities. For example, these towers can be mixed vertically, with office uses occupying the lower floors of the building and housing above. In other cases that involve large urban mixed-use projects (sometimes called "super blocks"), housing towers can be located above a much larger base structure of nonresidential uses. The towers can then have a private area for recreational facilities on the base structure's roof, which is well removed from the busy street below.

The architecture of sculptured towers stresses varied heights, articulated rooflines, changes of materials or texture, and other vertical and horizontal elements that can be used to dissolve the rectangular grid created by the units. Such towers are often inspired by vernacular architectural forms. A case in point—the colorful and decorative top of Seattle's Watermark Tower was inspired by the older art deco buildings found in this once seedy waterfront area. In another example, from St. Paul, the two residential towers of Galtier Plaza strike a balance between the brick warehouses of the Lowertown Historic District in which they are located and the nearby glass skyscrapers of the downtown. Each project blends architecturally with its particular urban context.

Other contemporary high rises achieve their sculptured qualities with less emphasis on the vernacular. At their best, these sleek, minimalist towers may be likened to an object of art. Perhaps no better example can be found than the residential tower built over the Museum of Modern Art in New York City. The tower's varied colors of glass and spandrel panels resembles a Mondrian painting. In this case, the merging of art with architecture is complete.

Robert Pisano

THE WATERMARK TOWER
SEATTLE, WASHINGTON

Mark Ashley

The scene of many peculiar pastimes and exotic endeavors over the course of a century, the skid rows of America constitute a class of marginal urban areas with origins in the frontier town of Seattle. The first "Skid Road" was a steep incline of greased log skids down which felled trees slid to the mill and the harbor. Around it

Mark Ashley is director of public relations for The Bumgardner Architects in Seattle, Washington. He is the editor of, and a frequent contributor to, ARCADE: The Northwest Journal for Architecture and Design.

emerged a district of taverns, tatoo parlors, brothels, and flophouses. By the mid-1970s, neglect had turned the waterfront warehouse district of woodsmen, sailors, and footloose fortune-seekers into a blighted hole in the city center. Urban nomads, drug pushers, pornographers, and prostitutes owned the streets and the street-level shops in the otherwise empty buildings along Seattle's First Avenue. Today, the last of the pawn shops, porn theaters, adult bookstores, and vacant transient hotels are being replaced by a more civilized, if less exotic, mix of activities that appeals to a wider segment of Seattle's population.

■ While the Watermark looms over its immediate neighborhood, its relatively modest height and downhill location diminish it in the city's thicket of 30- to 70-story office towers. The architectural form of the Watermark Tower (right) was influenced by the massing of Seattle Tower (left), which was designed as the Northern Life Tower in 1929 by Albertson, Wilson & Richardson, and which, for years, was Seattle's quintessential skyscraper.

Sandy Farrier

SITE LOCATION

The contemporary renaissance of Seattle's First Avenue began with the creation of Waterfront Place—developed by Cornerstone Development Company[1] and master-planned by The Bumgardner Architects and Cornerstone's Paul Schell and Harriet Sherburne—in the heart of downtown Seattle's Central Waterfront District. Located halfway between the city's two historic districts, Pioneer Square and Pike Place Market, Waterfront Place is a 1.4 million-square-foot, mixed-use development combining six historic structures (turn-of-the-century office buildings, warehouses, and hotels) with four new buildings in the redevelopment of the six blocks.

One of the largest projects of this type to be developed exclusively by the private sector, the $130 million Waterfront Place was carefully planned to mix low-rise rehabilitation; new mid-rise construction; and a variety of housing, office, recreational, and retail uses. The goal has been to create an urban neighborhood that would reweave the hole in the existing fabric of downtown Seattle.

Planning for Waterfront Place started in 1979, and construction began in July 1981 with the rehabilitation of the historic buildings. These buildings were available for occupancy in the fall of 1982. In July 1983, the $17.8 million Watermark Tower opened as the neighborhood's first new structure.

DEVELOPMENT STRATEGY

As originally proposed, the Watermark was not at all towerlike. It was to have 12 stories of condominiums and street-level shops on a single

[1]Now Cornerstone Columbia Development Company, a partnership of Weyerhaeuser Real Estate Company and Portland General Electric/Columbia-Willamette Development Company.

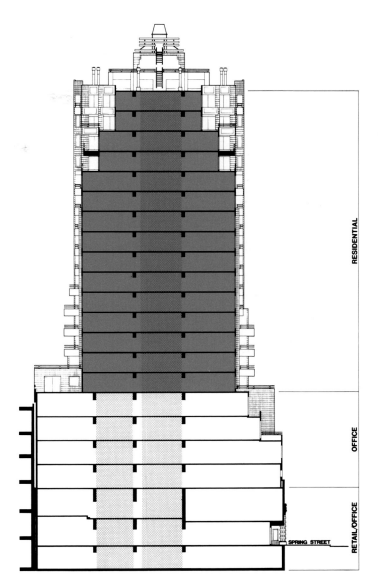

parcel of land. This plan, however, depended on a $13 million urban development action grant (UDAG) for Waterfront Place. And because of criticism of the neighborhood redevelopment plans by opponents wanting to prevent the gentrification of the last vestiges of Skid Road, the UDAG was not conferred, necessitating a reformulation and redesign of the project. Without the public loan commitment (for a project that surpassed the city's declared goals both for downtown housing and the preservation of historic areas), the developer chose to try to recoup some of the fixed development costs by changing the land use mix and increasing the density. Some rental

■ When the original plans for a 12-story residential building on this site fell through, the developer changed the land use mix and upped the density. The tower, as built, provides 94 condominiums—yielding a residential density of more than 300 units per acre—atop a seven-story base of office and retail uses.

housing evolved into the luxury Alexis Hotel, and the 12-story residential and retail building became the pricier half-block, 22-story Watermark Tower with 94 condominium units above seven floors of offices

■ The multicolored, tile crown to the tower frames balconies and provides visual interest. One Seattle architectural critic referred to the "Watermark's rumpled profile and polychrome icing" and called it "a ceramic anthill with Buck Rogers additions. Terrific."

■ The parapet of the 1932 Federal Building (center) served as the inspiration for the Watermark's crowning tile motif.

and retail space. Thus, the building grew into a tall, mixed-use tower that became the focal point of the neighborhood.

The Watermark Tower site lies in the center of the larger Waterfront Place project at First Avenue and Spring Street. The city's guidelines targeted Spring Street as a major downtown east-west axis between the uphill financial district and the waterfront two blocks from the site. A broad stairway, street trees, and widened sidewalks emphasize the pedestrian focus of the Spring Street corridor throughout the project. On the site of the Watermark stood two buildings. One of them—the Coleman Building—bore the

most dramatic element of any of the neighborhood's existing facades—a grand terra-cotta portal that became the signature of the neighborhood. This portal established the "friendly" architectural character of the Watermark Tower.

PLANNING AND ARCHITECTURE

The neighborhood's designers set out to integrate new buildings in Waterfront Place to mesh with the project's edges. The new buildings would serve as infill on vacant blocks or as replacements for insignificant structures. The mix of retail, office, and residential uses would help to define a small, articulated architectural scale.

With the increase to 22 stories, the top of the Watermark Tower would loom 14 floors above the historic buildings along First Avenue. Fitting this behemoth into the streetscape was (literally) a tall order for the building's designers. But as built, the Watermark Tower actually sums up the neighborhood's essence and serves as its icon, both at street level and from afar. The Watermark's recycled terra-cotta facade from the 1915 Coleman Build-

Because the Watermark Tower would block some of the views of the bay that pedestrians enjoyed as they walked up Seattle's hilly streets, the design team decided to offer a compensation. Thus it is that instead of staring at a barren rooftop landscape of mechanical equipment, pedestrians and others are treated to a view of the tower's charmingly ragged (articulated) top, which, with its large decks and distinctive colors, adds punch to its surroundings, particularly on the city's many gray days. The building was designed in the art deco style of neighborhood buildings, with a stepped-back form and a shimmery blue, brown, and black tile motif at the top. The tile motif is carried into the building entrance and elevator lobbies on each floor.

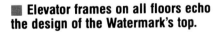

■ The terra-cotta facade of the Coleman Building, constructed in 1915, was preserved as a base for the tower and provides one entrance into the building (left). In a more contemporary but compatible style (right), another entrance to the building has been criticized favorably as being in the "Egyptian headdress motif."

■ Elevator frames on all floors echo the design of the Watermark's top.

ing—which was braced up until the new building rose behind it—is important for the image it brings to the streetscape as the portico icon of the neighborhood, and for its architectural heritage. The University of Washington's architecture building bears the name of the Coleman Building's designer, Carl Gould, the first dean of the School of Architecture.

The cornice line of the preserved facade continues the cornice line of adjacent buildings. Where the terra cotta of the old facade ends and the buff-colored tile of the new structure begins, the uses change from primarily retail to office. A few stories above that, the building pinches in noticeably, signaling the change to residential use. Vertical stacks of balconies give a third dimension to each facade. The deliberate breaking of symmetry on the building's shaft not only allows more freedom in the interior design of the residential units, but also was seen by the design team as clearly demonstrating the building's residential use. The typical residential floor was designed so that two to eight units could fit on a single floor, thereby allowing a marketable mix of different sized units.

At the time of its completion, the Watermark Tower was the tallest tile-clad building in the United States. It has a steel frame with a composite steel deck floor system and a slip-form concrete core. Exterior walls are prefabricated unglazed tile-clad panels. Office and residential uses are served by separate banks of elevators with access from the street through adjacent lobbies.

■ High ceilings and large windows that offer views of Seattle's waterfront and downtown skyline lend to a feeling of spaciousness. Most units have balconies off the living rooms. Although kitchens are located in the interiors of the units, pass-throughs allow views through the living areas and out windows.

Robert Pisano

Stewart Tilger

MARKETING

The Watermark Tower opened during the midst of the 1983 economic recession, with high mortgage interest rates and an ample supply of downtown condominiums in a flat downtown housing market. Cornerstone chose to hold the Watermark's condominium prices at their starting rate and lease the units until the market improved, rather than make drastic cuts soon after opening. During the first five years, 25 units were sold, while the remainder was leased. In January 1988, Cornerstone decided to sell the remaining units in the building by 1990. To achieve this, asking prices were reduced by 20 percent and a more aggressive advertising and sales campaign was initiated.

Amenities include an exercise room, a spa, a sauna, a community lounge and kitchen, a roof terrace, one secured covered parking space per unit with additional spaces available for purchase, a tennis court and a daycare playground on the roof of the adjacent parking structure, and storage lockers. There is a resident manager, as well as a concierge to help with deliveries and errands. Six different unit configurations are available, all with elegant kitchens. One particularly notable unit has two separate bedroom suites, each with its own bath, which allows a variety of options for unrelated individuals co-owning, for single parents and their children, or for separate study areas and home offices. The quality of materials is excellent: tile floors and splashes in bathrooms, hardwood floors in the entrances and kitchens, wood trim and wood windows throughout, and coffered nine-foot-high ceilings.

The success of the Waterfront Place neighborhood can best be demonstrated by its wide-ranging effects. Since its completion in 1984, additional development up and down First Avenue has gradually re-

APPROVALS

Review and approval by the Seattle Landmarks Board was one of 23 separate approvals that were obtained for subsurface, surface, and above-grade elements, including utility lines, traffic rights-of-way, and seasonal banners and flowers. The developer negotiated with neighboring property owners and financed the upgrading of facades of their buildings ($90,000 for painting and signage) to make them more compatible with Waterfront Place's new uses and physical improvements.

moved the seamy haunts of the district. First Avenue is on its way to becoming again one of downtown's liveliest streets. Since 1984, widespread preservation work has occurred in downtown Seattle and in neighborhoods nearby. Two recent buildings—a mixed-use residential building and a speculative commercial office tower—complement the Watermark's articulated top with their own. The Watermark is frequently cited in popular surveys as one of Seattle's favorite downtown buildings. Today, the chief criticism voiced about the rumpled building that grew from a modest 12-story concept to a 22-story reality is that it should have been taller.

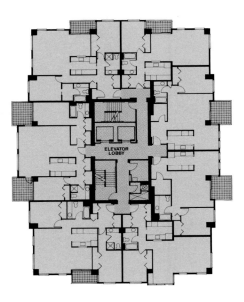

**TYPICAL RESIDENTIAL
FLOOR PLAN**

■ **Each of the 15 residential floors contains from two to eight units ranging from 761 to 2,220 square feet. To broaden the marketing range, floor plans were highly interchangeable. Unit interiors feature quality materials and nine-foot-high ceilings.**

PROJECT DATA

LAND USE INFORMATION:
Site Area: 0.3 acres (13,209 square feet)
Building Site Coverage: 100 percent
Parking: 94 spaces
Density: 300+ units per acre
Total Units: 94
Total Height: 272 feet; 22 stories

USES AS A PERCENT OF TOTAL FLOOR SPACE:
Retail: 6.5 percent
Office: 31.3 percent
Residential: 62.2 percent

UNIT INFORMATION[1]:

Program	Type	Square Feet	Number	Sales Price
A	2-bdrm./1¾-bath	1,042	28	$164,000–$207,000
B	2-bdrm./1¾-bath	1,012	14	$170,000–$218,000
C	1-bdrm./1-bath	761	22	$102,000–$167,000
D	1-bdrm./1-bath	804	24	$124,000–$162,000
E	2-bdrm./1¾-bath	2,220	2	$450,000–$500,000
F	2-bdrm./1¾-bath	1,638	4	$350,000–$500,000

ECONOMIC INFORMATION:
Site Value: $850,000[2]
Site Improvement Costs: $1,040,400[3]
Construction Costs:

Structural	$13,648,000
Carpentry	840,000
Electrical	1,115,000
Plumbing	1,340,000
HVAC	730,000
Other (fire protection)	160,000
Total	$17,833,000[4]

Homeowner Fee: $21,024 (total building) per month

Notes:
[1]Each unit has one secured parking space in adjacent building.
[2]$9,042.55 per unit.
[3]This work was done under a separate contract for total six-block project.
[4]$90.07 per square foot.

DIRECTIONS:
From Seattle/Tacoma Airport, take Interstate 5 north to the Madison Street exit. Follow Madison Street west for five blocks to First Avenue; the project will be on the right. Driving time is approximately 20 minutes in non-rush-hour traffic.

DEVELOPER:
Cornerstone Development Company
1011 Western Avenue, Suite 500
Seattle, Washington 98104

ARCHITECT/INTERIOR DESIGNER:
The Bumgardner Architects
101 Stewart Street, Suite 200
Seattle, Washington 98101

STRUCTURAL ENGINEER:
Chalker Engineers
950 S. Fawcett, Suite 301
Tacoma, Washington 98402

LANDSCAPE ARCHITECT:
Thomas L. Berger Associates
2021 Minor Avenue E.
Seattle, Washington 98102

CONTRACTOR:
Sellen Construction Company
228 Ninth Avenue N.
Seattle, Washington 98109

AWARD:
•Seattle Chapter AIA Merit Award

GALTIER PLAZA
ST. PAUL, MINNESOTA

Edwin M. Bell

The Lowertown Historic District of St. Paul, Minnesota, contains 180 acres of warehouse and vacant land bordered by the downtown skyline to the west, the state capitol to the north, and the Mississippi River to the south. To stimulate the redevelopment of this historic district, the Lowertown Redevelopment Corporation envisioned a large, mixed-use project that, through its design and uses, would act as an anchor for the area's revival. But developing a 1.3 million-square-foot mixed-use project on a single Lowertown block presented an array of challenges—not the least of which

Edwin M. Bell, AIA, is president of Miller Hanson Westerbeck Bell Architects, Inc., an architectural, planning, and design firm based in Minneapolis, Minnesota.

was coming up with a design concept that would blend with this varied urban context.

DEVELOPMENT STRATEGY

Galtier Plaza is the largest mixed-use development in St. Paul and features a significant concentration of residential, retail, commercial office, and recreation space. It is the result of a development strategy with multiple—and often difficult to mesh—objectives. Countering the desire to preserve the warehouse quality of the historic district was the desire to create a project that would have the size and density necessary to bring about Lowertown's economic rebirth. Throw into this the usual array of political, economic, and legal realities, and the complexities associ-

■ The eastern facade, which faces Mears Park, respects the need to have a six-story base along the streetfront and to preserve the cornice of the existing building. The residential towers that rise from the office/retail base are oriented to the western side of the block, which relates more closely to the modern downtown skyline.

ated with large urban mixed-use projects begin to emerge.

The catalysts for Galtier Plaza were both the city of St. Paul and the Lowertown Redevelopment Corporation (LRC). As a nonprofit coordinator of development in the Lowertown Historic District, LRC had sought to fill the block for several years. The site, located next to Mears Park and just east of the downtown business district, represented the keystone in the district's redevelopment. LRC's executive director had patiently wooed developers with the concept of a mixed-use center and had in hand one eager tenant—the downtown YMCA.

Efforts to put together a project by forming a development partnership among existing owners fell through, as had a modest plan for housing and service retail development proposed by a developer from Madison, Wisconsin. The city had already secured an urban development action grant (UDAG) from the federal government to develop the site, and, with a three-month deadline looming on the grant, it called upon new developers.

When these efforts failed, LRC brought together a local commercial developer, a local housing developer, and the YMCA to work together on a combined project. Planning was started on the complex with the agreement that it would be a single entity in its design and function, with each element complementing the others.

PLANNING AND DESIGN

The one-block site contained five structures of varying quality and value. Three of these structures were historic but only the facades of two of them were considered significant. The third structure was a Romanesque building with an ornate, multicolored marble interior. Because of the need to excavate for underground parking and the nature of the soil conditions (loosely compacted rocks), saving the three historic structures proved to be more costly than starting from scratch. However, the size, texture, and locations of the structures offered a strong context within which to begin developing a design and planning program for the new project.

The historic district made it necessary to integrate into the project the three existing structures. Ultimately, the economic feasibility of the project required that the two historic facades be dismantled and rebuilt, while the large Romanesque building was rehabilitated and preserved. An existing service alley running through the site was redesigned as a pedestrian spine. Working around this existing framework, the architect began to lay out the rest of the land use program.

The pedestrian spine is encased in a seven-story glass atrium that organizes the project vertically as well as horizontally. The first three levels form an enclosed retail strip running from one entrance to another; from floors four through seven, the atrium provides light to the offices on either side of the spine. The city's skywalk system ties into this glass-enclosed space, thereby providing easy pedestrian access from surrounding uses. The large and very successful YMCA serves as an anchor tenant to the pedestrian spine and generates activity during much of the day and evening.

Rather than running the length of the block uninterrupted, the atrium is divided into three distinct spaces by soaring elevator cages. The Palm Court is the most festive with space for public events, as well as lunching or playing chess at special tables. Steps, escalators, and elevators at the atrium's division points actually encourage confusion to force people through as much of the retail space as possible. The second level of the atrium has been detailed as an interior street and

■ The architecture strives to individualize each of the elements while also unifying them. The detailing of materials helps to identify each of the project's separate elements— dark brick at the base, primarily light brick on the residential towers, different window treatments on the condominium and apartment units, and glass on the retail spine and atop the towers.

functions as the major thoroughfare, in keeping with St. Paul's increasingly skyway-oriented circulation pattern.

Above the seven-story, block-square base of retail space, offices, and the YMCA, the atrium rises up to become a party pavilion surrounded by a rooftop garden for residents of the housing towers. There is also outdoor recreation space for the YMCA with a pool, tennis courts, basketball court, and running track.

The exterior facades of the office/retail base evolved out of respect for the surrounding land uses and the overall context of the historic Lowertown area. The residential towers, however, which rise out of the office and retail base, proved a design opportunity to bridge the social and aesthetic gap between Lowertown and the nearby central business district.

The housing units were split into two towers, one falling under the F.A.A. guideline of 452 feet and the other set back 60 feet from Mears Park to lessen its impact on the park. The towers are sheathed in blue reflective glass and brick to blend with both the glass curtain-wall skyscraper aesthetic of downtown and with the more personable articulation and texture of Lowertown's brick warehouses.

Galtier Plaza illustrates some basic approaches for dealing with new development within established and valued older urban areas. Through the careful consideration of forms, materials, articulation, and spatial sequences, the new development reinforces the fabric of both the existing city skyline and the re-emerging Lowertown Historic District.

■ Galtier Plaza is the largest mixed-use center in St. Paul, Minnesota; it contains a large YMCA, office and retail uses, 121 condominiums, and 347 apartments. The residential uses on this one-block redevelopment site achieve a density of almost 190 units per acre. The seven-story office/retail base relates chiefly to the Lowertown Historic District, while the 30- and 46-story housing towers relate to the nearby downtown skyline.

PROJECT DATA

LAND USE INFORMATION:
Site Area: 2.47 acres (107,623 square feet)
Total Units: 347 apartments and 121 condominiums
Density: 189.47 units per acre
Parking: 800 spaces[1]

PROGRAM INFORMATION:
Residential Area: 609,000 gross square feet
Office Area: 100,000 gross square feet
Commercial/Restaurant Area: 192,000 gross square feet
YMCA Facility: 75,000 gross square feet
One Building on Historic Register Retained (McColl Building)
Two Historic Building Facades Retained

LAND USE PLAN:

	Acres	Percent of Site
Open Space	0.070	2.8%
Buildings/Roads	2.400	97.2
Service/Drop-Off Areas	0.023	
Amenities/Rooftop Development	0.860	

RENTAL UNIT INFORMATION:

Type	Number	Square Feet	Rent
Studio	60[2]	439–469	$495–525
1-bdrm.	156	566–849	$620–730
2-bdrm.	124	912–1,238	$860–990
2-bdrm./den	7	1,186–1,221	$1,150–1,250

CONDOMINIUM UNIT INFORMATION:

Type	Number	Square Feet
Jackson Tower:		
1-bdrm./den	77	1,056–1,440
2-bdrm./den	24	1,450–2,440
3-bdrm./den	2	2,266–2,440
4-bdrm./den	1	3,273
Parkside Tower:		
1-bdrm.	4	845
2-bdrm./den	6	998–1,006
2-bdrm./den	6	1,310–1,580
2-bdrm/den/studio	1	1,705

Notes:
[1] In underground garage.
[2] 27 of which were subsidized.

ECONOMIC INFORMATION:
Total Estimated Development Cost: $107 million
Financing Sources:
• UDAG: $4.8 million
• Port Authority Revenue Bonds: $22 million
• HRA Revenue Bonds (for YMCA): $5.2 million
• Port Authority Revenue Bonds (for restoration of McColl Building): $5.2 million
• Equity: $6 million
• HRA Revenue Bonds for Rental Units: $34 million
• Conventional Financing for Condos: $20 million
• Tax Increment Financing: $3.15 million
• Lowertown Redevelopment Corporation Investment: $2 million

DIRECTIONS:
From the airport, take Highway 5 east over river and into downtown (about four miles) to St. Peter's Street. Turn right on Fifth Street and left on Jackson Street. Project occupies a block between Jackson and Sibley streets and Fifth and Sixth streets.

ARCHITECT:
Miller Hanson Westerback Bell Architects Inc.
1 Main Street, S.E., Suite 400
Minneapolis, Minnesota 55414

AWARDS:
• 1985 National Endowment for the Arts Presidential Design Award
• 1987 Award of Excellence, Post Tensioning Institute

MUSEUM TOWER
NEW YORK, NEW YORK

John A. Casazza

Amid the diversity and complexity of New York City, the development of a new luxury high-rise condominium apartment building typically generated little public interest. Museum Tower, however, represents a notable exception. Built above the new west wing of the Museum of Modern Art, the 263-unit

John A. Casazza is assistant vice president for education with the National Association for Industrial and Office Parks, based in Arlington, Virginia. Before joining NAIOP, Casazza was a senior associate in the Research and Education Division of ULI, where he was responsible for several publications.

luxury project played a crucial role in financing a major expansion and renovation of the museum. The development of Museum Tower resulted from a complex transaction and agreement between the developer, the Charles H. Shaw Company, and the Museum of Modern Art (MOMA), from which Shaw acquired the air rights to construct the tower above the museum building.

The 44-story tower provides more than 400,000 square feet of residential space and features a contemporary glass mosaic exterior that is integrated visually with the design of MOMA's expansion. Units range from 734-square-foot studios to two-, three-, and four-bedroom residences and duplex penthouses. The project is targeted to the upper end of the luxury market; sales prices range from $273,000 to nearly $5 million.

DEVELOPMENT STRATEGY

To assure a strong working relationship and mutually beneficial partnership, Shaw and MOMA entered into a complex development agreement that clearly established the obligations and responsibilities of both parties. Shaw acquired the air rights outright from MOMA in 1979 for $17 million. In addition, MOMA (through a special organization called the Trust for Cultural Resources) receives payment in lieu of real estate taxes from unit owners in Museum Tower; these payments subsidize the operating expenses of the museum. This enabled the Trust for Cultural Resources to issue two series of bonds, totaling $60 million,

■ **Museum Tower—built within 10,000 square feet of air rights acquired from the museum—rests on top of the new west wing of the Museum of Modern Art (MOMA). The sale of the air rights was a major factor in financing the museum's expansion and renovation.**

to pay for the museum's expansion and renovation.

The agreement between Shaw and MOMA also recognized that while the construction of the tower and the expansion of the museum were two separate projects, certain portions of both projects could be constructed more efficiently and more economically under a single construction plan. The agreement also required that the developer comply with the museum's design criteria for the tower's exterior and lobby areas. Under the agreement, the Museum Tower/MOMA project (52 stories overall) was divided into three sections: the six-story lower building containing the expanded museum's west wing; the 44-story Museum Tower; and two "transfer" floors housing mechanical equipment.

The agreement also established a development schedule for the overall project, a reciprocal easement agreement, and a joint review process for those design issues affecting both the tower and the museum. Both Shaw and MOMA agreed to pay their proportionate shares of the cost for the lower building and the transfer floors. They also agreed upon the standards for a "distinguished luxury residential building." Finally, the agreement provided for an arbitration mechanism to settle any disputes, a termination date for the completion of the lower building shell (exclusive of the facade), and the issuance of a certificate of occupancy for the tower. Shaw assumed responsibility for the construction of the lower building shell to assure that it was completed in a timely manner, allowing the 44-story tower above the shell to be constructed as scheduled.

SITE

Museum Tower stands in midtown Manhattan on the north side of West 53rd Street between Fifth Avenue and the Avenue of the Americas. It

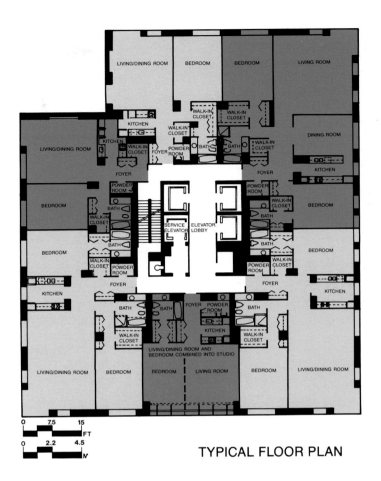

TYPICAL FLOOR PLAN

0   7.5   15
FT
0   2.2   4.5
M

■ Units range from a 734-square-foot studio/one-bath plan to a 4,741-square-foot duplex penthouse with four and one-half baths. The initial selling prices reflect this huge range—$273,000 to almost $5 million. Marketing efforts were directed at both local New York and international buyers. Foreign real estate brokers showed videos describing Museum Tower to their wealthy clientele.

is located within one of the few areas of midtown Manhattan that is residential in character, yet close to prime office space, shopping, hotels, restaurants, museums, art galleries, theaters, and concert halls. Prominent New York City attractions such as Rockefeller Center, St. Patrick's Cathedral, and Central Park are a short walk from the site. Museum Tower is bordered by a mix of uses including older brownstones on 54th Street, the Dorset Hotel to the northwest, and MOMA's well-known sculpture garden immediately to the north. The tower offers dramatic views of New York Harbor, the Hudson River, the East River, and Central Park.

ARCHITECTURE

MOMA selected Cesar Pelli as the architect for the tower's exterior and the museum expansion. As noted earlier, the museum thus maintained control over the basic massing of the tower and the concept of the curtain wall integrating the tower and the museum.

The tower has a reinforced concrete structural system supported by reinforced concrete flooring. Its exterior is a polychrome glass curtain wall consisting of over 18,000 separate pieces of ceramic glass in 680 different sizes and 11 different shades of gray, with light and dark shades interlocking in a geometric pattern. The tower is slender (to reduce the impact of its height on the midblock site and to maintain the openness of the museum's sculpture garden) and is set back at the top. It has its own private entrance (highlighted by a stainless steel canopy), lobby, concierge desk, and elevators, with no access to or from the museum. The lobby is finished in brass, granite, and wood and contains works of art selected under the guidance of noted art expert Andre Emmerich.

Edward Durell Stone designed the tower's interior. Units feature nine-foot-high ceilings (instead of the eight-foot-high ceilings customary in most high-rise apartments, teak herringbone floors, large walk-in closets, travertine marble bathrooms, and floor-to-ceiling windows. Setback duplex penthouses on the 51st and 52nd floors offer log-burning fireplaces, as well as terraces on the lower level.

For all units except the studios, which run up the center of the tower's south face, living rooms are set at the building's corners and feature floor-to-ceiling windows extending to a width of eight feet along each side. Residents thus have unobstructed views in two directions, and when the windows are lighted after dark, the building takes on a residential character.

Museum Tower stands out as an exception to the norm in high-rise residential architecture. The articulation of its exterior with glass mosaic in a variety of colors, shades, and sizes, sets the tower apart from the typical gridlike masonry structures most often seen in projects of

MECHANICAL EQUIPMENT

FLOORS 9–52, CONDOMINIUMS

FLOORS 7–8, MANAGEMENT SERVICES

THE MUSEUM OF MODERN ART

WEST

53RD STREET ELEVATION

EAST

■ Located in the heart of midtown Manhattan, Museum Tower contains 263 luxury condominium units. Standing 52 stories, it consists of six floors of museum space, two floors devoted to equipment and management services, and 44 floors of apartments. The upper floors contain a grouping of smaller studio apartments that define the top of the building.

its type, and integrates it with the art and sculptural center from which it rises.

MARKETING

Museum Tower was marketed throughout the United States as well as internationally. Approximately 50 percent of the buyers have been from the United States and 50 percent from abroad, primarily from South America, Europe, and the Far East. For many buyers, Museum Towers is not a primary residence.

The marketing program took a low-key approach, designed to create an appropriate image for the project and to appeal to a luxury market. A limited amount of direct mail advertising supplemented advertising in upscale monthly and weekly publications in both the United States and abroad. Brokers in major foreign markets also used an audiovisual program.

■ Unit interiors feature nine-foot ceilings and teak herringbone floors. All but 20 of the 167 corner apartments have floor-to-ceiling corner windows providing truly dramatic views of the cityscape.

■ Designed for Cesar Pelli and Associates, the tower's facade is covered by a glass-module mosaic of 12 shades of gray and blue. Through the interplay of warm and cool hues, and of opaque and transparent surfaces, the tower presents a continually changing reflection of sunlight and shadow.

PROJECT DATA

LAND USE INFORMATION:
Site Area: 0.25 acres
Total Units: 263
Density: 1,052 units
Gross Building Area (GBA): 500,00 square feet
Total Residential Space: 409,129 square feet
Parking: NA[1]

ECONOMIC INFORMATION:
Site Value: $17,000,000[2]
Construction Costs[3]: $52,000,000
Soft Costs: $62,000,000
Total Project Cost: $131,000,000
Operating Expenses:

Labor	$1,063,500
Electricity[4]	128,000
Gas	399,200
Water/Sewer	31,000
Window Cleaning	54,000
Building Services/Supplies	91,000
Building Repairs/Maintenance	88,000
Management	55,000
Legal and Audit	8,000
Insurance	64,000
Miscellaneous	5,000
Reserve for Contingencies	120,300
Total	$2,107,000

UNIT INFORMATION:

Type	Square Feet	Number[5]	Sales Price
Studio/1- or 1½-bath	734	10	$273,00–$278,250
1-bdrm./1½-bath	973–1,204	139	$410,000–$605,000
2-bdrm./2½-bath	1,917–2,248	86	$952,000–$1,235,000
3-bdrm./3½-bath	2,890–3,452	13	$1,630,000–$1,640,000
4-bdrm./4½-bath	2,890	8	$1,405,000–$1,565,000
Duplex penthouse/4½-bath	4,557–4,741	3	$4,750,000

Notes:
[1]The project has no parking facilities, but several private garages are located in the vicinity.
[2]Cost for acquisition of approximately 10,000 square feet of air space above a portion of the west wing of the Museum of Modern Art.
[3]Hard costs only; $104 per square foot.
[4]Electricity consumed in common areas. Units have individual electric meters.
[5]Some units were combined, resulting in fewer total units than the 263 that were initially offered.

DIRECTIONS:
From La Guardia Airport, take the Grand Central Parkway west (across the Triborough Bridge) to the F.D.R. Drive south. Continue on the F.D.R. Drive to the 63rd Street exit. Take 63rd Street west to Park Avenue south to 53rd Street west. Follow 53rd Street past Fifth Avenue and the project will be on the right.

DEVELOPER:
The Charles H. Shaw Company
676 St. Clair, Suite 2200
Chicago, Illinois 60611

ARCHITECT (EXTERIOR):
Cesar Pelli and Associates
1056 Chapel Street
New Haven, Connecticut 06510

ARCHITECT (INTERIOR):
Edward Durell Stone Associates
4 East 79th Street
New York, New York 10021

GENERAL CONTRACTOR:
The Leon D. DeMatteis Construction
  Corporation
820 Elmont Road
Elmont, New York 11003

AWARD:
• Urban Land Institute Award for Excellence, Large-Scale Development, 1985

THE CONTINUING EVOLUTION

James W. Wentling and Lloyd W. Bookout

The case studies in this book present a diversity of contemporary higher-density housing styles that have succeeded in their respective markets and locations. All of the projects examined have borrowed elements from their predecessors but have given them new interpretations to meet today's density and lifestyle needs. Despite the diversity of styles considered, the case studies contain some common design "threads" that lead in the direction of future, higher-density housing forms.

THE HUMAN DIMENSION

Design theory holds that the ability to comprehend the whole of one's environment depends on an ability to understand the individual parts. Architecture and planning that reduce large buildings and projects into comprehensive elements facilitates this objective. As residential buildings and housing clusters increase in size to accommodate higher densities, the need to reduce large building elements to an identifiable, human dimension increases.

In virtually all of the projects examined in the case studies, the scale of the projects was kept down either through site planning or architectural features. In Whitman Pond, potentially long rows of townhouses were broken up into small clusters with comfortable central courtyards that encourage interaction among residents. The mid-rise Barony on Peachtree and the high-rise Watermark Tower incorporated elements such as peaks and articulated rooflines to reinforce the residential character of the buildings. Reducing large building elements to an identifiable dimension will ultimately enhance the livability of the house.

SPATIAL QUALITY

The theme of quality over quantity of space pervades higher-density housing projects. In both interior and exterior spaces, efforts are being made to accomplish more with less. The case studies reveal some consistency in techniques that are being used.

In nearly all of the examples, open floor plans, volume ceilings, and extensive glazing are used to make interior floor space seem larger. Other techniques that are used for this purpose include rounded drywall corners and built-in niches for plants or sculpture (Barcelona in Westpark), soffits instead of walls to divide rooms (Casa del Cielo), and skylights to drop light into interior spaces (Lakemont). As demonstrated by Woodbridge Apartments, success in the rental housing market can also be enhanced by employing volume ceilings and other features that increase the perception of space. Increasingly, renters are demanding design and amenity features once found only in for-sale housing.

One method of expanding interior space that has proven extremely popular is to capitalize on the outdoors. Advances in energy-efficient construction practices and materials make it possible—even in harsher climates—to "open-up" the interior of houses. Contemporary designs incorporate generous amounts of glazing to expand views and emphasize outdoor activity areas. Fairway Pointe serves as an example with its use of decks and patios around the entire perimeter of many of the houses.

As lots for single-family houses become smaller, the need to make maximum use of the available yard area increases. The case studies indicate that the days of vast lawns may be giving way to more use-intensive spaces like patios and spas and to high-quality landscape treatments such as brick garden walls, courtyard fountains, trellises, and privacy screens. Villa D'Este illustrates how the needs of even the most discriminating residents can be met on relatively small lots. Gradually, the growing emphasis on interior luxury is finding its way to the outdoors and features once associated only with custom homes are being incorporated into production housing.

REDUCING MAINTENANCE

A growing segment of the population wants houses that are easy to care for. This trend is caused both by the increasing number of empty-nester households and by the maturing baby boom population that seeks more time to enjoy leisure activities. A growing percentage of households have two working adults, which leaves less time for household chores. Higher-density houses generally lend themselves well to low maintenance; designers and builders are incorporating features that can reduce time spent on maintenance even further.

One way to reduce maintenance time is to structure projects so that all or a part of the exterior area is maintained by a community association. This does not necessarily require condominium ownership. For example, the detached houses at Spinnaker Ridge are sold with fee simple lots but all exterior maintenance and repairs are conducted by a homeowners' association. The detached houses at California Meadows were sold with fully installed front yard landscaping that will also be maintained by a community association. Demographic and lifestyle trends suggest that designing for low maintenance, and establishing mechanisms for providing maintenance, will be important factors in future housing forms.

INTERNAL ORGANIZATION

Providing residents with a feeling of comfort and practicality goes to the essence of successful housing design. Comtemporary floor plans place more emphasis on rooms in which entertaining, relaxation, and family activity occur. In the single-family houses of Westgreen, for example, a formal living room with separate den proved less popular than a single "great room" that could accommodate large social gatherings as well as daily family functions. The case studies also show the growing emphasis on retreat-like master bedrooms and baths that often function as a separate, but very private, living area. Several of the projects feature flexible floor plans that can easily provide a mix of room types and sizes to accommodate the varied requirements of a diverse market.

TRADITIONAL CRAFTSMANSHIP

Contemporary housing often succeeds by achieving the "customized" quality readily found in older homes. Advancing construction technology and volume building favor machine production of building components over hand craftsmanship. In spite of these technological changes, manufacturers still seek to retain the aura of individual craftsmanship being involved in residential products. For example, windows often include muntin and mullion attachments that recall individual window panes, while doors and shutters often include raised panels.

Mass-produced construction materials that reinforce the customized image are popular in contemporary higher-density housing: lattices, shingles, shutters, wood siding, and brick are examples. Monolithic building materials such as stucco are broken up into articulated forms; arches and quoins are incorporated for relief and multiple color schemes are used. Even paving materials can assume craftsmanlike qualities with the use of stamped concrete walkways and entries designed to give the appearance of inlaid cobblestones.

Traditional materials such as hardwood floors, beveled glass, and marble foyers readily are found in the interiors of upper-range production housing—such as Villa D'Este—reinforcing the theme of quality over quantity. Crown moldings and chair rail trim are commonly used to represent the building craft even in moderately priced houses like those of Riverplace.

The integration of "technological craftsmanship" into modern housing recalls—somewhat nostalgically—past housing forms. The occupants of today's high-density housing overwhelmingly prefer their homes to show quality, attention to details, and human-scale materials.

REGIONALISM

The diverse geography and cultures of the United States have led to innumerable regional housing styles, which were shaped by available building materials, climate, social traditions, ethnic heritage, and other local influences. The incorporation of local precedents into contemporary housing acknowledges these regional building traditions.

The case studies illustrate the wide diversity of styles—from the simple forms of Puritan New England (Whitman Pond and The Boatyard), to the practical side house design of the South (Charleston Place) and the colorful Spanish Mission style of California (Barcelona in Westpark). Residents of essentially new housing forms take comfort in these familiar architectural traditions that have been preserved.

SITE CONTEXT

Higher-density housing can be appropriate for a variety of locations: downtowns, urban infill, and newly developing suburban areas. As with any development proposal, good design stems largely from sensitivity to the conditions of the site.

The duplex and triplex buildings of Lakemont evolved partially out of consideration for terrain, view opportunities, and the architect's desire to create a Spanish-style enclave amid the rolling northern California landscape. The design of the mid-rise Barony on Peachtree evolved in response to neighboring single-family houses, whose architectural features it incorporated. As demonstrated in the case studies, issues like massing, color, height, and detailing must be considered carefully within the context of the site if housing design is to succeed.

FACILITATING COMMUNITY

Individual housing units relate ultimately to a larger community, and design solutions should consider the opportunity for that community to grow and develop—particularly as density increases. Houses that are designed with an inward orientation, for example, may not be as likely to foster a sense of community as those that are oriented around a cluster (Spinnaker Ridge) or that relate to the street (Westgreen), both of which encourage interaction. Effective site planning can accomplish the mutual objectives of establishing a sense-of-neighborhood and of protecting privacy.

CURB APPEAL

The preponderance of the modern two-car household creates a design challenge for today's designer and builder of higher-density housing. This challenge is particularly evident in small-lot detached houses, where the automobile may be the only viable means of transportation and buyers expect a traditional two-car attached garage. In practically all of the case studies with densities below 20 units per acre, accommodating the automobile proved to be a major design dilemma.

Several methods were employed in the case study projects to reduce negative visual effects caused by garage doors. Barcelona in Westpark and California Meadows use a wider but shallower lot to "expand" the front elevation of the house. Other techniques include turning the garage at an angle to the street, placing the garage within the main structure of the house, placing a second-story room over the garage, and increasing architectural details around the garage door.

In both detached and attached houses, providing for a separate and identifiable entrance to the front of each house became a common objective. Entrance identity can be enhanced with architectural treatments (such as arches), entry gates, courtyards, and special landscaping treatments. Bringing back the front porch has also improved the curb appeal of contemporary houses. The street-friendly porch, reminiscent of quaint, small-town houses, is regaining popularity (as demonstrated by the houses of Westgreen and Fairway Pointe) and can be used successfully in both detached and attached designs.

Whatever the methods used, today's development teams need to consider how higher-density houses will look from the street. Long, monotonous rows of garage doors and poorly marked entrances should be avoided.

THE CONTINUING EVOLUTION

The currents of change in housing types and design gathered momentum during the 1980s. Along with changes in other segments of our technological culture, innovations in housing design were introduced at a furious pace.

The forces that drove the demand for higher-density housing in the 1980s are expected to continue—if not multiply—during the next decade. Shortages of infrastructure, limitations on suburban growth, increasing land and building costs, and issues of affordability will strongly affect the density of what is built. Changing lifestyles caused by factors such as a gradually aging population and a greater emphasis on leisure time will also necessitate higher densities.

Today's housing professional must be a student of history as well as a knowledgeable follower of current demographic and market trends. Despite the dynamics of economic and technological change, homebuyers and renters alike will rely largely on traditional values when making their housing choices. By continuing to reinterpret the values and housing forms of the past, planners and designers can better provide housing solutions for the future.